LAW, LIBERTY,
and PSYCHIATRY

/395

Other books by Thomas Szasz

Pain and Pleasure
The Myth of Mental Illness
Psychiatric Justice
The Ethics of Psychoanalysis
The Manufacture of Madness
Ideology and Insanity
The Age of Madness (Ed.)
The Second Sin
Ceremonial Chemistry
Heresies
Karl Kraus and the Soul-Doctors
Schizophrenia
Psychiatric Slavery
The Myth of Psychotherapy
The Theology of Medicine
Sex by Prescription
The Therapeutic State
Insanity

LAW, LIBERTY, AND PSYCHIATRY » *An Inquiry*

into the Social Uses of Mental Health Practices

THOMAS SZASZ

SYRACUSE UNIVERSITY PRESS

Copyright © 1963, 1989 by Thomas Szasz

All Rights Reserved

Syracuse University Press Edition 1989
94 93 92 91 90 89   6 5 4 3 2 1

The paper used in this publication meets the minimum requirements of American National Standard for Information Sciences—Permanence of Paper for Printed Library Materials, ANSI Z39.48-1984.∞™

Library of Congress Cataloging-in-Publication Data

Szasz, Thomas Stephen, 1920–
    Law, liberty, and psychiatry.
    Reprint. Originally published: New York :
Macmillan, 1963.
    Bibliography: p.
    Includes index.
    1. Insanity—Jurisprudence—United States.
2. Criminal liability—United States. I. Title.
KF9242.S937   1989   345.73′04   89-11294
ISBN 0-8156-0242-1   347.3054

Manufactured in the United States of America

They [the clergy] believe that any portion of power confided to me will be exerted in opposition to their schemes. And they believe truly, for I have sworn upon the altar of God eternal hostility against every form of tyranny over the mind of man.

—THOMAS JEFFERSON (1800)

Contents

Preface

EVER SINCE I first reflected on matters such as madness and madhouses and especially the incarceration of insane persons in insane asylums—long before I went to college, much less medical school—it has seemed to me that the entire edifice of psychiatry rests on two false premises, namely: that persons called "mental patients" have something others do not have—mental illness; and that they lack something others do have—free will and responsibility. In short, psychiatry is a house of cards, held up by nothing more, or less, than mass belief in the truth of its principles and the goodness of its practices. If this is so, then psychiatry is a religion, not a science, a system of social controls, not a system of treating illness.

But if I knew this long ago, why—I am often asked—did I enter psychiatric and psychoanalytic training? I did so for two reasons: because I wanted to practice psychotherapy, and because I wanted to see if I could mount a successful critique of the fundamental principles and practices of psychiatry.

After floating a few cautiously phrased articles in professional journals, in 1961 I published *The Myth of Mental Illness*,[1] and all hell broke loose. Psychiatrists greeted my assertion that there is no mental illness with as much enthusiasm as priests might greet a fellow clergyman's assertion that there is no God: not, mind you, because the assertion is clearly false, or because they are sure that it is false, but because the person making it is not supposed to say such a thing—especially if it is true.

The controversy about mental illness still rages, and the nature of the controversy is often still stubbornly misunderstood: Mental health professionals and lay persons alike seem to believe that the demonstration of a genetic defect or neurological lesion in some so-called mental patients proves that mental illness exists—"like any other illness." But this is silly: If mental illness is a metabolic or neurological disease, then

it is a disease of the body, not of the mind; and if mental illness is misbehavior then it is behavior, not disease. A screwdriver may be a tool
or a drink: no amount of empirical research on orange-juice-and-vodka
can establish that it is, in reality, an unrecognized manifestation of a
carpenter's tool. With the simple but uncompromising idea that mental
illness is a metaphor, I hoped to inflict a fatal blow, philosophically
speaking, on the conceptual foundations of psychiatry. Perhaps I succeeded. But then, given what Freud, the greatest scientist of the mind
who ever lived, considered to be a typical instance of mental illness, this
may not have been so difficult: "The moment a man questions the meaning and value of life, he is sick, since objectively neither has any existence; by asking this question one is merely admitting to a store of
unsatisfied libido to which something else must have happened, a kind
of fermentation leading to sadness and depression."[2]

Recognizing a metaphor—as well as a dangerous deception and self-
deception—when I saw one, I next turned my energies to constructing
a critique of psychiatric practices, especially those taking place outside
the privacy of the consulting room.

Once again, my basic idea could not have been simpler. In *The Myth
of Mental Illness*, I tried to clarify why mental illness is not, and cannot
be, a bona fide illness—because the mind is not a bodily organ, and
because, as everyone knows but few acknowledge, the term "mental
illness" is typically affixed to misbehavior, not brain disease. In *Law,
Liberty, and Psychiatry*, I set out to document two equally obvious observations: First, that mental hospitalization is not, and cannot be, the
same as medical hospitalization—because the mental patient is not free
to leave the building in which he is housed, whereas the medical patient
is. Second, that the two paradigmatic practices of psychiatry—involuntary mental hospitalization or civil commitment and the insanity defense
or the exculpation of persons guilty of crimes as not guilty by reason
of insanity—rest on a philosophically indefensible and morally odious
proposition, namely, that unlike the behavior of the sane person, which
is governed by free will, the behavior of the insane person is governed
by impulses which the subject finds irresistible and for which he is,
therefore, not responsible. With the rejection of these fundamental
propositions as well, my excommunication from psychiatry became complete and irreversible.

Why should such ideas cast one out of an ostensibly scientific, professional discipline? Because of their consequence: If mental illness is
like any other illness, and if psychiatrists are like other medical practi-
tioners, then psychiatrists ought to act like physicians. The individual
suffering from diabetes or multiple sclerosis is not hospitalized involuntarily, nor is he excused from punishment if he commits a crime. Why,

then, commit the mentally ill person innocent of lawbreaking, and why acquit him as not guilty by reason of insanity when he is, in fact, guilty of a premeditated crime?

After all, it is self-evident that the so-called mentally ill criminal has committed a crime. What psychiatrists contend, and what most people now accept, is not that such a person does not commit crimes, but only that he does so from psychotic motives, exemplified by the phrase "I heard God's voice and he told me to kill my child." But "crimes," asserted Sir Hartley Shawcross at the Nuremberg trials of the Nazi war criminals, "do not cease to be criminal because they have a political motive."[3] Obviously so. By the same token, I maintain that crimes do not cease to be criminal because they have a "psychotic" motive.

Thus, it was not just liberty that I sought for the mental patient unjustly deprived of it. More important, I sought to impose on him, if guilty of misbehavior or crime, the same responsibility and punishment we impose on the mentally healthy person. With respect to psychiatry and law, my whole argument can thus be condensed into a few paragraphs, exposing two phony psychiatric claims and their consequences. The claims are: "I can't/couldn't help it . . ." and "He can't/couldn't help it . . ."

In the first phrase, "it" may refer to eating too much or too little, drinking, smoking, gambling, having adulterous affairs, killing one's baby or someone else, and so forth. If such a claim about one's non-responsibility is legally and socially accepted, then the claimant is not only excused of his immoral or illegal behavior but is often also accredited as a person with special expertise in diagnosing and treating eating disorders, alcoholism, tobacco dependence, sexual addiction, and countless other (alleged) mental maladies.

In the second phrase—"He can't/couldn't help it . . ."—"it" may refer to hearing voices no one else can hear, seeing things no one else can see, expressing a desire to kill oneself or someone else, or virtually any other socially disturbing or illegal behavior. If such a claim about another person's nonresponsibility is legally and socially accepted, then the person so identified becomes a fit subject for imprisonment without trial (involuntary psychiatric hospitalization) and punishment without having been sentenced (psychiatric treatment).

But this is heresy: Psychiatrists have correctly perceived that if involuntary psychiatric interventions of all sorts along with the insanity defense were abolished, as I proposed, psychiatry as we know it would cease to exist.

My sustained critique of the conceptual foundations and legal-social uses of psychiatry have proved to be very influential, though not, at least not yet, in the ways I had hoped. My aim was, and still is, to usher in a new way of seeing and treating individuals who are called, or call themselves, mentally ill: Accord them the same rights, and impose on them the same responsibilities we accord and impose on other adults in our society. We have abandoned the tradition-sanctioned co-ercive-paternalistic control of blacks and women; we should similarly abandon the legally and psychiatrically sanctioned coercive-paternalistic control of mental patients.

I did not expect this to happen overnight, and it didn't. Maybe it will never happen. What did happen is that psychiatrists, and many others too, began to feel guilty about the mistreatment of the mentally ill and embarked on yet another cycle of so-called reforms. Mental patients, it became clear, were deprived of their rights. Okay, said the reformers, we'll give them some rights. Thus did it come about that since the publication of *Law, Liberty, and Psychiatry* in 1963, mental patients have become the involuntary recipients of rights they never dreamed of—such as the right to a lawyer, to treatment, to refuse treatment, to be incarcerated in the least restrictive setting, and so forth. This time the Potemkin's Village called Psychiatry was spruced up in earnest. Before the 1960s, the abuse of the psychiatric patient was un-disguised: the mental hospital was a "snake pit." Clearly, the snakes had to go. American psychiatry and the society it serves replaced the reptiles with lawyers and therapists:

The right to refuse antipsychotic medication [writes a psychiatrist in 1988] is now more than a decade old. . . . refusal is not uncommon, but refusing patients appear almost always to receive treatment in the end. These findings point up the essential illogic of allowing committed persons to refuse treatment that would permit their freedom to be restored. The future evolution of the right [to treatment] . . . will restore the equivalence between the power to commit and the power to treat.[4]

Exhilarated by the prospect of possessing not just one but two different powers over his patient, this author adds "That such a right to refuse treatment might exist was unimaginable before the 1970s."[5] But the practice of rulers giving meaningless rights to their subjects can hardly be called unimaginable in our century saturated with slogans of phony freedoms. Sadly, but not surprisingly, if the pillars of society go to enough trouble to conceal their dark deeds, they are likely to succeed. That the concealments practiced by legal and psychiatric reformers have, this time around, been more successful than heretofore is suggested by the fact that they now fool even seasoned, critical observers. How else are we to explain the views of Roger Scruton, Professor of Aesthetics at Birkbeck College in London and editor of the *Salisbury Review*? In a note appended to an essay entitled "Do Liberals

Love Liberty?" Scruton states: "It is worth pointing out that the thinking represented by Szasz has been so successful that US law has been revised so as to forbid compulsory hospitalisation of the insane. The chaotic and disturbing result of this change can be witnessed in every major American city."[6]

The assertion that "US law has been revised so as to forbid compulsory hospitalisation of the insane" is news, indeed. Does Scruton actually believe that John Hinckley, Jr., is staying at St. Elizabeths Hospital, the nation's premier madhouse, because he likes it there, and because the government likes him so much that it houses and feeds him at taxpayer's expense? I go to the trouble of refuting Scruton's absurd misstatement because it reflects the widespread perception, carefully cultivated by psychiatric propagandists, that involuntary mental hospitalization has become so rare in America as to be irrelevant. This is not so. As I write these lines there comes to my hand the February 1989 issue of *The American Journal of Psychiatry* featuring a "Special Section" containing four articles collectively titled "Dangerousness and the Civil Commitment Process."[7] An editorial introducing these studies states: "The most recent national data (1980) show that of 1,176,558 inpatient admissions, 26% were involuntary noncriminal commitments. More than 51% of admissions to state and county mental hospitals are, however, involuntary (noncriminal)."[8]

Moreover, these figures do not even begin to reflect the escalating ugliness of the American psychiatric scene, noted in an essay in the *Sunday Times Magazine* (London): "Thousands of [New York] homeless are former inmates of mental hospitals which [Mayor] Koch emptied, largely on economic grounds; on the other hand, he has decreed that a 'sidewalk dweller' should be carted off to a mental hospital, on the grounds that anyone sleeping rough and pestering passers-by must be mentally disturbed. New Yorkers see no method in what some of them call the mayor's madness."[9]

In the past, thousands of individuals were forcibly incarcerated in mental hospitals, often for life; that was bad enough, but at least many of these unfortunate persons could make the asylum their home. Now the situation is even worse, thousands of persons being not only forcibly incarcerated in mental hospitals but also forcibly evicted from them as soon as they show any sign of adapting to their new environment. Then the cycle of forcible hospitalization and dehospitalization is repeated over and over again, depriving the "mental patient" of a predictable and stable environment both within and without the insane asylum.

Thus, what Scruton observed "in every major American city" is not the triumph of my ideas as social policy but only a singularly unattractive feature of the American national character (if one can so generalize), otherwise often good and generous. Perhaps precisely because Americans strive so hard to be good and generous, they don't like to be told that they have done wrong. Dickens' observation on just this point is unerring: "I believe [he wrote in 1842] there is no country, on the face of the earth, where there is less freedom of opinion on any subject in reference to which there is a broad difference of opinion than in this [the United States]. . . . I write the words with reluctance, disappointment, and sorrow; but I believe it from the bottom of my soul. . . . The wonder is that a breathing man can be found with temerity enough to suggest to the Americans the possibility of their having done wrong."[10]

Dickens was right. Instead of simply acknowledging their wrongdoing, Americans prefer to deny it with a dramatic gesture of undoing. Indians on reservations, blacks on plantations, epileptics in colonies, the mentally ill in snake pits—all these embarrassing wrongs must be quickly righted and forgotten: the Indians are treated like citizens of fictitious independent nations; the blacks get reverse discrimination; epileptic colonies are written out of medical and psychiatric history; the men and women imprisoned in mental hospitals for years and decades are suddenly and forcibly evicted.

The result, pretentiously called "deinstitutionalization," proves not only how very respectful psychiatrists really are of the civil rights of mental patients, but also how very right psychiatrists have been all along in stigmatizing and segregating mental patients as dangerous deviants. The failure of the quick cure then justifies the re-repression of the mad: Mental illness exists and the mentally ill are dangerous; ergo, mental patients, lacking free will and responsibility, have a right to be hospitalized against their will, treated against their will, lawyered against their will, even aquitted of crimes against their will; and if they commit mayhem and murder, then, suffering as they do from mental illness, they cannot be held responsible for their actions, need to be hospitalized against their will, treated against their will, and so on . . . ad nauseam and ad infinitum.

In short, I interpret Scruton's howler (and its making it into the pages of so prestigious a publication) as evidence that psychiatry is a religion and that Voltaire was right: If mental illness did not exist, it would be necessary to invent it. Clearly, people now passionately believe in psychiatric explanations, excuses, and coercions—the educated perhaps even more than the uneducated, the latter stubbornly clinging to Jesus and the televangelists, refusing to embrace Freud and the soul-doctors.

"Analyzing humor," remarked E. B. White, "is like dissecting a frog.

Few people are interested and the frog dies of it." The same goes for dissecting a popular delusion, such as psychiatry today: Few people are interested and the delusion dies of it—except people don't let it die. Indeed, why should they, if they want it to live? Freedom of belief lies at the heart of individual liberty and dignity. That is why I maintain that the "deluded" patient is as entitled to his belief as the "enlighted" psychiatrist is to his. Like clergymen of different faiths, or believers and unbelievers, each should be protected from being coerced by the other. To insure our protection from unwanted saviors—whether clerical or clinical—is a fundamental duty of the American government.

In the United States, the pursuit of happiness is an opportunity and an obligation that belongs to each and every individual. We are supposed to chase and catch that elusive quarry ourselves. We can delegate the task to experts, but no one—no pope, no prince, no politician, not even a psychiatrist—should be able to take it away from any of us. For, after all is said and done, is justifying the armed hunt for the happiness of the Other not the most dangerous delusion to which we can succumb?

Syracuse, New York   Thomas Szasz
March 1989

Notes

1. Thomas S. Szasz, *The Myth of Mental Illness: Foundations of a Theory of Personal Conduct* (New York: Hoeber-Harper, 1961); rev. ed. (New York: Harper & Row, 1974).
2. Sigmund Freud, Letter to Marie Bonaparte, 13 August 1937, in Ernst L. Freud, ed., *Letters of Sigmund Freud*, trans. by Tania and James Stern (New York: Basic Books, 1960), 436.
3. Sir Hartley Shawcross, *Trial of the Major War Criminals Before the International Military Tribunal*, Nuremberg, Germany. Proceedings 19 July–29 July 1946, vol. 19, 26 July 1946, 467.
4. Paul S. Appelbaum, "The Right To Refuse Treatment with Antipsychotic Medications: Retrospect and Prospect," *American Journal of Psychiatry*, 145 (April 1988): 413–19.
5. Ibid., 414.
6. Roger Scruton, Editorial note, in Ryszard Legutko, "Do Liberals Love Liberty?" *Salisbury Review*, September 1988, 30.
7. Special Section: "Dangerousness and the Civil Commitment Process," *American Journal of Psychiatry*, 146 (February 1989): 170–93.

8. Loren H. Roth, "Four Studies of Mental Health Commitments" (Editorial), ibid., 135–37.

9. Cal McCrystal, "The Big Apple Turns Sour," *Sunday Times Magazine* (London), 12 February 1989, 24–37.

10. Charles Dickens, quoted in John Forster, *The Life of Charles Dickens* (2 vols.; London: Dent/Everyman's Library, 1966), vol. 1, 194.

Preface to the First Edition

LIKE A versatile actor, the modern psychiatrist plays many roles on the stage of social action. One of these roles—that of the psychoanalyst or psychotherapist engaged in a private, two-person relationship with his patient—has received undue emphasis. I say this not because I do not consider this sort of psychotherapy the most important function of the psychiatrist, but because, in actuality, it constitutes a very small part of the professional work of present-day psychiatrists.

Psychiatric activity is medical in name only. For the most part, psychiatrists are engaged in attempts to change the behavior and values of individuals, groups, institutions, and sometimes even of nations. Hence, psychiatry is a form of social engineering. It should be recognized as such.

This being the case, it is important to know what sorts of behavior and values psychiatrists promote. But it is widely maintained that psychiatrists are not social engineers but doctors and therapists. Further, that insofar as they are social engineers, their goal is to advance not ethical but health values. Instead of remaking individuals and society to give greater scope, say, to individualism and critical rationalism, as the philosophers of the Enlightenment sought to do, the modern psychiatrist tries to remake individuals and society to promote mental health. So-called health values have thus tended to replace moral and political values. This explains why, in the voluminous psychiatric publications on many subjects, the reader will rarely, if ever, encounter the idea of liberty.

This present book has two major aims: first, to present a critical inquiry into the current social, and especially legal, uses of psychiatry; second, to offer a reasoned dissent from what I consider the theory and practice of false psychiatric liberalism. Most of the legal and social applications of psychiatry, undertaken in the name of psychiatric liberalism, are actually instances of despotism. To be sure, this type of despotism is based on health values, but it is despotism nonetheless. Why? Because the promoters of mental health do not eschew coercive methods but, on the contrary, eagerly embrace them. Just as in democracy there lurks the danger of tyranny by the majority, so in mental-health legislation there lurks the danger of tyranny by therapy.

The book is addressed not only to lawyers, psychiatrists, and social scientists but also to the intelligent layman. Indeed, the last may find it especially useful, for organized psychiatry poses a much graver threat to him than it does to the professionals.

Like any knowledge, psychiatric knowledge may be made to serve almost any cause. I shall try to show that today psychiatry in the United States is all too often used to subvert traditional political guarantees of individual liberty. Benjamin Franklin warned us, "They that can give up essential liberty to obtain a little temporary safety, deserve neither liberty nor safety." Yet today Americans seem ready to sacrifice liberty to obtain a little temporary "mental health." To complicate matters, "mental health" is a vague, almost meaningless term. Probably it is only a new name for our age-old longing for security.

Today we are confronted not so much by the specter of political tyranny as by the specter of personal responsibility for a decent and meaningful life. Trying to escape this danger by pursuing the mirage of "mental health" is moral suicide. For Franklin was right. Regardless of how we define "mental health," if we sacrifice essential liberty for it, we shall deserve—and in fact have—neither liberty nor "mental health."

THOMAS S. SZASZ, M.D.

Syracuse, New York
October 1, 1962

Acknowledgments

I SHOULD like to express my thanks to all who have helped me with this book. In particular, Dr. Ernest Becker, Dr. Edward Engel, and Dr. Charles Reed, for their critical suggestions concerning various parts of the manuscript; the staff of the Library of the State University of New York, Upstate Medical Center in Syracuse, for untiring effort to secure the references consulted in the preparation of this volume; Mrs. Arthur Ecker, for conscientious editorial assistance; Mr. Peter Ritner of The Macmillan Company, for excellent suggestions for organizing the manuscript; and last but not least, my secretary, Mrs. Margaret Bassett, for her devoted labors, far beyond the call of any secretarial code of duty.

I wish also to thank the National Institute of Mental Health, United States Public Health Service, for a research grant (No. M–5706A), which partially supported the work for this book.

Earlier drafts of some of the material presented here have appeared in various journals and collections of essays. Chapters 1 and 2 were adapted from articles in *The American Psychologist*, volumes 15 and 16, 1960 and 1961. Passages in Chapter 3 have appeared in *The American Journal of Psychiatry*, Volume 114, 1957, and in *The Psychiatric Quarterly*, Volume 33, 1959. Parts of Chapters 4 and 6 were first published in *The Journal of Nervous and Mental Disease*, Volume 125, 1957. Chapter 7 contains material published in *Mental Hygiene*, Volume 45, 1961, and in Helmut Schoeck and James W. Wiggins (Editors), *Psychiatry and Responsibility* (Princeton, N.J.: Van Nostrand, 1962). Passages in Chapter 9 have appeared in the *Columbia Law Review*, Volume 58, 1958. Chapter 10 was adapted from an essay in Hans Toch (Editor), *Legal and Criminal Psychology* (New York: Holt, Rinehart and Winston, 1961). Parts of Chapter 11 were published in *The Journal of Nervous and Mental Disease*, Volume 131, 1960. Chapter 13 was adapted from an article in *The American Journal of Psychiatry*, Volume 119, 1962. Parts of Chapter 14 have appeared in *The Cleveland-Marshall Law Review*, Volume 9, 1960. Passages in Chapters 16 and 17 were published in *The Yale Review*, Volume 49, 1960, and in *The American Journal of Psychiatry*, Volume 115, 1958. I am grateful to the editors and publishers for their permissions to reprint and rework these articles for this book.

Finally, I wish to thank the many authors, editors, and publishers for permission to quote from copyrighted material. The sources indicated in the text are fully identified in the Bibliography.

LAW, LIBERTY,
and PSYCHIATRY

Introduction

> *The spirit of liberty is, indeed, a bold spirit. . . . It demands checks; it seeks for guards; it insists on securities; it entrenches itself behind strong defences, and fortifies itself with all possible care against the assaults of ambition and passion. This is the nature of constitutional liberty; and this is our liberty, if we will rightly understand and preserve it.*
>
> DANIEL WEBSTER (1834)

The Concept of Liberty and the Origin of Psychiatry

MOST SCIENTIFIC disciplines have grown from a single stock, by a kind of progressive enlargement of a primitive nucleus of knowledge and skills. Biology, chemistry, and physics have developed in this fashion. But not psychiatry. This discipline was born of two parents, by a kind of cross-fertilization.

Before the Freudian revolution, psychiatry was both a medical enterprise, concerned with people who were considered *sick,* and a legal and penological enterprise, concerned with people who were *imprisoned.* During the eighteenth and nineteenth centuries, psychiatry and law were much more closely intertwined than at present. Most of the prominent pre-Freudian psychiatrists were experts in "medical jurisprudence." Today this is no longer true. In fact, many psychiatrists have little or no contact with or interest in legal matters. Nevertheless, psychiatry still bears evidence of its dual heritage.

1

There are still many significant connections between law and psychiatry, even though they are frequently obscured by regarding legal actions as punitive and psychiatric actions as therapeutic. This is a false dichotomy. Actually, law and psychiatry are similar in that both disciplines are concerned with *norms of conduct* and *methods of social control.* Curiously, although liberty is often discussed in legal and political writings, it is seldom mentioned in psychiatric works. Probably the main reason for this is that liberty sounds too unlike anything on which doctors of medicine ought to have a professional opinion. Thus, instead of liberty, modern psychiatric authors use words like "maturity" and "independence" as if they referred to notions of psychological health having nothing to do with liberty. But this is not so. The ill-defined concepts of mental health and illness are a hiding place for certain moral values, among them liberty.

Psychiatric history sustains this argument. Modern psychiatry was born a few years after the founding of the United States of America. On May 24, 1798, Philippe Pinel removed the chains from one of the most feared patients at the Bicêtre, the Paris asylum for male lunatics. Thus, the historical paradigm of psychiatric treatment is neither prescribing medicines nor performing operations, but giving an imprisoned human being a measure of freedom. Esquirol and Ferrus, the two outstanding French psychiatrists of the first half of the nineteenth century, were both students of Pinel. More than anything else, they were prison-reformers.

Despite the fact that efforts to liberate mental patients began in 1798, they are still not free. "It should not be thought, however, that with the action of Pinel's the liberation of patients was complete. . . . Again and again the patient had to be freed of chains, though the chains were no longer visible ones, and again and again there resulted a new psychiatry from such a liberation" (van den Berg, 1955, page 86). Either society must seek to deprive mental patients of their freedom, or mental patients themselves must seek to be enslaved, or both. Later we shall analyze each of these possibilities. For the present, these reflections are intended only to suggest why I think liberty is a crucial concept for both psychiatry and law.

Health Values and Moral Values

Before we can understand the present-day connections between psychiatry and liberty, we must be clear about exactly how health values have usurped the place of moral values. Let me illustrate this point with a few typical quotations.

According to Hartmann (1960), the purpose of psychoanalytic treatment is "the aim of every therapy, and the value of this therapeutic aim is not questioned; moral considerations are kept from interfering with it" (page 20). Elsewhere Hartmann stated: "I suppose we should leave out of our discussion the problem of 'choice' which we meet here" (page 49). We could hardly wish for a more striking example on the part of a psychiatrist, and in this case, a psychoanalyst, of avoiding the issue of liberty in its simplest sense, that is, freedom to choose among alternative courses of action.

Hartmann's views exemplify the position of those psychiatrists who refuse to look at moral issues and instead accept unquestioningly certain health values. Another common position is to acknowledge the significance of moral and political values, but to define as mental health that which one considers morally good, and as mental illness that which one considers morally evil. Brock Chisholm's (1946) writings illustrate this approach. He asks why we fight wars, and answers:

Many of them are easy to list—prejudice, isolationism, the ability emotionally and uncritically to believe unreasonable things, excessive desire for material or power, excessive fear of others, belief in a destiny to control others, vengeance, ability to avoid seeing and facing unpleasant facts and taking appropriate action. These are probably the main reasons we find ourselves involved in wars. *They are all well known and recognized neurotic symptoms* [italics added; page 5].

Does Chisholm express himself loosely or metaphorically? No. Apparently he means what he says quite literally. Moreover, his views are typical of the psychiatrist turned social reformer. Writes Chisholm:

The necessity to fight wars, whether as aggressor or as a defender who could have, but has not, taken steps to prevent war occurring, is as much a *pathological psychiatric symptom as is a phobia or the antisocial behavior of a criminal* who has been dominated by a stern and unreasonable father [italics added; page 7].

This is pacifism disguised in psychiatric jargon. It is especially interesting that this is the view of a man who distinguished himself as a general in the Royal Canadian Medical Corps during the Second World War.

Implicit in Chisholm's writings is an attack on the morality of others, from the vantage point of his own morality. Chisholm, however, commits the traditional mistake of the naïve moralist, considering his own system of values not morality but rationality. Chisholm attacks morality as a general evil, and calls the concept of right and wrong a "perversion" (page 7). Further, he asserts that the "reinterpretation and eventual eradication of the concept of right and wrong . . . are the belated objectives of practically all effective psychotherapy" (page 9). And he adds: "The fact is that most psychiatrists and psychologists and many other respectable people have escaped from these moral chains and are able to observe and think freely. . . . If the race is to be freed from its crippling burden of good and evil it must be psychiatrists who take the original responsibility. This is a challenge which must be met" (page 9).

These are appalling suggestions. I believe, as do many others, that the burden of good and evil lies not too heavily but too lightly on the shoulders of modern man. All too often, modern man tries to shed the burden and to delegate moral leadership to others. The major Western religions—except, perhaps, the most enlightened brands of Protestantism —have always advocated this. In our own day, Fascists and Communists have built their empires on this basis. And now Chisholm and many of his colleagues advocate not that every man should assume more responsibility, but, on the contrary, that he should delegate his responsibility to psychiatrists.

Here is another example, this one from Overstreet's book *The Great Enterprise* (1952), of social engineering disguised as mental health promotion:

A man, for example, may be angrily against racial equality, public housing, the TVA, financial and technical aid to backward countries, organized labor, and the preaching of social rather than salvational religion. . . . Such people may appear "normal" in the sense that they are able to hold a job and otherwise maintain their status as members of society; but they are, we now recognize, well along the road toward mental illness [page 115].

My aim, of course, is not to judge the moral values of the psychiatrists cited. I merely wish to show that moral and political values may be redefined as health values. This sort of redefinition will play an important part in many of the issues to be considered in this book.

This brief discussion of health values and moral values should warn the reader of a recurrent problem about psychiatry. I refer to the persistent confusion between two distinct psychiatric roles—namely, the psychiatrist as an *analyzer* of life-games and meanings, and as a *giver* of games and meanings. This distinction is displayed in two ways. One is the posture of the psychiatrist *offering* his wares—call it analysis, help, therapy, or what not—to self-responsible, adult buyers. The other is the posture of the psychiatrist *coercing* others, with police power if necessary, to submit themselves to his control. His is not the role of vendor vis-à-vis buyer, but rather of civil servant imposing conduct and values on those who are subject to him.

The Psychiatrist's Dilemma: Autonomy, Coercion, and Mental Health

As long as the psychiatrist or psychotherapist confines his efforts within the walls of his private consulting room—as Freud did, for the most part—he may be able to avoid certain moral dilemmas. When he steps outside, however, he can escape them no longer. When he does this, the psychotherapist must give up his role as analyzer of the games people play and of the meanings they attribute to their actions, and must instead become a social engineer. His dilemma is this: What methods should he use to promote mental health? Specifically, he must decide what values to attach to personal freedom and responsibility, and when to justify the use of force.

What do psychiatrists mean when they advocate large-scale protection of mental health? Ostensibly this is a sort of public health venture, like smallpox vaccination. Usually an effort is made to enlist public cooperation. If this fails, however, it is considered justified to resort to coercive measures. The morality of such coercion rests on the premise that although the measure violates the wishes of particular persons, it is needed to protect the health of the majority.

Health values are thus treated differently than ordinary moral, political, or religious values. This is exemplified by the attitude of the government toward public health hazards and its attitude toward moral dangers.

The American people approve of the right of the government to compel people to be vaccinated against smallpox, for the unvaccinated person is a potential danger to the community. It is important, also, that vaccination against smallpox is a safe procedure. However, spreading infection is not the only way for people to harm one another. For example, deeply religious persons may consider atheistic ideas "poisonous" and may feel justified in demanding that the spread of such toxins also be controlled by the state. Conversely, atheists may regard religious ideas as harmful, especially for children, and may wish to see such teachings banned.

What is the American political ethic about matters like these? Simply stated, it demands that people should be free to advocate values of all kinds. The government is expected to maintain a laissez-faire attitude about this, so long as people act peacefully; it is expected, however, to step in and prevent individuals or groups from imposing their values on others by coercive means. In other words, all types of ideas and values may be *offered*. The promoters may also try to *persuade* others to buy their ethical merchandise. But they may not use force to *compel* the buyer to take something he does not want.

Much of this book centers upon this issue. For in psychiatry the burning question is: Which methods are justified, and which are not, for promoting and enforcing so-called mental health? I am opposed to coercive methods in the mental health field. I also believe it is important for lawyers, psychiatrists, and the public to think about this problem and to reach conclusions of their own.

The redefinition of moral values as health values will now appear in a new light. If people believe that health values justify coercion, but that moral and political values do not, those who wish to coerce others will tend to enlarge the category of health values at the expense of the category of moral values. We are already far along this road.

Liberty Against Psychiatry

Liberty, declared the Founding Fathers, is an unalienable human right, second in importance only to the right to life. Unfortunately, emotionally powerful symbols tend to have intellectually imprecise meanings. Although we cannot easily define liberty, we can, with a little effort, understand what people mean by it.

In its most elementary sense, to be at liberty—or to be free—means to be unfettered. Hence, the exact content of liberty will depend on the impediments a person or group wishes to overcome. When the impediment is political oppression, liberty is political freedom. When the impediment is feudalism, liberty is Socialism or Communism. When the impediment is theological tyranny, liberty is religious freedom. And when the impediment is starvation, liberty is adequate nutrition. It need not surprise us that although all people assert their love of freedom, to each person it means something different (De Jouvenel, 1953).

The impediment I want to consider here is restraint on persons exercised by psychiatrists by virtue of the powers vested in them by law. For those oppressed by psychiatrists, liberty means freedom from psychiatric coercion.

This may seem startling. We are accustomed to thinking of psychiatrists as physicians who help people. Of course, they do that too. But let us not forget that organized groups have always tried to dominate and exploit others. For this historical reason it is characteristic of Anglo-American polity to distrust any group entrusted with power. We owe many of our cherished personal and political freedoms to this attitude.

In this book I am concerned with the psychiatric abuses of power, and also with possible ways of combating them. Many specific suggestions for reform in the mental health field will be offered. A basic remedy may be summed up in three words: "Liberty against psychiatry." I use this phrase in the sense in which Professor Corwin (1928–1929), the great historian of the Constitution, spoke of "liberty against government." As used by Corwin (1948), and presumably as understood by the framers of the Constitution, liberty is a juridical concept. Primarily it means a constitutional limitation of the legislative branch of government, enforceable by the courts. In addition, liberty "always implies the distinct and independent identity of the individual from the political order of which he is a member" (page 3). And, more specifically:

Liberty signifies the absence of restraints imposed by other persons upon our own freedom of choice and action—that and nothing more recondite. But once again the subject dichotomizes itself, namely, along the line which separates *private* persons, our neighbors, as possible sources of restraints upon our freedom of choice and action from persons who are clothed with authority to restrain us— *government,* in short. Or to approach the subject from the opposite angle, we enjoy *civil liberty* because of the restraints which government imposes upon our neighbors in our behalf and *constitutional liberty* because of the constitutional restraints under which government itself operates when it seeks to impose restraints upon us [italics in the original; page 7].

Constitutionalism has aptly been called an "experiment in ordered liberty" (Rossiter, 1955). According to this system, the liberty we enjoy, as well as the necessary limits on it, are not regulated by the opinions of experts, but by laws rationally conceived, carefully formulated, and impartially administered. This principle, best known as the rule of law, is threatened by many contemporary psychiatric practices. I shall try to show exactly where and how it is threatened. But let us remember, throughout the discussion that follows, that unless we favor a therapeutic tyranny that knows no restraints in the pursuit of its interests, we must consider, more seriously than we have thus far, the controls under which psychiatric power should operate.

PART ONE » *Psychiatry as a Science*

CHAPTER 1 » *What is*
Mental Illness?

A myth is, of course, not a fairy story. It is the presentation of facts belonging in one category in the idioms belonging to another. To explode a myth is accordingly not to deny the facts but to re-allocate them.

—GILBERT RYLE (1949, page 8)

AT THE core of virtually all contemporary psychiatric theories and practices lies the concept of mental illness. This is especially so in forensic psychiatry—that is, in those areas of life where psychiatrists seek to influence the legal process. For example, although anthropologists, political scientists, psychologists, social workers, and sociologists all address themselves to problems of human conduct, only psychiatrists are considered experts on mental illness. We shall begin, therefore, with a critical examination of this concept.°

Let us launch our inquiry by asking, somewhat rhetorically, whether there is such a thing as mental illness. My reply is that there is not. Of course, mental illness is not a thing or physical object. It can exist only in the same sort of way as do other theoretical concepts. Yet, to those who believe in them, familiar theories are likely to appear, sooner or later, as "objective truths" or "facts." During certain historical periods, explana-

---

° In my book *The Myth of Mental Illness* (1961), I traced in detail the origin and evolution of the concept of mental illness. My present aim is to present certain less technical considerations which lead to the same conclusions as I have reached there.

tory conceptions such as deities, witches, and instincts appeared not only as theories but as *self-evident* causes of a vast number of events. Today mental illness is widely regarded in a somewhat similar fashion, that is, as the cause of innumerable diverse happenings.

As an antidote to the complacent use of the notion of mental illness—as self-evident phenomenon, theory, or cause—let us ask: What is meant by the assertion that a person is mentally ill? In this chapter I shall describe briefly the main uses of the concept of mental illness. I shall argue that this notion has outlived whatever usefulness it may have had and that it now functions as a myth.

Mental Illness as a Sign of Brain Disease

The notion of mental illness derives its main support from such phenomena as syphilis of the brain or delirious conditions—intoxications, for instance—in which persons may manifest certain disorders of thinking and behavior. Correctly speaking, however, these are diseases of the brain, not of the mind. According to one school of thought, *all* so-called mental illness is of this type. The assumption is made that some neurological defect, perhaps a very subtle one, will ultimately be found to explain all the disorders of thinking and behavior. Many contemporary psychiatrists, physicians, and other scientists hold this view, which implies that people's troubles cannot be caused by conflicting personal needs, opinions, social aspirations, values, and so forth. These difficulties—which I think we may simply call *problems in living*—are thus attributed to physicochemical processes which in due time will be discovered (and no doubt corrected!) by medical research.

Mental illnesses are thus regarded as basically no different from other diseases. The only difference, in this view, between mental and bodily disease is that the former, affecting the brain, manifests itself by means of mental symptoms; whereas the latter, affecting other organ systems—for example, the skin, liver, and so on—manifests itself by means of symptoms referable to those parts of the body.

In my opinion, this view is based on two fundamental errors. In the first place, a disease of the brain, analogous to a disease of the skin or bone, is a neurological defect, not a problem in living. For example, a *defect* in a person's visual field may be explained by correlating it with certain definite lesions in the nervous system. On the other hand, a person's *belief* —whether it be in Christianity, in Communism, or in the idea that his internal organs are rotting and that his body is already dead—cannot be explained by a defect or disease of the nervous system. Explanations of this sort of occurrence—assuming that one is interested in the belief itself and does not regard it simply as a symptom or expression of something else that is more interesting—must be sought along different lines.

The second error is epistemological. It consists of interpreting communications about ourselves and the world around us as symptoms of neurological functioning. This is an error not in observation or reasoning, but rather in the organization and expression of knowledge. In the present case, the error lies in making a dualism between mental and physical symptoms, a dualism which is a habit of speech and not the result of known observations. Let us see if this is so.

In medical practice, when we speak of physical disturbances we mean either signs (for example, fever) or symptoms (for example, pain). We speak of mental symptoms, on the other hand, when we refer to a patient's communications about himself, others, and the world about him. He might state that he is Napoleon or that he is being persecuted by the Communists. These would be considered mental symptoms *only* if the observer believed that the patient was *not* Napoleon or that he was *not* being persecuted by the Communists. This makes it apparent that the statement "X is a mental symptom" involves rendering a judgment. The judgment entails, moreover, a covert comparison or matching of the patient's ideas, concepts, or beliefs with those of the observer and the society in which they live. The notion of mental symptom is therefore inextricably tied to the *social,* and particularly the *ethical,* context in which it is made, just as the notion of bodily symptom is tied to an *anatomical* and *genetic* context (Szasz, 1957b).

To sum up: For those who regard mental symptoms as signs of brain disease, the concept of mental illness is unnecessary and misleading. If they mean that people so labeled suffer from diseases of the brain, it would seem better, for the sake of clarity, to say that and not something else.

Mental Illness as a Name for Problems in Living

The term "mental illness" is also widely used to describe something very different from a disease of the brain. Many people today take it for granted that living is an arduous process. Its hardship for modern man, moreover, derives not so much from a struggle for biological survival as from the stresses and strains inherent in the social intercourse of complex human personalities. In this context, the notion of mental illness is used to identify or describe some feature of an individual's so-called personality. Mental illness—as a deformity of the personality, so to speak —is regarded as the cause of interpersonal or social disharmony. It is implicit in this view that social intercourse between people is regarded as something inherently harmonious, its disturbance being due solely to the presence of mental illness in many people. Clearly, this is faulty reasoning, for it makes the abstraction "mental illness" into a *cause,* even though this abstraction was originally created to serve as a shorthand expression for certain types of human behavior. It now becomes necessary to ask: What kinds of behavior are regarded as indicative of mental illness, and by whom?

The concept of illness, whether bodily or mental, implies deviation from a clearly defined norm. In the case of physical illness, the norm is the structural and functional integrity of the human body. Although the desirability of physical health, as such, is an ethical value, what health is can be stated in anatomical and physiological terms. What is the norm deviation from which is regarded as mental illness? This question cannot be easily answered. But whatever this norm may be, we can be certain of only one thing: namely, that it must be stated in terms of psychosocial, ethical, and legal concepts. For example, notions such as "excessive re- pression" or "acting out an unconscious impulse" illustrate the use of psychological concepts for judging so-called mental health and illness. The idea that chronic hostility, vengefulness, or divorce are indicative of mental illness is an illustration of the use of ethical norms (that is, the desirability of love, kindness, and a stable marriage relationship). Finally, the widespread psychiatric opinion that only a mentally ill person would commit homicide illustrates the use of a legal concept as a norm of mental health. The norm from which deviation is measured, when one speaks of a mental illness, is a *psychosocial and ethical* one. Yet, the remedy is sought in terms of *medical* measures which—it is hoped and assumed— are free from wide differences of ethical value. The definition of the dis- order and the terms in which its remedy is sought are therefore at odds with one another. The practical significance of this covert conflict between the alleged nature of the defect and the remedy can hardly be exaggerated.

Having identified the norms used for measuring deviations in cases of mental illness, we shall now turn to the question: Who defines the norms and hence the deviation? Two basic answers may be offered. First, it may be the person himself—that is, the patient—who decides that he deviates from a norm. For example, an artist may believe that he suffers from a work inhibition. He may implement this conclusion by seeking help *for* himself from a psychotherapist. Second, it may be someone other than the patient who decides that the latter is deviant—for example, relatives, physicians, legal authorities, society generally. A psychiatrist may then be hired by persons other than the patient to do something *to* the patient in order to correct the deviation.

These considerations underscore the importance of asking the question, "Whose agent is the psychiatrist?" and of giving a candid answer to it. The psychiatrist (or nonmedical psychotherapist) may be the agent of the patient, the relatives, the school, the military services, a business organization, a court of law, and so forth. In speaking of the psychiatrist as the agent of these persons or organizations, it is not implied that his values concerning norms, or his ideas and aims concerning the proper nature of remedial action, must coincide with those of his employer. For example, a patient in individual psychotherapy may believe that his salvation lies in a new marriage; his psychotherapist need not share this hypothesis. As the patient's agent, however, he must not resort to social or legal force to prevent the patient from putting his beliefs into action. If his *contract* is with the patient, the psychiatrist (psychotherapist) may disagree with him or stop his treatment, but he cannot engage others to obstruct the patient's aspirations (Szasz, 1962). Similarly, if a psychiatrist is retained by a court to determine the sanity of an offender, he need not fully share the legal authorities' values and intentions in regard to the criminal, nor the means deemed appropriate for dealing with him. The psychiatrist cannot testify, however, that the accused is not insane, but that the legislators are—for passing the law which decrees the offender's actions illegal. Such an opinion could be voiced, of course, but not in a courtroom, and not by a psychiatrist who is there to assist the court in performing its daily work.

Clearly, psychiatry is much more intimately related to problems of ethics than is medicine. I used the word "psychiatry" here to refer to the contemporary discipline concerned with problems in living, and not with diseases of the brain, which belong to neurology. Difficulties in human relations can be analyzed, interpreted, and given meaning only within specific social and ethical contexts. Accordingly, the psychiatrist's socio-ethical orientations will influence his ideas on what is wrong with the patient, on what deserves comment or interpretation, in what directions change might be desirable, and so forth. Even in medicine proper, these factors play a role, as illustrated by the divergent orientations which physicians, depending on their religious affiliations, have toward such things as birth control and therapeutic abortion. Can anyone really believe that a psychotherapist's ideas on religion, politics, and related issues play no role in his practical work? If, on the other hand, they do matter, what are we to infer from it? Does it not seem reasonable that perhaps we ought to have different psychiatric therapies—each recognized for the ethical positions which it embodies—for, say, Catholics and Jews, religious persons and atheists, democrats and Communists, white supremacists and Negroes, and so on? Indeed, if we look at the way psychiatry is actually practiced today, especially in the United States, we find that people seek psychiatric help in accordance with their social status and ethical beliefs (Hollingshead and Redlich, 1958). This should occasion no greater surprise than being told that practicing Catholics rarely frequent birth-control clinics.

To recapitulate: In contemporary social usage, the finding of mental illness is made by establishing a deviance in behavior from certain psychosocial, ethical, or legal norms. The judgment may be made, as in medicine, by the patient, the physician (psychiatrist), or others. Remedial action, finally, tends to be sought in a therapeutic—or covertly medical—framework. This creates a situation in which it is claimed that psychosocial, ethical, and/or legal deviations can be corrected by medical action. But is this rational?

Choice, Responsibility, and Psychiatry

While I argue that mental illnesses do not exist, obviously I do not wish to imply that the social and psychological occurrences *so labeled* do not exist. Like the personal and social troubles people had in the Middle Ages, they are real enough. What concerns us is the labels we give them, and, having labeled them, what we do about them. The demonologic conception of problems in living gave rise to therapy along theological lines. Today, a belief in mental illness implies—nay, requires—therapy along medical or psychotherapeutic lines.

I do not here propose to offer a new conception of "psychiatric illness" or a new form of "therapy." My aim is more modest and yet also more ambitious. It is to suggest that the phenomena now called mental illnesses be looked at afresh and more simply, that they be removed from the category of illnesses, and that they be regarded as the expressions of man's struggle with the problem of *how* he should live. By problems in living I refer to that explosive chain reaction which began with man's fall from divine grace by partaking of the fruit of the tree of knowledge. Man's awareness of himself and of the world about him seems to be a steadily expanding one, bringing in its wake an ever larger *burden of understanding* (an expression borrowed from Susanne Langer, 1942). This burden is to be expected, and must not be misinterpreted. Our only rational means for easing it is more understanding, and appropriate action based on it. The main alternative is to behave as if the burden were not what we perceive it to be, and to take refuge in an essentially theological view of man, whether this parades in scientific guise or not. But today is not a propitious time in human history for obscuring the issue of man's responsibility for his actions, by hiding it behind the skirt of an all-explaining conception of mental illness.

Conclusions

I have tried to show that the notion of mental illness has outlived whatever usefulness it may have had and that it now functions as a convenient myth. As such, it is a true heir to religious myths in general, and to the belief in witchcraft in particular.

When I assert that mental illness is a myth, I am not saying that personal unhappiness and socially deviant behavior do not exist; but I am saying that we categorize them as diseases at our own peril.

The expression "mental illness" is a metaphor which we have come to mistake for a fact. We call people physically ill when their body-functioning violates certain anatomical and physiological norms; similarly, we call people mentally ill when their personal conduct violates certain ethical, political, and social norms. This explains why many historical figures, from Jesus to Castro, and from Job to Hitler, have been diagnosed as suffering from this or that psychiatric malady.

Another way of highlighting the distinction between physical and mental sickness is to emphasize that physical illness is usually something that *happens* to us, whereas mental illness is something we *do* (or feel or think). Brown (1961) expressed the same idea when he wrote that "Neurosis is not a disease in the medically accepted sense; . . . it is not something a person *has* but rather something that he *is*" (page 81).

It may be objected that whether or not we choose to call certain events in the universe "mental illness" is chiefly a semantic issue. Yes and no. The point is that when a scientific judgment becomes the basis for social action, the consequences are far-reaching. For example, when equal protection of the laws is withdrawn because a person has been labeled "mentally ill," we are confronted with an act of discrimination. Surely, from the victim's point of view, it makes little difference whether his right to vote is denied because of his race, or whether his right to stand trial is denied because of his mental illness (Chapter 13). In the past, discrimination has been based chiefly on nationality, race, religion, and economic status; today, there is a mounting tendency to base it on psychiatric considerations. Since these practices rest on allegedly scientific grounds, and are implemented by professional persons, the ethical issues they pose are especially delicate.

Finally, the myth of mental illness encourages us to believe in its logical corollary: that social intercourse would be harmonious, satisfying, and the secure basis of a "good life" were it not for the disrupting influences of mental illness or "psychopathology." However, universal human happiness, in this form at least, is but another example of a wishful fantasy. I believe that human happiness is possible—not just for a select few, but on a scale hitherto unimaginable. But this can be achieved only if many men, not just a few, are willing and able to confront frankly, and tackle courageously, their ethical, personal, and social conflicts.

CHAPTER 2 » *Mental Illness:*
Disease or Derogation?

> *The psychiatric vocabulary and definitions, which once seemed such
> a liberating instrument for modern man, have now woven a tight and
> strangling noose around the neck of the brain.*
> —SEYMOUR KRIM (1959)

The Uses of Language

LANGUAGE HAS three main functions: to transmit information,
to induce mood, and to promote action (Reichenbach, 1947). It should be
emphasized that conceptual clarity is required only for the cognitive, or
information-transmitting, use of language. Lack of clarity may be no handi-
cap when language is used to influence people. Indeed, it might even be
an advantage.

The social sciences—psychiatry among them—are devoted to the study
of how people influence one another. The promotive use of language is,
therefore, a significant aspect of the observations the social sciences seek to
describe and explain. A major difficulty in this enterprise is that the social
sciences have no specialized idiom of their own. They use everyday language, which is often logically obscure, and which lends itself readily to
promotive usage. Thus, psychiatric and sociologic descriptions and explanations may offer promotive statements in the guise of cognitive asser-
tions. In other words, while allegedly *describing* conduct, psychiatrists
often *prescribe* it. To call someone sick—especially mentally sick—is an

18

example. When social science functions in this fashion, its own formulations present a barrier against the recognition of the very phenomena it seeks to elucidate and comprehend.

During the second half of the nineteenth century—when modern neurology and psychiatry originated—the rules of the game of living made it advantageous for a disabled person to be called sick. Confronted with such people—regardless of why they were disabled—physicians had two choices. They could classify, or rename as "sick," all who were disabled in any way, so as to improve their lot. Or they could have examined the rules, and could have extended the humane treatment accorded the sick to other members of society. Invariably, physicians adopted the first course. It was the morally expedient alternative.

The pioneer neuropsychiatrists—Charcot, Janet, Bernheim, Kraepelin, Freud, and others—were faced with the problem of labeling persons disabled by certain kinds of neuromuscular and sensory symptoms. Should they be called malingerers, hysterics, physically or mentally ill patients, or something else? Before Charcot, all those without demonstrable physical illness were usually diagnosed as malingerers. Thus, one of Charcot's alleged discoveries was not a discovery at all. Rather, it was a reclassification of malingerers as "hysterics" (Freud, 1893; Guillain, 1959; Szasz, 1961).

Semantic Conversion and Reconversion

Changing the name of "malingering" to "hysteria" left untouched the basic rule that physicians could treat some disabilities with kindness, others with hostility. The renaming was simply a useful maneuver for certain heretofore handicapped participants. In other words, the conversion of malingerers into hysterics was merely a device for transforming members of the outgroup into members of the ingroup.

Such a maneuver, it seems, invites its converse. For each step of "conversion," there is a corresponding step of "reconversion." This has occurred in the relationship of psychiatry to medicine in America.

During the first half of the twentieth century, human disabilities formerly called "malingering" (or sometimes "sin") were renamed as "mental illnesses." In part, this gave the bearers of the labels new citizenship in the land of the sick. Perhaps, for a while, this maneuver was effective. But soon, people bearing the titles of mental illnesses began to reacquire their former ill repute. Thus, the new label "mental illness" (and its variants) became only a substitute for the abandoned words of denigration. This is not to say that in some psychoanalytic writings, words such as "hysteria" or "schizophrenia" may not have a more precise, technical meaning. They sometimes do, and to that extent have a limited scientific usefulness.

Frequently, however, these terms are used, even by psychiatrists and psychoanalysts, only for their instrumental-promotive effect. When it is asserted, for example, that "Mr. A. is mentally ill," it may mean, "Do not pay any attention to what Mr. A. says"; or, "Don't take Mr. A. seriously"; or, "I suggest that you deprive Mr. A. of his civil liberties"; and so forth. If the person so labeled is a fellow psychiatrist, psychologist, or psychoanalyst, the assertion may mean, "Dr. A. is all wrong"; or, "Dr. A. is a poor psychotherapist; do not send him any patients"; and so forth. The expression "mental illness" as a convenient term of- derogation, denigration, or thinly veiled attack, has thus become part of everyday life.

This thesis may be illustrated by considering Ernest Jones's (1953–1957) biography of Freud, and some reactions to it. Fromm (1958) decried as unjust Jones's description of Ferenczi and Rank as mentally ill. The gist of his argument was that they were healthy mentally (whatever he meant by that) and that Jones called them sick only to impugn their stature. Fromm went even further. He implied that it was not Ferenczi and Rank who were sick, but Freud and Jones. Fromm could not have been unaware of the derogatory meaning of the expression "mental illness." And so, the cognitive function of a word is replaced by the instrumental. Instead of science, there is advertising. Instead of diagnosis, there is name-calling. And the game of psychiatric name-calling goes on and on, with new players aspiring to denigrate and injure others by finding them insane.

It is consistent with this view that not only did Freud, Jones, and others use the expression "mental illness" to belittle and injure others (particularly fellow professionals); they also employed its converse, "mental health," to promote those whom they liked and respected. For example, Freud found no signs of mental illness in his analysand, Frink, even though Frink behaved in a socially disordered manner before his analysis and "passed through a psychotic phase" during it. Wrote Jones (1957):

This year brought Freud a keen personal disappointment, second only to that concerning Rank. Frink of New York had resumed his analysis in Vienna in April, 1922, continuing until February, 1923, and Freud had formed the very highest opinion of him. He was, so Freud maintained, by far the *ablest American he had come across, the only one from whose gifts he expected something.* Frink had passed through a psychotic phase during his analysis—he had indeed to have a male nurse with him for a time—but Freud considered he had quite overcome it, and he *counted on his being the leading analyst in America.* Unfortunately, on returning to New York Frink behaved very arrogantly to the older analysts, particularly Brill, telling everyone how out of date they were. Frink's second marriage, which had caused so much scandal and on which high hopes of happiness had been set, had proved a failure, and his wife was suing for a divorce. That, together with the quarrels just mentioned, must have precipitated another attack. Frink wrote to me in November, 1923, that for reasons of ill health he had to give up his work for the Journal and also his private practice. In the following summer he was a patient in the Phipps Psychiatric Institute, and he never recovered his sanity. He died in the Chapel Hill Mental Hospital in North Carolina some ten years later [italics added; pages 105–106].

The Frink affair exemplifies the typical problems which arose in the subsequent course of psychoanalytic education and which are rampant today. Training analysts, especially those with proselytizing tendencies, are prone to see evidence of mental health in candidates they favor and consider worthy disciples. Contrariwise, candidates disliked by their training analysts, or who are in serious disagreement with them, are in danger of being found mentally unhealthy, and of requiring prolonged and repeated analyses. I do not imply that this is the only criterion for assessing "psychopathology" in training candidates. But it is a significant bias, and one that is inherent in the present organization of the psychoanalytic training system (Szasz, 1960a, 1961). Similar biases operate in other situations where the therapist is not solely the patient's agent.

In this connection, the criteria governing admission to psychoanalytic institutes are pertinent. Eisendorfer (1959), who served for many years as chairman of the New York Psychoanalytic Institute's committee on selection of candidates, stated: "Such factors as overt psychopathology, perversions, homosexuality, and antisocial psychopathic acting out automatically eliminate the candidate" (page 376). One paragraph later he noted, "A not uncommon characteristic of a considerable number of candidates (about ten percent) is a facade of normality.—A dogged determination to present himself as being normal, more often than not, serves as veneer to conceal chronic pathology" (page 377). Apparently Eisendorfer did not regard these two requirements—namely, presenting no overt psychopathology on the one hand, and presenting no facade of normality on the other—as mutually contradictory. But what else is left for the candidate to present, except, of course, "precisely the right kind of psychopathology" (my formulation). Eisendorfer's statements exemplify that psychoanalytic training organizations use the notion of psychopathology, and the process of naming, to promote their particular ends, rather than to communicate verifiable observations.

Eisendorfer stated that candidates diagnosed as having "perversions" or "overt psychopathology" are automatically excluded from acceptance. He did not specify the definition of perversion or psychopathology that was used. This makes for a convenient arrangement for the admissions committee, but gives no clue to the actual practices employed. Inasmuch as analytic training organizations have adopted this negative attitude toward psychopathology, it may not be a coincidence that their applicants present a facade of normality. At the same time, this allegedly pseudonormal attitude of present-day candidates is resented by many analysts. The possible connections between the prevailing psychoanalytic position toward so-called psychopathology and the candidate's facade of normality are, curiously, never discussed.

A final illustration of the contemporary usage of the term "mental illness" may be found in a portion of *Time* magazine's (June 23, 1958) commentary on Taft's (1958) biography of Rank. It read, in part, as follows:

In Rank's later years his behavior was more appropriate to the role of patient than of therapist. He went through one emotional crisis after another (diagnosed by famed Freud Biographer Ernest Jones as a mild manic-depressive psychosis), even suffered artist's and writer's block—a symptom that analysts claim to relieve most effectively. One thing certain from Biographer Taft's candid pages: In the post-Freud patter of the cocktail hour, Otto Rank was "sick, sick, sick" [page 68].

In this context, the word "sick" is used very differently than when the patient develops, for example, arteriosclerosis and coronary heart disease. Like malingering formerly, mental illness now implies not ordinary sickness but obnoxious and socially deviant behavior. There is a parallel between this and the revival of anti-Semitism in Central Europe after the First World War. The period of improvement in the life of the Jews resulting from religious and social conversion was soon followed by one of reconversion of the semantic and social changes to their original form. Thus, certain people who bore German names and professed belief in Christianity were—under the Nazi rules—once again treated as Jews, and with the conviction that persecuting Jews was the patriotic and right thing to do. Those who sought to improve their lot in life by semantic and religious conversion never challenged this rule. Indeed, many converted European Jews became identified with their aggressors. Thus, not only was this type of conversion an unsuccessful revolt against anti-Semitism—it was a covert way of fanning the flames of racial and religious intolerance. Accordingly, anti-Semitism was not given up by the ingroup. All that happened was that some Jews removed themselves from the "hated" and joined the "haters."

The events sketched have their parallels in medical psychology. The psychiatrists of the late nineteenth and early twentieth centuries—the former alienists—were regarded as outcasts by their medical colleagues. Contrast this with the public image and social role of the mid-twentieth century psychiatrist in the United States of America. His prestige often outranks that of other physicians. He has become a kind of supertherapist. And this is not all. He eulogizes his togetherness with his medical colleagues, and proudly proclaims his loyalty to medicine (Felix, 1961). And how is the loyalty of the present-day psychiatrist to medicine demonstrated? By an attitude of aggressive condescension toward psychologists and other nonmedical psychotherapists.

Relabeling and the Problem of Professional Integrity

The Nazis removed converted Jews from the class of nonpersecutables, and returned them to the class of persecutables, which they formerly occupied. Similarly, modern medical and psychiatric customs and opinions have removed the "mentally ill" from among the class of fully respectable patients, and returned them to the class of social deviants and troublemakers, which they formerly occupied. This is particularly evident in the present-day psychiatric posture toward patients who are stuck with labels such as "passive-aggressive personality," "psychopathic or sociopathic personality," "dependency reaction," and the like.

It behooves physicians, psychologists, jurists, social scientists—and intelligent laymen as well—to examine carefully both scientific and everyday attitudes toward so-called mental illness and its alleged victims. This does not gainsay the progress that has been made in psychiatry since the days of Charcot. Yet, in this very progress may lie the seeds of its destruction. For psychiatry—in contrast to the nonmedical branches of social science—has acquired much social prestige and power through an essentially misleading association with the practice of medicine.

In order to incorporate into psychiatry the scientific advances that have been made, I believe that our knowledge should be recast in a psychosocial, linguistic, and ethical framework. This would reemphasize the differences, rather than the similarities, between man the social being and man the mammal. It would also result in abandoning the persistent attempts to convert psychologists and sociologists to physicians and physicists. In turn, these people themselves would no longer need to aspire to these roles.

The psychosocial disciplines must establish their rightful place among the sciences. This cannot be done by imitating other, better established, sciences. Newly developing sciences, like youthful persons, can establish their integrity only by frankly recognizing their historical origins and by fearlessly searching out their unique characteristics and potentialities.

CHAPTER 3 » *Classification in Psychiatry*

Seeing then that truth consists in the right ordering of names in our affirmations, a man that seeks precise truth, has need to remember what every name he uses stands for; and to place it accordingly; or else he will find himself entangled in words, as a bird in lime-twigs; the more he struggles, the more belimed.
—THOMAS HOBBES (1651)

IF SO-CALLED mental illnesses are diseases, it should be possible to classify them as we classify other diseases. Although psychiatrists have tried hard, their efforts to construct systems of psychiatric nosology have been notably unsuccessful. Why? Because all such systems have attempted to encompass various methods and tasks, some of which were incompatible with others. Critical examination of the problem of psychiatric classification, which is the purpose of this chapter, should help us further to clarify the nature of the psychiatric enterprise.

What Does Psychiatric Nosology Classify?

There is ambiguity about the scope and limits of psychiatry. Is it a branch of medicine? If so, is it principally a diagnostic and therapeutic discipline, based on and utilizing the methods of physics and chemistry?

Or is psychiatry a social science, concerned with the study of human relationships? If so, it must be closely related to anthropology, psychology, and sociology, and must employ the concepts and methods of the social sciences. We can have two psychiatries, but not a combination of both, despite the insistence in many quarters that man is a psychosomatic unity.*

Consider, for example, general paresis. This diagnosis refers to a physicochemical phenomenon. The term does not describe any particular behavioral event. How then can we hope to bring it into a meaningful relation with other psychiatric diagnoses that refer only to behavioral events, such as hysteria, reactive depression, or situational maladjustment? Yet many such dissimilar concepts are now subsumed under the general category called "psychiatric diagnosis." It is as if, in the periodic table of elements, we would find coal, steel, and petroleum interspersed among items such as helium, carbon, and sulfur. This is the main reason the taxonomic system known as psychiatric nosology does not work, and why attempts to improve it, which have not considered this basic fact, have failed to satisfy anyone but their creators.

A second source of difficulty lies in the implications of the word "nosology," which means the classification of diseases. This immediately casts psychiatry into the medical mold. In this view, psychiatry is the study of diseases of the mind; psychopathology is the nosology based on this concept. This introduces the troublesome concept of mind (Ryle, 1949). Still others believe that psychiatric nosology should classify disorders of behavior. Thus, there is a tendency to combine three classes of concepts—brain, mind, and behavior. Not only do different psychiatrists use different categories, usually without specifying their respective schemes, but often they combine concepts from each to form a single taxonomic system. Illustrative is the *Standard Nomenclature* of the American Psychiatric Association, which recognizes, as mental illnesses, such diverse phenomena as general paresis, reactive depression, and homosexuality.

Although the term "psychiatric nosology" means the classification of psychiatric diseases, modern developments in psychiatry have led to new taxonomic possibilities. This has come about as psychiatry has developed into both a basic science and a set of clinical techniques. It is only as a clinical science that psychiatry is oriented toward diseases, diagnoses, and treatments. As a basic science, psychiatry, like other sciences, is oriented toward a nonjudgmental understanding of the phenomena it studies. Taxonomic systems of this type aim at ordering data to increase our sense of clarity, and at helping us master or control our subject matter. Classifications designed solely for the purpose of diagnosis and treatment represent a special type of taxonomic system. When we apply them to other, non-

---

* Religious faith and political action are more useful for producing unity in the midst of diversity than is science, which, as it progresses, reveals diversity where before there was unity.

therapeutic (for example, judicial) situations, the results are likely to be disastrous.

The principal categories to which the term "psychiatric nosology" is commonly applied are summarized in Table I.

An Operational Approach to Classification in Psychiatry

Classification is a special case of category formation. This process depends on the psychological characteristics of the person forming categories and on the social situation in which he participates. The dependence of the psychological variable on brain function was impressively demonstrated by Kurt Goldstein (1951). The effect of the social situation on category formation is so obvious that it may escape attention and explicit understanding. For example, it would be trivial to emphasize that from the point of view of an economist, there are no significant similarities between coal and

Table I FOUR BASIC CATEGORIES OF PSYCHIATRIC CLASSIFICATION

Psychiatry: its subject, method, and aim	Nosology
I. Diseases of the brain; physicochemical method; prevention and cure of brain disease.	Neuropathology: a part of medical diagnosis; e.g., general paresis, toxic psychosis.
II. Diseases of the mind; physicochemical and/or psychosocial methods; prevention and cure of mental illness.	Psychopathology: a part of medical diagnosis, yet different from it; the classification of so-called functional illnesses; e.g., conversion hysteria, schizophrenia.
III. Diseases of social behavior; psychosocial method; prevention and cure of social pathology.	Sociopathology: a system based on the medical model, with assumed or explicit norms of social conduct; e.g., crime, homosexuality.
IV. Human behavior and relations; group behavior and personal conduct; psychosocial method; scientific mastery and behavior change.	An hypothetical, nondiagnostic system of classification; identification of significant recurrent patterns; e.g., transference.

diamond. The economist is eager to distinguish diamond, gold, platinum, and money as different members of the same class—class membership being assigned on the basis of fiscal considerations. The chemist, on the other hand, may classify diamond and coal as chemically similar members of the class called carbon.

This example illustrates what I mean by an operational approach to classification. The word "operational" is used to denote not only the characteristic methods of observation but also both the social situation in which the observation is made and its purposes. Let us look at psychiatric nosology in this light.

The social situations in which psychiatric observations are made are diverse. Nevertheless, it is generally assumed that the same system of classification should apply to all. Here is a list—by no means exhaustive—of the major psychiatric situations: the mental hospital, private psychiatric practice, the psychiatric clinic for adults, the child-guidance clinic, the psychoanalytic training system, the military service, the court of law, and the prison. Psychiatric diagnoses are made and used in each of these settings. However, the methods of examination employed, and the purposes for which diagnoses are made, differ. I submit that a system of psychiatric nosology developed in one situation cannot be expected to be meaningful and serviceable in another.

The fact remains, however, that items from different systems of psychiatric classification are shuffled about with abandon on the current American social scene. For example, concepts applicable, perhaps, to mental hospitals are used in politics and law, while others are transferred from psychoanalysis to general psychiatry. This practice has penetrated into every aspect of psychiatry, and has affected psychoanalysis no less than forensic psychiatry (Weinstock, 1957).

I shall not try to analyze the characteristics of the various psychiatric situations mentioned. It should suffice for our purposes to be aware of the differences among them. The salient features of each are presented in Table II.

A few comments about the data summarized in Table II may further clarify the purely situational relevance of psychiatric diagnostic terms. Let us focus our attention on the meaning of the term "psychosis" in three situations—the state hospital, private psychoanalytic practice, and the courtroom.

In the state mental hospital, the principal diagnostic issue is whether or not the patient is psychotic (Bowman and Rose, 1951; Diethelm, 1953). The diagnosis of psychosis is employed to justify the patient's forcible retention in the hospital, and also to legitimize punishing him in the name of therapy.

In the psychoanalytic situation, the patient may be considered psychotic if he exhibits certain types of resistances to being analyzed. Or the analyst may use this term to describe the "excessive" use of certain mental mechanisms—for example, "too much" projection. Thus, the concept of psychosis

Table II CHARACTERISTIC FEATURES OF THE PRINCIPAL PSYCHIATRIC SITUATIONS ON THE CURRENT AMERICAN SCENE

Social Setting	Object of Observation	Observer	Principal Aims of the Classification	Principal Action Patterns
I. Mental Hospital				
a. State Mental Hospital	Hospitalized mental patient; may be confined voluntarily or involuntarily; usually in overt conflict with social norms.	State hospital psychiatrist: an employee of the state; mainly an agent of society.	To justify patient's retention in, or discharge from, the hospital; to explain patient's conduct by naming it.	Segregation and forcible restraint; "defacement"; coercion into compliance with hospital authorities.
b. Hospital for the Criminally Insane	Hospitalized mental patient; always confined involuntarily; always in overt conflict with social norms and with the law.	Same as above; the psychiatrist's role as guard conflicts sharply with his role as therapist.	Same as above; also to prevent patient from standing trial, or to justify his indefinite incarceration.	Same as above; also custodial care for social outcasts.
c. Private Mental Hospital	Hospitalized mental patient; may be confined voluntarily or involuntarily; usually in conflict with social norms.	Psychiatrist is an employee of private hospital; his allegiance is divided between the needs of the hospital and the needs of the patient.	To explain patient's disorder; to justify the treatment; to communicate with others.	Segregation and sometimes forcible restraint; treatment of mental disorder; recreation, etc.

28

Table II—Continued

II. Private Psychiatric Practice			
a. Organic-Directive Practice	The patient; members of his family; records; information from other sources, e.g., medical colleagues, employers, etc.	The private psychiatrist; his allegiance is split between the needs of the patient and the demands of the patient's family.	To facilitate the psychiatrist's thinking; to justify the treatment; to communicate with colleagues and others.	Various types of organic-directive psychiatric treatments; manipulation of the environment; commitment.
b. Psychoanalytic Practice	The patient only.	The psychiatrist is the agent of the patient only.	To facilitate the psychiatrist's thinking; to organize and present data for scientific purposes.	The psychoanalytic method of therapy; limited to verbal communications with patient.
III. Psychoanalytic Training System	The candidate-patient; his training activities.	Training analyst; his allegiance is split between the needs of the patient and the demands of the psychoanalytic training system.	To judge the candidate's fitness for progress in the institute; to justify his acceptance or rejection.	An attempt to combine psychoanalytic therapy with decision making about the patient's fitness for his chosen occupation.
IV. Mental Health Clinic	The adult psychiatric outpatient; members of his family; records; information from other sources, e.g., medical colleagues, employers, etc.	Employees of the clinic: psychiatrist, clinical psychologist, social worker; their allegiance is divided between the needs of the patient and the demands of the community.	To serve as a guide for treatment; to communicate with colleagues and others; to justify acceptance for or rejection from treatment.	Various types of psychiatric treatment; environmental manipulation; reports to other social agencies; commitment, etc.

Table II—Continued

Setting			
V. Child Guidance Clinic	The child patient; his parents who are potential patients; other sources of information, especially the school.	Employees of the clinic: child psychiatrist, clinical psychologist, social worker; they try to balance the often conflicting needs of the community, the parents, and the child.	Same as in IV above.	Same as in IV above; also, treatment of one or both parents, in addition to the child.
VI. Military Service	Military personnel; the patient and his entire social environment.	The military psychiatrist; primarily an agent of the military service, only secondarily an agent of the patient.	To justify disposition of the "case"; to communicate with other military agencies, e.g., compensation board.	Psychiatric treatment; return to duty; discharge from service.
VII. Courtroom	The defendant; sometimes others, e.g., a witness, or society itself.	The psychiatrist as a legally recognized expert in "mental diseases" and "mental treatments"; an agent of the defense, of the prosecution, or of the court.	To justify particular recommendations about defendant; e.g., that he should or should not be permitted to stand trial, etc.	Decision making about the defendant; e.g., commitment to hospital for the criminally insane; acquittal by reason of insanity, etc.
VIII. Prison	The prisoner; his records; other sources of information.	Employees of the state or federal government: prison psychiatrist, psychologist, or social worker; agents of society first, of the prisoner, second.	To classify antisocial conduct as if it were a disease; to justify quasi-medical treatment of social and moral problems.	Decision making about the prisoner; e.g., recommendations for early parole or for prolonged incarceration.

does not codify significant phenomenological similarities between patients so labeled by psychoanalysts and those so labeled by state hospital psychiatrists (Szasz, 1957a).

In the legal situation, where the psychiatrist functions as expert witness, the diagnosis of psychosis may mean that the accused should be considered not guilty by reason of insanity; or that he should be "sentenced" to mental hospitalization and involuntary psychiatric treatment (see Part IV).

A Situational Analysis of Psychiatric History

Thus far, we have been concerned with the various contemporary psychiatric situations, examining each in terms of whom we study, where, and with what methods. Let us now apply these questions to the activities of the leading psychiatric personalities since Emil Kraepelin.

Kraepelin (1855–1926) chiefly studied inmates of mental hospitals, both private and public. His method was direct commonsense observation. However, there were two inexplicit assumptions underlying Kraepelin's work. First, that the patients suffered from diseases similar to those familiar to physicians. Second, that physicians, and society generally, were "normal." The behavior of the psychiatrists was the standard against which the behavior of the patients was measured. Accordingly, patients were subsumed under categories ("diagnoses"), based on the behavioral phenomena ("symptoms") considered to be dominant. The spirit of the inquiry precluded emphasizing what was specifically personal in the patient's illness. This approach was at once humane and inhuman. Kraepelin was interested in man in general, but not in the patient as an individual.

Eugen Bleuler (1857–1939) worked in a psychiatric situation similar to Kraepelin's. The main difference was that Bleuler was more interested in the patient as a person. He recognized, for example, that patients with dementia praecox were not really demented.

Freud (1856–1939) worked under very different circumstances than did his predecessors. I think this was one of the reasons why he saw more. In other words, Freud was not engrossed with the problems of involuntarily hospitalized mental patients. On the contrary, he limited his practice to voluntary patients who consulted him as a private practitioner. Moreover, he proceeded to enlarge his field of observation and soon included in it everyone who came within his purview. His methods of observation were more imaginative too. He thus shifted from clinical observation, with or without hypnosis, to free association and dream analysis. And in addition to patients, he studied himself, other socially normal individuals, and the biographies of artists and psychotics.

Like his predecessors, Freud used society and the observer as the norms against which the patient's conduct was measured. He, however, made the standard explicit. Nevertheless, Freud's ideas about nosology were chaotic. He retained the Kraepelinian scheme of diagnostic terms, but used them as he pleased. This resulted, among other things, in repeated attempts by subsequent workers to reclassify his cases (for example, Reichard, 1956). Obviously, Freud cared little about the diagnostic labels he used. He concentrated instead on accurate description, reconstruction, and the formulation of new abstractions to account for what he observed.

There have been repeated attempts to create new psychiatric nosologies on the basis of psychoanalytic concepts (for example, Menninger, 1954). None of them has proved useful. Such attempts could succeed, if at all, only by limiting their range of applicability, and by adhering to operational criteria. An example would be to classify patients in accordance with their reactions to the analytic situation (Eissler, 1953).

Adolf Meyer (1866–1950) did not believe that mental disorders are basically similar to physical diseases. In this, his approach to psychiatry was a significant departure from Kraepelin's and Bleuler's. However, in keeping with psychiatric tradition, he worked mainly with hospitalized mental patients. This tended to limit his attention to those who are considered mentally ill by social criteria. Though his observational method was only "common sense," in his teaching and writing he combined biological, historical, psychological, and social perspectives (Lief, 1948; Meyer, 1926, 1933). He developed a system of classification, not of mental diseases, but of "reaction types." The technical terms, the "ergasias," which Meyer coined for these categories, were never widely accepted, despite his great personal influence in American psychiatry. Within a few decades his system of nosology became a historical relic.

Like Freud, Kurt Goldstein (1878–) worked in a novel psychiatric setting. He studied the brain-injured, combining in his approach the methods of neurology, clinical psychiatry, and psychological testing. In addition, he introduced important philosophical and linguistic considerations into psychiatry. Although his name is not usually associated with nosological innovation, he did create two new categories—the concrete and the abstract attitudes (Goldstein and Scheerer, 1941; Goldstein, 1948). These grew out of the particular situation in which he made his observations.

It is significant that the nosological categories of Kraepelin, Bleuler, Freud, and Goldstein continue to be used. Each makes sense in the setting in which it originated. However, these categories have since been combined with one another, and are now used in every conceivable situation. Is it surprising then that our current psychiatric nosology is a modern Tower of Babel?

Eclecticism is no doubt a healthy antidote to factional fanaticism. But in modern psychiatry, it may have been carried too far, assuming, perhaps, that it is without dangers of its own. Yet, our chaotic nosology may well be part of the price we have unwittingly paid for excessive eclecticism.

Modern psychoanalytic research throws fresh light on the interrelations of methods of observation, schemes of classification, and the uses of psychiatry in various social situations. Increasingly, workers have abandoned traditional nosological categories and developed new concepts of their own. For example, Sullivan's (1953) contributions cannot be fitted into our current official nosology without doing violence both to Sullivan and to our nosology. This is true also for newer contributions to the psychology of object relations (Fairbairn, 1952).

In sum, there is an obvious and pressing need for us to develop new systems of classification, adequate for our present needs, rather than to continue paying lip service to an outmoded nosology.

Panchrestons in Psychiatry

Perhaps there is a lesson to be learned from the persistent failure to create a workable system of psychiatric nosology along medical lines. By looking more searchingly at the problem of naming and classifying the things we observe, we may learn to avoid some of the dangers inherent in this kind of enterprise.

Let us first consider a similar problem in biology. In a study of the concept of protoplasm, Hardin (1956) called attention to the danger of words that "explain everything":

> Such enemies of thought, like all enemies, may be easier to spot if we label them. Such "explain alls" need a name. As we borrow from the Greek to call a "cure-all" a *panacea,* so let us christen an "explain all" a *panchreston.* The history of science is littered with the carcasses of discarded panchrestons; the Galenic *humours,* the Bergsonian *élan vital,* and the Drieschian *entelechy* are a few biological cases in point. A panchreston, which "explains all," *explains nothing* [page 112].

In Turton's *Medical Glossary* (1802), "panchrestus" is defined as an "epithet of a collyrium described by Galen, and so named for its general usefulness" (page 488). How can a collyrium—a liquid to be applied to the eyes—be generally useful in all types of illness? There can be only one answer: Because a highly respected medical authority claims that it possesses magically curative properties. We know that Galen was, indeed, such a charismatic healer:

> Galen knows everything, has an answer for everything; he confidently pictures the origin of all diseases and outlines their cure. He is the incarnation, per-

haps for the first time in history, of the physician who regards himself as omniscient and whose attitude of authority emanates from every act and every word [Castiglioni, 1941, pages 220–221].

Cure-alls and explain-alls satisfy the common human craving for omniscience and omnipotence. Equipped with such weapons, man need no longer feel helpless.

Panchrestons have played, and continue to play, an enormous role in psychiatry and psychoanalysis. Many terms—some diagnostic, like schizophrenia, others nondiagnostic, like libido—function as panchrestons. Thus, the term "schizophrenia" is supposed to explain so-called insane behavior just as the term "protoplasm" was supposed to explain the nature of life, and "ether" the transmission of energy through space. Not only have these words failed to explain the phenomena in question, but, as Hardin (1956) rightly emphasized, they hindered our understanding. We realize today that words like "ether" and "protoplasm" obscured important problems in physics and biology; but we fail to realize that words like "schizophrenia" and "psychosis" might obscure important problems in psychiatry.

To assert that a concept is a panchreston is, of course, to judge it. The question arises: When, in the history of a science, does a concept *become* a panchreston? In physics, for example, ether did not function as a panchreston in the days of Newton. It became a panchreston in the days of Michelson, Morley, and Einstein. Similarly, schizophrenia was a useful concept when it was first introduced by Bleuler, and remained so for some time afterward. The question is: Is it still useful, or has it become, in our day, a panchreston? Only the future historian of science will be able to answer with assurance. Yet despite our uncertainty, our work will depend heavily on our answer to this question.

Whether or not we consider schizophrenia a panchreston, it is clear that the concept hinders scientific work in two important respects. First, as a so-called nosological entity, schizophrenia has grown too large: it now encompasses too many diverse phenomena. Second, the concept has become reified: it has come to mean that there exists in nature a mental "illness" recognizable by specific "symptoms."

Many psychiatrists regard schizophrenia as the core problem of psychiatry today. It seems to me, however, that the problem of schizophrenia is comparable to the problem of ether. In effect, there is no such problem. Rather, the task is to redefine our questions by relating them to the conceptual and observational tools at our command. For the problem of schizophrenia, this means, first, clarifying the manifold meanings of the word. This must be followed by elucidating specific facts and relations. For example, biochemical studies may throw light on disorders of brain function in so-called schizophrenics, just as the discovery of the histological lesions of general paresis confirmed the hypothesis that paretic patients had syphilis. We cannot be certain that some patients now labeled schizophrenic do not suffer from diseases of the brain. Similarly, psychological and social studies could add to our knowledge of the uses of language and symbolization, learning, role-playing, and other aspects of the behavior of such patients. It is unlikely, however, that either type of research, even though successful, would "explain" schizophrenia. What seems more likely is that various behavioral processes would be better understood and that the need for the word "schizophrenia" would disappear.

Some Implications of the Situational Approach to Psychiatric Classification

The effort to use the same system of psychiatric nosology in several different social situations has failed. Our energies should now be directed toward constructing several classificatory schemes, each one applicable to a particular situation.

In actuality, there are several psychiatric classifications of people and of mental diseases. For example, the distinction between sane and insane is relevant only in a judicial context. Indeed, psychiatrists often protest that these terms have no "medical meaning." Paradoxically, this does not prevent them from offering their services in situations where these terms are used. The point, I think, is not whether the term "insanity" has or has not a medical meaning, but rather that it is relevant only in a legal situation. The adjectives "medical" and "legal" should qualify "situation," not "meaning."

My thesis is that the significance of a psychiatric label depends more on the social situation in which it occurs than on the nature of the object labeled. This may be illustrated by the different meanings that may be attached to the diagnosis of psychopathic personality. In a courtroom where the M'Naghten rule prevails, psychopathic personality is not considered a mental disease; in another, in which the Durham rule prevails, it is.

Social pressures, together with a kind of primitive psychiatric common sense, act as constant encouragements to psychiatrists to use all available psychiatric notions in every conceivable situation. Partly as a result of this, the psychiatrist has become widely accepted as an expert capable of offering sound scientific advice on problems ranging from child rearing to criminology. This is a propagandistic, not a scientific, view of psychiatry.

Each science, especially after it has developed beyond the initial stages of simple description and correlation, must guard against two dangers: first, not to be swayed by common sense; second, not to confuse expectation with fact, propaganda with truth. Psychiatry can be no exception.

I shall have more to say later about psychiatric propaganda. As to common sense, we must deny and transcend it in psychiatry, just as physicists and biologists have had to in their sciences. Why? Because, for example, common sense has taught us to apply insights gained in the psychoanalytic situation to others, like rearing children in the family or disposing of criminals in courts of law. Experience, however, has taught us that this does not work. But instead of psychiatry becoming a more empirical social science, with knowledge increasing through actual observations—people prefer to criticize, in turn, psychoanalysts, parents, and lawyers. We thus tend to lose sight of the fact that many psychoanalytic concepts make good sense in the psychoanalytic situation; it is only their relevance to other situations that ranges from problematic to nil. Similar considerations apply to concepts developed and used in other settings, such as the state hospital (chronic schizophrenia), the prison (Ganser syndrome), or the military service (malingering).

PART TWO » *Psychiatry as a Social Institution*

CHAPTER 4 » *Commitment*
of the Mentally Ill

I wish to stir up an intelligent and active sympathy, in behalf of the
most wretched, the most oppressed, the only helpless of mankind, by
proving with how much needless tyranny they are treated—and this
in mockery—by men who pretend indeed their cure, but who are,
in reality, their tormentors and destroyers.

—JOHN PERCEVAL (1838)

COMMITMENT IS compulsory or involuntary detention of a
person in an institution designated as a mental hospital. Like imprisonment in jail, commitment entails the loss of basic civil liberties. Unlike imprisonment, commitment ostensibly serves a medical-therapeutic, rather
than a judicial-punitive, purpose. We shall have occasion to examine this
distinction and the problems it poses.

In this chapter, I shall try to show that commitment serves the institutional values of psychiatry as a system of social control. Yet, psychiatry is
not explicitly defined as an agency of social control as, for example, is the
police. Its controlling function is hidden under a facade of medical and
psychiatric jargon, and is buttressed by a self-proclaimed desire to help
or treat so-called mentally ill persons.

Types of Commitment and Their Scope

I shall not discuss the legal regulations governing commitment in various parts of the United States.* Instead, I shall examine the actual operation of commitment procedures, the opinions of psychiatrists about them, and the inference we can draw from the existence and uses of contemporary commitment laws.

Each year approximately 250,000 patients are committed to mental institutions. The total number of committed patients on the rolls of these institutions at any one time is in excess of one million. (Some of these patients may be on convalescent leave or temporary discharge.) Approximately 90 percent of the patients in public mental institutions are in a committed status.

Truly voluntary hospitalization is virtually nonexistent in public mental institutions in the United States. In some jurisdictions patients may be admitted on a "voluntary commitment," which means that they enter the hospital voluntarily rather than because of legal coercion. However, such persons are not free to leave the hospital, and their commitment is readily converted into an "involuntary" type. The distinction between voluntary and involuntary commitment is therefore not a significant one. I shall use the term "commitment" to refer to any procedure by which a person is detained involuntarily in a mental institution.

There is, however, another, more important distinction between two types of commitment. One—emergency commitment or compulsory hospitalization for observation—is for a limited period, usually ten to sixty days. The other—regular or indefinite commitment—is for an unspecified term.

Whether commitment is effected by means of civil or criminal procedure creates still another distinction. Criminal commitment applies to persons charged with crimes awaiting trial and to defendants acquitted by reason of insanity. The civil procedure applies to persons who have not broken any laws and, occasionally, to minor offenders who are committed instead of tried. Civil commitment is usually to a state mental hospital, criminal commitment to a state hospital for the criminally insane.

The committed patient suffers a serious loss of civil rights. In many jurisdictions he is automatically considered legally incompetent: he cannot vote, make valid contracts, marry, divorce, and so forth. In others, incompetency is a separate matter. In either case, the committed person is incarcerated against his will, must suffer invasions of his person and body,

* For a comprehensive analysis of the legal aspects of commitment, the reader is referred to Ross's (1959) masterly review of the subject, and to the American Bar Foundation's recent study (Lindman and McIntyre, Jr., 1961).

cannot communicate freely with the outside world, usually loses his license to operate a motor vehicle, and suffers many other indignities as well.

Because of the large number of persons affected by commitment procedures, and because of the extensive deprivations of civil rights which commitment entails, the compulsory hospitalization of mentally ill persons is a matter of considerable legal, moral, and social—as well as psychiatric—significance.

Psychiatric Positions on Commitment

Since commitment is a significant social fact in the life of the hospitalized psychiatric patient, one would expect that, for this reason alone, it would be of great interest to psychiatrists. And yet, we find either a complete disregard of the problem, as if it were of no consequence, or a very slanted presentation of it.

In the fourth edition of the standard American textbook, *Modern Clinical Psychiatry* (Noyes, 1953), there is no mention of commitment procedures or involuntary hospitalization. This omission is all the more remarkable since for several decades Noyes had been the superintendent of a state hospital, and had therefore dealt predominantly with committed patients. What are we to make of this omission, and of others like it? To me, such silence speaks eloquently. It suggests that many psychiatrists would like to ignore the circumstances under which people become their patients and would prefer to focus only on their patients' alleged mental illnesses. Presently, we shall have an opportunity to see whether this supposition is an unfounded criticism or whether there is evidence to support it.

Masserman's textbook, *The Practice of Dynamic Psychiatry* (1955), reveals an equally complete omission of the subject of commitment.

So much for psychiatric efforts to disregard or ignore commitment. I shall now comment on efforts to embellish it, and shall then turn to the few forthright and undistorted psychiatric accounts of this subject which I have been able to find.

In the fifth edition of *Modern Clinical Psychiatry* (Noyes and Kolb, 1958), a new chapter on "Psychiatry and the Law" has been added. Procedures for hospitalizing the mentally ill are discussed, and the following opinion is offered:

One of the important differences between the psychiatrist and the lawyer is in their respective attitudes toward the admission of the mentally ill person to a hospital. The psychiatrist urges that the *dignity* of the patient be respected and that the *obstacles to his admission* be no greater than those experienced by the physically ill [italics added; page 666].

This view, though often held by psychiatrists, is not only propagandistic and self-congratulatory but also false. Its implication, that the psychiatrist is interested, but that the lawyer is not, in preserving the patient's dignity and welfare, is not true. The history of Anglo-American law is one of unremitting striving for liberty and dignity in human affairs. Can organized psychiatry match this proud legal heritage? Hardly. The treatment of mental patients in public institutions during the past hundred years or more offers no grounds for self-congratulation.

Another reason for objecting to the foregoing claim is that it relies on a misleading analogy between bodily and mental illness. This argument is constantly invoked by psychiatrists in urging easier ways of getting patients into mental hospitals. However, they usually forget, as have Noyes and Kolb, demanding provisions for equally easy means of leaving mental hospitals.

In his book on hospital psychiatry, Linn (1955) tried to gloss over the coercive features of commitment. He justified the hospitalized patient's loss of rights as follows:

These rights are taken from them in the words of the Iowa Supreme Court "to aid and assist the individual, to provide means whereby the state may protect its unfortunate citizens, to furnish hospitalization so that the insane will have an opportunity for rehabilitation and readjustment into *useful* and *happy* citizens. It is not a criminal proceeding in any way. The restraint placed upon them is only until they have recovered so that they may again take their places in the communities from which they came. *The confinement is not intended as a punishment* but solely and only to provide the mentally sick with that environment which may possibly cure the disease and return them to society as *useful* citizens." One might wish to add that we also take into consideration the dangers to society which sometimes ensue from the actions of the mentally sick, although admittedly the importance of this factor has often been exaggerated, and it may certainly be given second place in our thoughts [italics added; page 420].

Linn failed to scrutinize this pious and paternalistic pronouncement by the Iowa Supreme Court. He accepted it as a valid position on commitment and urged the reader to accept it also. The emphatic assertion that commitment is not intended as punishment betrays its actual social function.

What, then, is the real point of the position advocated by Linn? It is a justification of the demands by the holders of power in society for certain role performances by the powerless. Linn's emphasis on the restoration of the psychotic to usefulness and happiness is particularly significant. Throughout history, those in power have always sought to justify their control over the weak and oppressed by claiming to act in their interests. This was the slaveholder's attitude toward slaves, and the crusading Christian's toward the heathen. Today the psychiatrist adopts a similar attitude toward the mental-hospital patient (see Chapter 12).

Linn, and other psychiatrists who favor easy commitment, are identified with the aspirations of the society to which they belong. They prefer to see no significant conflicts between serving the needs of society and those of the patient. The following passage exemplifies the attempt to reconcile or perhaps deny the potentially conflicting needs of society and patient:

> In general, proceedings to commit a patient are initiated at the request of relatives or other *responsible* individuals in the form of a petition. The patient is then examined by one or two doctors to ascertain if he is a *danger to himself or those about him.* If so, they complete a certificate which endeavors to explain to a court of law why it is necessary to deprive the patient of his liberty. The patient is then brought to a court hearing at which time judicial approval may be given or withheld at the judge's discretion. If the doctors feel that the appearance of the patient in court may be detrimental to his health, this appearance may be waived in many states. *In fact, court approval is usually given as a matter of routine on the basis of the considered opinions of properly qualified physicians.* The responsibility for a psychiatric patient's treatment begins in the psychiatrist's initial contact with him, even when this takes place during a commitment proceeding. *Any semblance of a punitive attitude should be avoided.* The existence of quasi-criminal proceedings for the hospitalization of the mentally ill is a holdover from the dark ages when thousands of innocent people were burned at the stake because of symptoms clearly recognizable today as manifestations of mental illness [italics added; page 422].

It should be evident that the psychiatrist who recommends commitment, or who accepts involuntary patients for "treatment," acts neither as a scientist nor as an ordinary physician (who treats only consenting patients). What, then, is such a psychiatrist's role? His role is to exert social control on a socially deviant person (Lemert, 1946), and as such it is similar to the roles of policeman, judge, or prison warden.

One technique for denying that commitment is punishment is to clothe it in a mantle of therapeutic paternalism. Another is to rename it. Orwell (1949) could hardly have asked for a better example of "newspeak" than that contained in the following proposal by the Group for Advancement of Psychiatry (1948):

> The Committee believes that all statutes should delete the term "commitment" in place of which should be substituted the term "certification"; "insanity" and "lunacy" should be replaced by the term "mental illness," and the terms "feeble-minded" or "weak-minded" should be abandoned. The Committee believes that the term "parole" should be abandoned and in its place the term "convalescent leave" should be substituted [page 3].

It is not clear how such semantic manipulation of the English language will help mental patients. The new terminology, while deceiving patients and public, can serve only to diminish the psychiatrists' guilt for their coercive control over the inmates of mental institutions.

It may be pertinent to note here that, in contrast to the coercive and paternalistic attitude so characteristic of the hospital psychiatrist in relation to his patient, American law assumes a far more dignified and constructive posture toward the blind (Cahn, 1956):

> In the law's appraisal, a blind man is not of a different species from one who has the sight of his eyes. A blind man is simply another member of the total society; he must take suitable and reasonable precautions for his and others' safety. So must a man who is too short or too heavy, or whose reflexes are slowing with the years; so also must every one of us.—*Persons who are afflicted and disabled must not be categorized even by themselves as an inferior or pitiable species.* They are, on the contrary, men in all essentials like their neighbors—with the needs, duties, dignities, and singular potentialities of the genus [italics added; pages 220–221].

Although there are several forthright discussions of commitment in the sociologic literature (Belknap, 1956, Goffman, 1961a), few can be found in the psychiatric literature. One is in Henderson and Gillespie's (1950) textbook. These authors emphasized the desirability of voluntary hospitalization, and stressed also the role of nonmedical and nonpsychiatric factors in commitment: [*]

> Apart from the medical side, the social and economic circumstances are often deciding factors for and against certification. Certification is desirable where no adequate accommodation at home or in a special nursing home is available or where money is a consideration. Certification is unnecessary where adequate arrangements for treatment can be made outside of mental hospitals, and undesirable where the patient occupies an important public position, e.g., director of a company, partnership, etc. [page 684].

From this statement we might conclude that commitment is largely a social and economic matter. Compare this with Davidson's (1952) views:

> Hospitalization proceedings should involve a *maximum reliance on medical judgment*. The *basic question* in deciding whether a person should be hospitalized is his *health* and his *medical* needs. The model law follows the current trend of placing major emphasis in any admission procedure on the conclusions of *qualified physicians* who have *examined the patient* [italics added; page 181].

Either Henderson and Gillespie's view or Davidson's must be false. Both cannot be true, although it is possible that both may be false.

Davidson's emphasis on the importance of the physician's personal examination of the patient deserves special attention. This is exactly the procedure which forensic psychiatrists cheerfully abandon when asked to pass judgment on a deceased person's testamentary capacity (see Chapter 6).

---

[*] In recent years, far-reaching changes have taken place in British mental-hospital practices. Today more than 90% of the patients in Great Britain are hospitalized informally, although not necessarily voluntarily. For current hospitalization procedures in Great Britain, see the (British) Mental Health Act (1959).

An excellent analysis of some aspects of the conflict between the hospitalized mental patient and society may be found in Stanton and Schwartz's book, *The Mental Hospital* (1954). They wrote:

> But, however much or little he knew about the community, the *psychiatrist either submitted to being an agent of the community or he abandoned work with the really seriously ill. He had no other choice.* The community had strong and effective techniques of maintaining order; it might be stupid or enlightened, brutal or friendly, closely integrated with the hospital or distant, and occasionally it was all of these. But it protected itself. The license for the hospital to operate was granted by the town government and had to be renewed each year. There was never any serious question about its renewal, but the license dramatized the fact that, regardless of the personal values of the psychiatrist, *protection of the community would take priority over the therapeutic purpose of the hospital,* if there was an obvious conflict between the two. The hospital had to be successful in this purpose, and it was [italics added; page 48].

I agree with Stanton and Schwartz. When a physician commits a patient to a mental hospital, he is mainly an agent of the community. Whether and to what extent commitment interferes with psychotherapy is a complex question. It cannot even be considered without a clear understanding of what is meant by psychotherapy. According to one view, it is a form of upbringing and social control. According to another, it is a form of education of the patient about himself and the world about him, whose purpose it is to increase his choices for action (Szasz, 1961, 1962). Coercive hospitalization will interfere little or not at all with psychotherapy stressing socialization, but will seriously hinder psychotherapy stressing autonomy and self-control.

Justifications for Commitment

Let us now analyze the justifications for commitment. Usually one or more of the following reasons are mentioned: (1) the person is psychotic or insane; (2) he is dangerous to himself; (3) he is dangerous to others; (4) he is mentally sick and needs hospital care and treatment, but does not understand his condition and the need for treatment.

As a rule, no single reason can account for the commitment of a particular person at a given time. Even all four, taken together, fail to explain some of the most essential features of this social phenomenon.

The so-called psychotic state of an individual is neither a necessary nor a sufficient cause for his commitment. Impecunious elderly persons, addicts, and offenders are committed; yet, they are not usually considered to be psychotic. Conversely, many persons whom psychiatrists regard as psychotic remain at liberty.

A person's dangerousness, to himself or others, is a more relevant consideration. However, dangerousness is undefined. Hence, this criterion also fails to offer a reliable guide for explaining the commitment of one person and the noncommitment of another equally as dangerous.

In the "Draft Act Governing Hospitalization of the Mentally Ill" (Federal Security Agency, 1952), involuntary hospitalization is considered to be justified if the following conditions are met:

(A) He [the patient] is mentally ill, and
(B) because of his illness is likely to injure himself or others if allowed to remain at liberty or
(C) is in need of care or treatment in a mental hospital, and because of his illness, lacks sufficient insight or capacity to make responsible application therefor [Section 5].

What constitutes dangerousness is left unspecified, perhaps intentionally, to allow for administrative decisions by lawyers and psychiatrists.

In my opinion, whether or not a person is dangerous is not the real issue. It is rather *who* he is, and *in what way* he is dangerous. Some persons are allowed to be dangerous to others with impunity. Also, most of us are allowed to be dangerous in some ways, but not in others.

Drunken drivers are dangerous both to themselves and to others. They injure and kill many more people than, for example, persons with paranoid delusions of persecution. Yet, people labeled paranoid are readily committable, while drunken drivers are not.

Some types of dangerous behavior are even rewarded. Race-car drivers, trapeze artists, and astronauts receive admiration and applause. In contrast, the polysurgical addict and the would-be suicide receive nothing but contempt and aggression. Indeed, the latter type of dangerousness is considered good cause for commitment. Thus, it is not dangerousness in general that is at issue here, but rather the manner or style in which one is dangerous.

Commitment as Social Restraint

Let us now analyze commitment from a sociopsychological standpoint. In general, that conduct tends to lead to commitment which appears abnormal to the layman. Such crudely offensive social behavior cannot, however, be readily correlated with psychiatric diagnoses. Nevertheless, psychiatrists tend to label this sort of behavior psychotic. Thus, the expressions "psychosis" and "behavior justifying commitment" overlap, and in effect often mean the same thing. Indeed, persons whom psychiatrists may consider psychotic are usually left undisturbed so long as they do not annoy others. Ezra Pound, for example, was released from psychiatric confinement with the explanation that although he was still seriously ill mentally, he was no longer dangerous (see Chapter 17).

A crucial consideration is the issue of social disturbance. If a person is old and cannot care for himself, he creates a social disturbance and may be committed. If a person threatens to kill himself—but does not do so— he too creates a social disturbance and, in a way, asks to be committed. If a person lays claim to ideas or beliefs or sensations that threaten society —for example, beliefs of being persecuted (called "delusions"), or sensations of seeing and hearing (called "hallucinations")—he too creates a social disturbance and may be committed. Finally, if a person commits acts which violate social rules—for example, by engaging in forbidden modes of sexual gratification—he too creates a social disturbance and may be committed.

The similarities between committable mental illness and crime thus emerge. In both, the person "offends" society, and is therefore restrained. The motives for restraining the mentally ill person are ostensibly therapeutic, whereas for the criminal they are allegedly punitive. This distinction, however, cannot be defended satisfactorily. State hospitals have been notorious for their neglect, and indeed abuse, of the mental patient. There is evidence that incarceration in a mental hospital may be more harmful for the personality than incarceration in a prison (see Chapter 14).

If so, irrespective of the motives that animate those who commit, the actual effect of mental hospitalization may still be punishment.

Another crucial factor in commitment is social role. Our problem may now be formulated by asking: Who annoys whom? It is a fact that the vast majority of committed patients are members of the lower classes. Upper-class persons are virtually immune from this sort of social restraint. This point deserves emphasis.

Before the law, all men are equal. This at least is the intention of the law. We know, however, that when in legal jeopardy, the wealthy and well educated often fare better than the poor and uneducated. Nevertheless, the whole tradition of Anglo-American law has been to support efforts to make the judicial process "fair." No such considerations of fair play enter into the game of commitment. Indeed, commitment is, in part, a symptom of class struggle—not exactly in Marxist terms, but a class struggle nonetheless. Let me illustrate what I mean. In the military service, an officer may send an enlisted man to the hospital for psychiatric observation. This may appear to be a request for medical study, but it is not. Rather it is a charge of probable mental illness, similar to an accusation of wrongdoing. In effect, the person requesting the examination says: "This man is probably crazy. See if it is so." The roles in this situation cannot be inverted. The enlisted man cannot request a psychiatric examination of his officer.

Since commitment is a grossly discriminatory sanction, injuring lower-class persons much more than upper-class persons, the participation of psychiatrists in its enforcement poses an especially significant moral problem. By participating in commitment practices, psychiatrists perpetuate a type of social injustice. Kecskemeti's (1952) criticism of this kind of behavior (although not specifically in psychiatry) is pertinent:

> The moment "principled" behavior is taken to imply the assumption that one group alone can do or suffer wrong, it ceases to be ethical behavior; and those who act on such maxims betray the principle of the open society, no matter how righteous and progressive they consider themselves to be [page 312].

The assumption that members of one group can do wrong but members of another cannot, can frequently be detected when the issue of a person's mental condition is raised. In the school, administrators and teachers may regard students as posing psychiatric problems, but not vice versa. Similarly, in psychoanalytic education, training and supervising analysts may decide that candidates need further analysis. Here too, the student is powerless to do anything about the training analyst's "mental health," even when the latter is obviously disabled, for example by senility. In courts of law, the same rule prevails: only the sanity of the defendant can be questioned, not that of the prosecutor or the judge.

The Case of King Ludwig II of Bavaria

Commitment is an everyday occurrence. Thus, the data necessary to support or refute my thesis are easily available. To illustrate the role of social power and status in commitment, I chose an unusual case history—that of a "psychotic" king who was "committed." This case has the advantage of historical distance. Thus, the reader need not be distracted by the emotional impact of current political events, as he would surely be if the issue of mental illness were raised about men like Eichmann or Trujillo.

In 1864, Ludwig II became King of Bavaria. Raised without affection or parental guidance, he was totally unprepared for the role of a modern ruler.

Although Ludwig longed for intimate relationships, he could never have any. He was an overt homosexual, but suffered keenly because his sexual cravings violated the teachings of his Roman Catholic faith.

Ludwig's reign was a steady descent into self-abasement and self-destruction. He had no family, no friends, no work. His chief contacts with reality were his love of music, chiefly Wagner's, and his love of ornate castles. He built three magnificent ones. Had it not been for these interests, he would undoubtedly have become desocialized and "schizo-phrenic" even sooner than he did.

For several years before the fateful final events, Ludwig failed to dis-charge any but the most minimal functions of a monarch. The country was run by the Prime Minister and his Cabinet. Finally, in June 1886, Prime Minister Lutz and his Cabinet appointed a commission of four eminent psychiatrists for the purpose of declaring the King mentally incompetent.

In his biography of Ludwig II, Werner Richter (1954) described the initial psychiatric intervention as follows:

In the morning hours of June 8, 1886, Dr. Bernard von Gudden, Director of the District Asylum for the Insane in Upper Bavaria, and Professor of Psychiatry at the University of Munich, finished the draft of a medical finding on which he had been working most of the night. An hour or so later, he went into closed session with two other directors of public institutions for the insane, Dr. Hagen and Dr. Hubrich, and with Professor Grashey. Around noon all four distinguished psychiatrists signed Gudden's finding which ended on these three conclusions.

"1) His Majesty is psychically disturbed in an advanced degree, suffering from the kind of mental sickness which psychiatrists know well and call paranoia (insanity).

"2) In view of this form of sickness and its gradual and progressive develop-ment over a great number of past years, His Majesty must be declared incurable, for a further deterioration of his mental powers appears certain.

"3) Because of his sickness the exercise of His Majesty's free will is rendered completely impossible and His Majesty must be considered hindered in the execu-tion of government, which impediment will last not only longer than a year, but for his entire lifetime."

These unequivocal sentences of the psychiatrists signified the removal of Ludwig II not only from Bavaria's throne but from community with the living [pages 250–251].

What was the basis for certifying the King as insane, at that particular time? His peculiar behavior was well known and there was nothing new about it. Moreover, as Richter cogently pointed out, "The money Ludwig wasted on his fantastic projects was, strictly speaking, no concern of the Bavarian government" (page 258). Unlike many other royal wastrels, Ludwig did not indulge himself at the cost of public funds. As to homo-sexuality, it had never before disqualified a European monarch from ruling.

Ludwig's commitment, then, like most commitments today, was initiated because he was in the way of more powerful persons—in this case, the Prime Minister and his Cabinet. Lutz was also supported by high-ranking Prussian politicians who saw in Ludwig a barrier to Bismarck's ambition to unify the German states. Richter, a historian and novelist, not a psy-chiatrist, was himself struck by what he considered the "shortcomings" in the judgment and action of the psychiatrists in this case. (It seems to me that the psychiatrists were lacking in self-judgment, rather than in professional judgment: they were unaware that although ostensibly employed to "diagnose" Ludwig, they were actually used to depose him.) What were these shortcomings?

First, all four of the psychiatrists were public officials. They were thus "closely affiliated with the bureaucracy whose authority their finding was supposed to bolster" (page 254).

Second, none of them had ever examined Ludwig. Grashey later tried to explain this by arguing that, had the psychiatrists first examined the King, "action would have had to be postponed for some time." To which Richter countered: "In this particular case, postponement of action would have merely meant that publicly known conditions, tolerated for years, would have continued for a few more weeks" (page 255).

Third, though Gudden's evidence was entirely indirect, he considered it "overwhelming." It was nothing of the kind. The evidence consisted partly of depositions taken from persons in the King's entourage, and partly of some of Ludwig's own writings. The latter, said Bismarck, "were picked up from wastebaskets and toilets and *cannot possibly justify a death sentence for Ludwig*" (italics added; page 255).

Fourth, the most damaging information against Ludwig came from the stablemaster and other lackeys. Having catered to the King's peculiarities for years, they may have felt that here was their chance to vent their grievances against him; or they "may have sensed that unusually juicy depositions were expected from them and might improve their careers" (page 255).

Having pronounced the King insane and thus incapable of governing, the commission faced the problem of carrying out the actions implicit in the diagnosis.

The psychiatrists, together with members of the Cabinet, proceeded to Neuschwanstein, where the King was staying. At first, they were not permitted to see the King. Indeed, they were arrested by the royal Bavarian gendarmes, who were still under the King's orders, and were held overnight.

The next day, the psychiatrists and their companions were released. They then took the King into their custody, and, on June 11th, moved him to Berg Castle, which had been converted into a psychiatric hospital for his exclusive use. According to Richter, Ludwig must have realized "that his captivity would never end, if only because his jailers would forever be afraid of his revenge; and so they would finally kill him" (page 277).

Only two paths were open to Ludwig. One was to resign himself to his fate, and permit his doctors and attendants to keep him alive as a harmless, chronic lunatic. His captors would then have succeeded in destroying him as a human being without actually killing him. Thus, they would be considered innocent of any wrongdoing.

The other possibility was to revolt—to assert himself in a final act of self-determination, by killing himself. Ludwig chose this course. Two days after arriving at the Berg Castle, he went for a walk with Dr. Gudden. At an unguarded moment, he tried to drown himself in the lake adjoining the castle. When his psychiatrist interfered, he killed him and then drowned himself.

What Can We Learn from the Case of King Ludwig? King Ludwig's mental illness and confinement exemplify many present-day problems of psychiatric diagnosis and treatment. Since Leo Alexander's (1954) views on this matter are almost diametrically opposite to mine, his comments should prove illuminating.

While traveling to Neuschwanstein, the psychiatrists acted as if the King were already a psychiatric patient. Their sole purpose, as they saw it, was to transfer him to a "hospital." However, Ludwig objected to being cast in the role of psychiatric patient—first, by refusing entrance to the psychiatrists, then, by killing himself. Alexander commented:

> Since the commission (composed of four psychiatrists) had arrived without military escort in order to show respect for the King, and *in order to eliminate any and all semblance of coercion,* the commission then returned to Hochenschwangau for further consultation, without its purpose having been accomplished [italics added; page 101].

The psychiatrists' wish to avoid showing evidence of coercion betrays the problem of power, to which I alluded earlier. Although the psychiatrists did not succeed in deceiving the "patient" about the role of coercion in this situation, they did apparently deceive themselves, and with tragic results. There was, of course, a good nonmedical reason in this instance for dissimulating a direct show of force. Ludwig was still King. Direct aggression against him might have proved physically dangerous to the members of the commission.

Alexander also thought that the King's suicide could have been prevented, had he been handled differently:

> . . . the major cause of the disaster perhaps was the basic attitude of making special concessions to a highly placed patient. . . . Removal of the King to a well-organized and well-staffed mental hospital would probably have been the better course. After all, the *basic reason for commitment is the expert's finding* and conclusion that the patient does not have sufficient independent judgment to carry out his affairs in his own best interests. Perhaps a great many other suicides of highly placed persons were not prevented because the same error was made as in the case of the sick King of Bavaria [italics added; page 106].

It seems to me that Alexander missed the whole point of this story, and the continuing dilemma it exemplifies. In the tradition of the authoritarian psychiatrist, he would like to strip the King of his special prerogatives and treat him like any other psychiatric patient. But how are ordinary psychiatric-hospital patients treated? First, they are subjected to what Goffman (1957) aptly calls a "stripping process," in which the patient is "defaced." The patient's authority is thus replaced by that of the psychiatrist and of the mental hospital as an institution.

Why Alexander would have liked to treat Ludwig in this fashion is understandable. It would have eliminated the problem of Ludwig's troublesome grandiosity—at least so long as he accepted the patient role, or so long as that role could have been imposed on him by force. But getting Ludwig to *accept* the patient role was precisely the task that faced the psychiatrists called on to treat him. It continues to be the problem of contemporary psychiatrists called on to treat prominent persons who are unwilling to accept the role of psychiatric patient. Secretary of Defense James Forrestal, for example, was never openly treated as a psychiatric patient. He committed suicide under circumstances similar to Ludwig's by jumping from an upper-story window of the hospital in which he was confined.

Alexander's solution for what to do about the prospective mental patient's power is simple: take it away from him. He wrote:

I am reminded of an experience during the recent war when as a newly activated medical officer I was faced with admission to the ward of a suicidal Major-General. One of my assistants, a lieutenant, called our commanding officer, a regular Army Colonel, to ask if there were any special things we were to do in the circumstances. The colonel curtly replied: "Take off his uniform and you will outrank him." This was promptly done and the patient made an uneventful recovery under the right form of treatment in a ward which contained all ranks and which provided the best treatment facilities the Army can provide [page 106].

Unfortunately, some of the most important facts have been omitted from this anecdote. Did the patient go to the psychiatrist of his own accord, or was he coerced? If force was employed, who used it? Who assigned to the general the social role of psychiatric patient? In both military and civilian life, this must be done by someone who outranks the patient. If attempted by a subordinate, the hapless "diagnostician" risks being accused of insubordination, disobedience of orders, mutiny, or some similar offense. *The Caine Mutiny* (Wouk, 1951) was a fictional account of this sort of problem aboard a Navy vessel. The point is that neither Alexander nor the lieutenant he mentioned encountered a power problem in their experience with the suicidal major general. When they met him, he had already been demoted to mental patient.

For Alexander, psychiatric treatment is apparently impossible unless the doctor outranks the patient. The case he cited is a striking example. In my view, however, the physician's superiority as regards power is not only unnecessary for psychotherapy, but positively harmful for it. In psychoanalysis, and especially in autonomous psychotherapy (Szasz, 1962), the therapist must eschew any coercive influence over his patient.

In sum, not only do Alexander's comments fail to acknowledge the historical and social circumstances of Ludwig's case, they also obscure the lessons we may learn from it.

In the first place, special concessions are regularly made to highly placed persons. This is true in medical and surgical cases, and it is especially so in psychiatric cases. The thesis that doctors treat all patients alike, irrespective of social circumstances, may be an aspiration, but it is not a fact. To acknowledge inequalities does not mean that one approves of them. Such recognition, however, is essential for social science.

Second, it seems unrealistic to advocate, as Alexander has, that the King should have been removed to an ordinary mental hospital. How could this have been accomplished? By what legal authority could he have been held there? It is pertinent to recall the case of Governor Earl Long of Louisiana. When his wife tried to commit him to a public mental hospital in his own state, he freed himself by dismissing the hospital superintendent. The fact that Ludwig was not committed, and could not be, is important evidence of the role of power in this procedure.

Third, Alexander's assertion that the "basic reason for commitment" is the expert's judgment—in other words, that it is essentially a medical matter—is a restatement of the official position on commitment. Ludwig's tragic story, in my opinion, demonstrates that commitment is chiefly a social and legal affair, not a medical one.

Finally, Alexander's comments about the prevention of suicide by those in high positions raise fundamental questions of a moral and social nature. Why limit dangerousness to suicide? Why not include homicide, an activity in which politically prominent persons have always had a great deal of license? Political opposition, revolt, and war, each could, in this way, become psychiatric problems of "dangerousness" which psychiatrists would be called on to "prevent" or "treat." This is preposterous. Yet such problems of "dangerousness" do exist. They must not be obscured by attempts to transmute them into what might seem like purely psychiatric problems.

The Mental Hospital as a Total Institution

The term "commitment" denotes a network of complex regulations and events pertaining to the manner in which a patient enters, stays in, and leaves a mental hospital. An exhaustive description of commitment would therefore entail a complete description of the mental hospital. Some observations about the mental hospital as a social establishment are therefore necessary at this point.

Mental hospitals must not be thought of as ordinary medical hospitals.

Inasmuch as the activities of the inmates of state hospitals are largely controlled and supervised by the staff, such establishments must be compared to others in which such inmate control is typically exercised. Tuberculosis hospitals, prisons, POW camps, work camps, and Army barracks are of this type. In an important analysis of the social structure of the mental hospital, Goffman (1957) called these institutions "total," because of their far-reaching control over the activities of the inmates. He listed the following features as characteristics of total institutions:

1. All aspects of life are conducted in the same place, and under a single authority.

2. There is little or no room for private activity and effort. The inmate is always in the company of others: "all are treated alike and required to do the same thing together" (page 6).

3. There is a strict schedule of daily activities which does not issue from the inmates' interests or wishes, but are imposed from above.

4. The contents of the various enforced activities are brought together as parts of a single overall rational plan purportedly designed to fulfill the official aims of the institutions.

Commitment, then, must be viewed as only one aspect—albeit a very important one—of the mental hospital as a total institution.

The Role of Deceit in Involuntary Mental Hospitalization. Total institutions, though similar to one another in the scope and degree of control which staff exercises over inmates, can be divided into two groups. In one group the inmate is expected to live up to and incorporate into himself a staff-sponsored ideal of himself and of his correct behavior. Mental hospitals and "brainwashing camps" illustrate this type of institution. In the other type—a prison, for example—this is not expected of the inmate.

This significant distinction between two types of total institutions may also be formulated in terms of honesty and deceit. It seems to me that prisons—evil as they may be—must be credited with addressing their inmates honestly. The nature of the imprisonment is clearly defined. It is as if society were to say to the inmate: "You are confined here for such-and-such reasons. As long as you are incarcerated, you must behave thus. After you have spent a certain number of months or years here, you will be set free again."

In contrast, the relationship between the mental hospital and its inmates is suffused with dishonesty and deceit. Usually, the patient is not told the true reason for his detainment. Nor is he given explicit directions about the way he must behave. Finally, his discharge is not predicated upon objective criteria, such as confinement for a given period of time. It depends instead upon the judgment by the staff of a transformation of his personality.

Much of the renaming that has characterized the history of modern psychiatry—like calling insane asylums hospitals—has served to disguise the actual functions of the institution behind a facade of benevolence toward the patients. Attention was thus diverted from the conflicts of interest between staff and inmates. Nearly one hundred years ago, in Mrs. Packard's famous fight against her false commitment, we find this issue displayed quite nakedly.

Mrs. Packard (1873b) quotes Dr. McFarland, the superintendent of the Jacksonville (Illinois) Insane Asylum where she was confined, as having commented on her manuscript as follows:

> I should like to remark here, that I don't like your calling this place a *prison*, so much; for it isn't so. And as I'm to superintend these manuscripts for the press, I'm not willing you should call it a prison. You may call it a place of confinement, if you choose, but not a prison [italics in the original; page 132].

This problem has hardly changed since then. Psychiatrists still resort to the tactic of mislabeling in order to mislead both patients and public. Only the rationalizations, the grounds given for the mislabeling, have changed somewhat. A century ago it was justified by humanitarian motives; today by modern *medical* knowledge.

Commitment and Slavery. The committed mental patient is disenfranchised and subjected to coercive "treatments." His relationship to his superiors invites comparisons with other types of oppressor-oppressed relationships. The master-slave pattern is one of the most extreme forms of this type of relationship and, perhaps for that reason, one of the most illuminating.

Let us consider the traditional attitudes of psychiatrists and lay persons toward the insane in this light. Even today, many people regard hospitalized mental patients as Plato regarded slaves. They are treated as if they did not know how to be anything but patients, and as if the psychiatrist-patient arrangement served their needs. Occasionally, there is protest. The misery of the patients is exposed. But the basic pattern of oppression continues. Like slavery, commitment is justified by appeal to the public interest. Mental patients annoy "normal" people. They are often said to be "dangerous." Hence, their confinement is required for the public good.

What is the evidence for this? First, there are the constant semantic efforts to embellish psychiatric oppression as benevolence. Words like "patient," "hospital," and "treatment" instead of "inmate," "prison," "asylum," and "punishment" are examples. Second, there is the violence—indeed the brutality—and also the completely unproved efficacy, of such "treatments" as lobotomy, convulsions induced by insulin, metrazol, and electricity, and most recently, the chemical straitjackets. Do the patients so treated feel that they have been helped? Rarely. Could it be that this was never the intention? Or if it was, help meant teaching them to accept their oppressed, submissive status uncomplainingly.

I believe that, like slavery, the entire oppressive-coercive pattern inherent in present-day involuntary mental hospitalization is an evil which must be done away with.

CHAPTER 5 » *False Commitment*

*Adequate remedies are not likely to be fashioned by those who are
not hostile to evils to be remedied.*

—FELIX FRANKFURTER (1947)

IMPROPER COMMITMENT of persons to mental institutions—
formerly called railroading—was much in the public eye during the
nineteenth century. This is no longer true today.

Of course, whether a particular commitment is proper or not depends
upon the standards by which it is measured. One of these is the law
regulating commitment. However, we shall presently see that in the most
flagrant cases of railroading in the history of American psychiatry no laws
were violated. The most "unjustly" hospitalized persons were committed
according to proper legal procedure. If we consider their commitment
improper, it is because our standard differs from the laws then in effect.

How should we judge today which commitment is proper, and which is
improper? Should we be satisfied with legality, or should we insist on more
searching criteria?

False Commitment in the Nineteenth Century

It was not until the 1830's that an appreciable number of state hospitals
began to operate in the United States. At that time, commitment laws were

either nonexistent or so lax that a person could be incarcerated in an asylum simply on the recommendation of a physician.

Many people who were committed claimed that they should not have been. Newspaper publicity of these cases helped promote legislation to safeguard the rights of people against too easy confinement in mental hospitals.

One of the most famous early American cases of railroading was that of Mrs. E. P. W. Packard. This lady, the wife of the Reverend Theophilus Packard, was committed by her husband to the Illinois State Hospital at Jacksonville, in 1860. Three years later she gained her release. Mrs. Packard claimed that she was sane and that her husband committed her so as to be rid of her. Her crusade for better commitment laws led to the enactment of new legislation in Illinois as well as in other states. Although the details of this case, and of Mrs. Packard's subsequent activities, are exceedingly interesting (Packard, 1868, 1873a and b), our task here is only to discover whether her commitment was improper. The statute under which she was committed read (Deutsch, 1949):

> *Married women* and *infants* who, in the judgment of the medical superintendent of the state asylum at Jacksonville are evidently insane or distracted, may be entered or detained in the hospital at the request of the *husband of the woman* or the guardian of the infant, *without the evidence of insanity required in other cases* [italics added; page 424].

Thus, Mrs. Packard's commitment was legal. In analyzing this case and others like it, Deutsch, I think, made a serious error. He remarked that this law "was so grossly discriminatory and unjust as to arouse the resentment of all fair-minded people" (page 424). However, this law must have reflected the views of the Illinois lawmakers of 1851 on the subject of women, children, and the insane. Had it been as abhorrent to them as it was to Deutsch, they would not have enacted it. By ascribing Mrs. Packard's incarceration to bad laws, we commit the error of ethnocentrism: we scrutinize and judge the standards of others, and glibly assume that ours are good.° I have tried to show in Chapter 4 that, although not as barbarous as the Illinois commitment law of 1851, our present legal orientation to so-called mentally ill persons is still discriminatory and harmful to their best interests.

Deutsch's acceptance of the standards of contemporary psychiatry is also revealed by his discussion of the question of Mrs. Packard's sanity. He seemed to doubt it, because as a girl she was said to have suffered from "delusions," and had been a patient at the Worcester State Hospital in

---

° The law under which Mrs. Packard was committted was no more (or less) discriminatory toward women than, say, current divorce laws in New York State are discriminatory toward poor people. Since in this state it is exceedingly difficult to obtain a divorce, most couples wishing to end their marriages avail themselves of out-of-state divorces. Obviously, this arrangement places a far greater hardship on the poor than on the well-to-do.

Massachusetts. This illustrates a bias in contemporary psychiatric thinking. How does Jones know that Smith is insane? He infers this from Dr. Psychiatry's opinions and actions. Dr. Psychiatry has examined Smith, judged his behavior improper, and committed him to a mental institution. Henceforth, the fact that Smith was confined in a mental hospital will be considered evidence of his mental illness. Let us recall, however, that, according to the Illinois statute of 1851, a married woman could be incarcerated in a state hospital without any evidence of mental illness. Moreover, then even more than now, there was no satisfactory definition of insanity or mental illness.

Bad as it was, the old Illinois statute was at least honest. The inferior status of women and children, like that of Negroes, was openly recognized. Wives were at the mercy of husbands, as Negroes were at the mercy of white men. The state did not attempt to protect these people from their self-appointed guardians. Today, women and children, and gradually Negroes too, are protected by law—while mental patients remain at the mercy of their "loved ones" and of psychiatrists.

False Commitment Today

Since the turn of the century, and especially since the end of the Second World War, American psychiatrists have tried very hard to create a favorable public image of themselves. According to this image, psychiatrists are: first, physicians, not wardens or administrators; second, like all good physicians, altruistic and overworked; third, their hospitals are overcrowded and understaffed.

Each of these emphases is important. Each is intended to assure the public that psychiatrists are not looking for business. No one need fear that he will be treated, in or outside a hospital, unless he "requires" treatment. Psychiatrists as a body insist that no one in America today is confined unnecessarily in a mental institution: no one is committed improperly, or detained longer than necessary. The standards of proper commitment and of necessary length of hospitalization are left unspecified. The public is expected to take the word of "responsible psychiatrists" for what is proper and improper in these matters. The following quotations, which reflect the views on false commitment of several prominent psychiatrists, illustrate what I have summarized above.

At a hearing before a Senate Subcommittee on the *Constitutional Rights of the Mentally Ill,* Overholser (1961) stated:

In a discussion of the rights of the mentally ill, unfounded fears have been created regarding possible unlawful deprivation of liberty of the patient. Actually, the public mental hospitals, as instrumentalities of the State, may reasonably be expected to send patients back to the community as soon as their condition warrants, and always habeas corpus is available.

After 45 years in mental hospitals and their administration, I am convinced that the basis for the belief that persons are improperly sent to mental hospitals is, for practical purposes, entirely without foundation [page 21].

It is perhaps significant that of the 7,000 patients in St. Elizabeths Hospital in 1960 only 265 were there voluntarily.

Testifying at the same hearing, Braceland (1961) also asserted that railroading no longer exists:

It is well known that there are legal safeguards against what is commonly called railroading of people into mental hospitals, and we contend that people are very well protected in all of the States. I have never in 30 years of constant living with this problem seen anyone whom I thought was being railroaded.

The opposite is true, however. People are railroaded out of mental hospitals before they should be, because these institutions are so crowded that in many instances they can't be given proper care [page 65].

Additional excerpts from Braceland's testimony are of interest, for they illustrate that, in the eyes of many psychiatrists, the standard of proper commitment is the psychiatrist's *own judgment:*

It is evident to you that we do not want to circumvent the law but there are *human aspects* of this problem which need to be considered. You will find us law abiding and *just as much interested in people's rights as anyone else.*

In general, *we favor a simple commitment procedure* entailing an application to the hospital by a close relative or friend and, as in some places, then a certification by two qualified physicians, and if judicial procedures are brought into play, the court should have the discretionary power to eliminate notification if they feel that it should be eliminated and also not have to require the patient to be present in person [italics added; page 67].

There is no mention here of the right of the patient to resist commitment. But if he has no such right, there can be no such thing as improper or false commitment. The psychiatrist can always claim that he acted in good faith and considered the commitment necessary. And, in fact, this *is* always his claim.

Mr. Creech, chief counsel for the Subcommittee, asked Braceland if he was familiar with the case of *Maben* v. *Rankin*, in which "the court found that the plaintiff had been forcibly administered an injection and taken to a hospital where she was detained for 15 days against her will" (page 70). Braceland said he was not familiar with this case, and then, in reply to another question on the use of restraints, answered:

I haven't seen anyone restrained for some time, and now with the drugs, there is rarely need for it.

I don't think that we ought to have absolute statements, for instance, that all hospitals must be open. I am not sure of that.

If a man brings his daughter to me from California, because she is in manifest danger of falling into vice or in some way disgracing herself, he doesn't expect me to let her loose in my hometown for that same thing to happen [page 71].

The cat is now out of the bag. Though not so stated in psychiatric textbooks, this is the standard actually used by many psychiatrists to justify coercive hospitalization. Is it accidental that in the example cited by Braceland, and in the Maben case cited by Creech, the "patient" was a woman? In Braceland's hypothetical case, we even have a father who engages a psychiatrist to do something to his daughter to prevent her from "falling into vice." The Illinois statute of 1851 was probably designed for just this sort of situation. This was the law under which Mrs. Packard was committed, which Deutsch considered absurd, but whose spirit still animates psychiatric thinking today. Does Braceland, who claims to be "just as much interested in people's rights as anyone else," dilate on the daughter's rights —yes, on her rights to remain at liberty, and possibly even to engage in sexual activities of which her father and *his* psychiatrist disapprove?

It is the official position of the American Psychiatric Association that physicians should have unrestricted power to commit. This is an ominous sign—for patients and psychiatrists alike—because it advocates large-scale deprivation of human liberties by members of a scientific and professional body. Consider the following statement from a document entitled, "Excerpts from Testimony Presented on Behalf of the American Psychiatric Association" (Braceland and Ewalt, 1961), which was submitted to the Senate Subcommittee on Constitutional Rights, in Washington, March 28, 1961:

We, as doctors, want our psychiatric hospitals and outpatient facilities to be looked upon as treatment centers for *sick people* in the same sense that general hospitals are so viewed. We want people in need of our services to come to them in the expectation of being benefited, *not incarcerated. We want to be considered doctors, not jailers* [italics added; page 80].

This is an odd disclaimer. First, if physicians do not want to be jailers, why do they accept that role? No one can force a psychiatrist to behave like a jailer against his will. Second, one might assume, from the above-quoted statement, that psychiatrists would want to do away with commitment. But this is far from what Braceland and Ewalt had in mind:

In recent decades, however, the new medical science of psychiatry, fighting an uphill battle, has sufficiently advanced that the public has become more sympathetic with the view that *accepts mental illness as an illness* which is correctable. It is in this context that psychiatry now seeks to modify legal procedures which will facilitate and not hinder prompt access to treatment by all citizens who need it, and this without the embarrassment, the stigma, and the deprivation of civil rights all too often associated with obtaining such treatment.

In general, *psychiatrists favor a simple commitment procedure* entailing an application to the hospital by a close relative or friend and a *certification by two qualified physicians* that they have examined the subject and found him to be *mentally ill.* . . . It is of great importance that laws should provide for emergency commitments for limited periods of time *without involving any court procedure* [italics added; page 81].

Thus, the American Psychiatric Association does not oppose commitment as such, but only commitment as a legal procedure. To subscribe to this view involves, it seems to me, scuttling our traditions of safeguarding our personal and political liberties.

Illustrative Examples of False Commitment. Since my psychiatric practice is limited to office patients, I encounter few instances of improper commitment. Nevertheless, during the past few years, I have personally observed two. In each case, commitment took place in the context of a mutually intolerable marriage which was about to disintegrate. Instead of allowing this to happen, the more aggressive and controlling marital partner committed the more passive one. Although ostensibly this step was taken to preserve the marriage, in both cases commitment resulted in the dissolution of the union by divorce.

Two pertinent cases were described by Professor Ross (1961), who had conducted a study of the legal aspects of mental hospitalization:

A well-adjusted postal employee was divorced from a rather difficult wife, but regular in his alimony payments. Incidentally, I use the word "patient" here as anyone who has been hospitalized, is going to be, or is possibly subject to it. The patient heard that his wife was about to be evicted from her apartment for nonpayment of the rent even though he has paid her the rent money as alimony. He goes to the landlord, an elderly man with symptoms of senility, and offers to pay the rent. The landlord has already been told by the ex-wife that the husband is crazy and violent. The landlord will not talk to the patient, calls the police, and files an affidavit for commitment. The patient is kept in the receiving hospital for several weeks before his hearing comes up, and at that time, everyone agrees that he is not now and never has been mentally ill [page 189].

The second case resembles the sort of situation I have observed personally:

The patient and his wife had some marital difficulties. Without telling her husband what she was up to, the wife took steps to file for divorce, and at the same time, she filed an affidavit of commitment. There was no allegation that the patient was violent or dangerous, yet he was arrested in his own home in a residential neighborhood by two policemen, who knocked at the door and told him he was wanted at the police station. They did not show a warrant. He was told it was probably in connection with some automobile accident he had some time ago. Now, most of us at one time or another have been involved in some kind of minor accident. Sometimes one is a victim, sometimes not. This meant something to him, so he left, telling his wife he would be back shortly.

Incidentally, there were two other policemen in uniform parked out in the driveway. Two cars, four policemen, the red flashing lights on, and, of course, a curious neighborhood crowd gathered and they all saw this man, a small businessman, respected in the community, being hauled away by the police.

The patient was taken to the hospital. He was told by the resident on duty that he could make one telephone call. He called his wife, who said, "Oh, that is terrible that you have been picked up. I shall take care of everything."

She did not. The patient was not told of his right to an immediate hearing in the probate court. When he did get to the probate court, I believe it was either 14 or 17 days after his detention. By this time, everyone had agreed that he was not subject to compulsory hospitalization [pages 189–190].

Here is a story excerpted from *The New York Times,* July 27, 1960:

A 64-year-old registered nurse who had been held in Hudson County mental institution since 1956, even though she had been considered sane, won her freedom today. Superior Court Judge David A. Pindar ordered her release on a writ of habeas corpus.

The woman, Miss Mae Dean, was admitted to the Jersey City Medical Center on July 4, 1956, while suffering from a severe attack of asthma. Twenty days later she was transferred to the Hudson County Hospital for Mental Disease in Secaucus on commitment by members of the medical center staff. The commitment papers were signed August 12, that year, by Hudson County Judge Paul J. Duffy.

At today's hearing in Judge Pindar's court, Dr. John J. Scott, assistant medical director of the county mental hospital, testified that as far back as 1957, at a hospital staff conference, Miss Dean had been adjudged sane.

Asked why she had not been released in view of her many requests for her freedom since that time, Dr. Scott said that the woman was without relatives and *it had been feared that she would become a public charge.*

While a patient at the hospital, Miss Dean performed the duties of a registered nurse, without pay.

Miss Dean's release was effected through the efforts of a friend, who remembered that Raymond H. Chasan, a lawyer, had won the release of another mental hospital patient in 1947, under somewhat similar circumstances [italics added].

This story speaks for itself. I should like to point out, however, that Miss Dean was denied release on her own request, despite the fact that she was considered "sane." Not much imagination is required to realize in what an exceedingly difficult situation a patient considered insane is, should *he* wish to protest his hospitalization. His very protest is likely to be construed as "lack of insight into his illness," and thus interpreted as fresh justification for his confinement. And yet, the availability, in principle, of habeas corpus is considered by Overholser and others adequate protection of the rights of persons involuntarily hospitalized.

At the hearing of the Senate Subcommittee mentioned earlier, Chasan (1961) described several other cases of improper commitment. This was one of them:

I had another case some years ago in which a man was committed by his wife. He had a human failing which is not too unfamilar to us. He drank to excess. And she wanted to put him away for that reason, and I think there were also some marital problems which could be resolved readily for her by having him out of the way.

He had the DT's when he was put in. He recovered from them within a period of 7 to 10 days. He was in there for 4 or 5 years, and he was talking to stone walls. Nobody would pay any attention to him until he got through to me somehow.

I had a habeas corpus issued. He was released immediately [page 223].

What can one say about these cases? Surely, the least is that psychiatry is as open to misuse as any other social institution. Perhaps more. Hence there is need for more, not less, nonmedical vigilance over the deployment of psychiatric power.

Mr. Chasan's views on the problem of improper commitment may be inserted here:

In practice, the mental institutions in my State [New Jersey] are jealous of their control over patients. They will release patients only conditionally in the custody of others and subject to reinstitutionalization, without further recourse even to such commitment procedures as now exist. In the case of a person who is without family or who, after a long period of confinement, has lost contact with friends, the commitment becomes tantamount to a life sentence. When people thus confined long beyond any necessity for treatment or restraint can bring their plight to the attention of counsel, and ultimately to the courts, then remedies are available. However, institutional restraints on correspondence to the outside severely restrict such prospects. And I might add parenthetically that in one of the institutions of which I am aware, the mail, ingoing and outgoing, is censored. By what right, I don't know. So that it is relatively impossible for one confined in such an institution to make his plight known to anyone on the outside [pages 220–221].

An amazing case of railroading, involving a psychiatrist on the staff of St. Elizabeths Hospital, was reported by the American Civil Liberties Union (Arens, 1961):

Only recently . . . a 34-year-old Falls Church, Va., trash collector was held in the Southwestern State Hospital for the Criminally Insane in Marion, Va. He had previously been taken into custody upon suspicion of murdering the Carroll Jackson family when Peter Herkos, an alleged "mind reader" with "clairvoyant" powers, pointed to him as a suspect. Mr. Herkos was invited to this area and had his expenses paid by a psychiatrist on the staff of St. Elizabeths Hospital, Dr. Regis Riesenman. Without any evidence to make a formal charge, *the police, acting upon the recommendation of Dr. Riesenman,* who in turn relied upon the recommendation of the "mind reader" for his evaluation of the case, picked up the unfortunate trash collector for questioning. After it was determined he was not the murderer he was not released, but instead, was subjected to civil commitment proceedings. Again Dr. Riesenman entered the case. He even sat as the sole psychiatrist of the three-member hastily convened commitment board which adjudged that the man be committed to a mental hospital for the *criminally insane*. The hearing was convened at 3:30 A.M. and within a few hours the man was on his way to a hospital hundreds of miles from his family and friends. He was represented by a court-appointed attorney who was summoned out of bed by the judge. The judge and the *jail physician* were the other two members of the commitment board. Needless to say, there was no opportunity for the attorney to consult with his client nor to give him the effective assistance of counsel. Parenthetically, a man named Melvin Rees has since been convicted for murdering two members of the Jackson family in Maryland, and has been indicted in Virginia for murdering two other members of the family.

The victim of this mockery of justice finally secured his liberty after protracted delay—after the intervention of the American Civil Liberties Union, which succeeded in finding a volunteer attorney near the mental hospital, who instituted habeas corpus proceedings. Under his pressure the hospital staff came into court with a psychiatric analysis that the man was neither criminally insane nor in need of psychiatric treatment. The fact remains, however, that the Commonwealth of Virginia succeeded in depriving a citizen of his liberty under mental health auspices for no reason which could stand the scrutiny of impartial and rational investigation, and in a manner which did violence to every factor considered essential to due process of law [italics added; pages 213–214].

Braceland and Ewalt declared that "We [that is, psychiatrists] want to be considered doctors, not jailers." These cases do not support their assertion. Undoubtedly, many psychiatrists do not want to be jailers, and refuse to be. But it is clear that many enjoy that role. Others may want to be detectives, judges, or even executioners.

Here is an example, reported in the *Bridgeport* (Connecticut) *Herald* on January 8, 1953, of a psychiatrist wishing to be a jailer. The offense against society by Max "The Actor" Laibman was that "he imagined himself to be a great actor and craved the footlights.' He had, however, only done bit parts on television. Following his fourth escape in less than two years from the Middletown (Connecticut) State Hospital, one of the hospital physicians was quoted as follows: "Dr. Russman stated that Max is harmless. 'He'll be back again,' the hospital official said, 'and the next time we'll just throw the key away.' "

The Legal Nonrecognition of False Commitment. It would be absurd to expect the practice of psychiatry to be an exception among human activities. Only by believing that in this field men are superhuman can we maintain that psychiatrists are never dishonest, never make mistakes, never act foolishly, and hence never commit a person falsely. If there is doubt about the reality of false commitment, I hope the cases cited will dispel it (see also Goldman and Ross, 1956).

Is there any legal redress for improper commitment? No, there is not. If the commitment forms are properly executed, the plaintiff has no valid claim.

In *Guzy* v. *Guzy* (1959), the plaintiff sued his wife and two examining physicians for having detained him in a state hospital for 115 days. The court dismissed the action, arguing:

> The gist of an action for false imprisonment is unlawful detention . . . so that *imprisonment which is authorized by process regular on its face and which is issued by a court of competent jurisdiction is lawful,* and cannot give rise to a cause of action for false imprisonment, *even though the process was erroneously or improvidently issued. . . .* In short, where the court authorizes an arrest or confinement, it is the act of the court and not of the complainant, and there can be no charge against him for false imprisonment . . . [italics added].

This position is accepted by the courts in all the States. A North Carolina court (*Baily* v. *McGill*, 1957) decided that even if the two psychiatrists who certify the patient to the hospital act in bad faith, they cannot be held liable for damages in a civil suit:

> The rule in this jurisdiction is that a defamatory statement made by witnesses in the due course of a judicial proceeding . . . is absolutely privileged, and cannot be made the basis of an action for libel or slander, *even though the testimony is given with express malice and knowledge of its falsity* [italics added].

The case of *Brecka* v. *State of New York* (1958) is another example of commitment that was legally proper but factually false. In this case, the Court of Claims dismissed a claim for false imprisonment because the health officer's certificate was found valid. This court, however, was not satisfied with the situation, for it stated that it was

. . . not happy that it took forty-nine days to find out that the patient was not actually one who would be dangerous to herself and others. . . . What other remedies, if any, are available to her against those who took claimant into custody and certified her condition as herein indicated, is a question upon which another tribunal must pass.

It is obvious that people who are improperly committed are legally impotent. Reform is necessary, and it can be achieved only through legislative action.

Is Habeas Corpus an Adequate Remedy Against False Commitment?

There are only two ways for a committed mental patient to gain his release. One is to cooperate with the medical staff of the hospital, in the hope of being judged sane and discharged. Some of the difficulties in securing release by this method have already been illustrated, and will be documented further in Chapter 14. Another is for the patient to bring suit against the hospital superintendent for a habeas corpus hearing, thus defining him and his staff as adversaries. Habeas corpus is the classic legal safeguard for every person deprived of his liberty. However, because of a complex interplay of educational, legal, psychological, and socioeconomic reasons, most mental patients cannot avail themselves of this protection against false commitment. And even when they can, it is not an effective remedy.

As protection against improper commitment, habeas corpus is especially inadequate for the indigent and the poorly educated. This requires emphasis, because the supporters of "easy" medical, as against "cumbersome" judicial, commitment always point to it as affording ample protection. For example, having asserted his belief that the rights of the mentally ill are well protected, Overholser (1961) added, ". . . and always habeas corpus is available" (page 21). Actually, however, the people most affected do not know how to use it, and no effort is made to teach them. On the contrary, psychiatrists usually consider it "good therapy" to keep from the involuntarily hospitalized patient information about his legal rights and recourses, lest he thereby deprive himself of needed "treatment."

Furthermore, it is unrealistic to expect too much from the writ of habeas corpus in a modern psychiatric setting. As originally conceived, the purpose of this legal measure was to protect victims of political harassment. It was never intended to protect people from deprivations of liberty at the hands of physicians and psychiatrists. Hence, it need not surprise us to find that habeas corpus is a grossly inadequate measure to protect the victims of psychiatric imprisonment.

Guttmacher is another prominent advocate of medical commitment. In Maryland (where Guttmacher works), the law provides that two physicians can legalize the involuntary confinement of a patient in either a private or public psychiatric hospital. In his testimony before the Senate Subcommittee, Guttmacher (1961) quoted the following statistics about the Spring Grove State Hospital, which has a patient population of 2,500:

> By far the greatest number of them were admitted and are held on the basis of the two medical certificates. And there has never been any kind of court action in their cases.
> During the past 8 years the total number of sanity and habeas corpus hearings was 73. Forty-seven were remanded back to the institution and 26 were released. Forty percent of the patients released were able to adjust satisfactorily outside of the hospital, the rest had to be readmitted [page 145].

Without knowing the turnover rate, or the total patient population during the eight-year period, we cannot be sure what proportion of the patient-population 73 individuals represent. In any case, the proportion is certain to be less than 1 percent. In Guttmacher's opinion, this is because "most patients when they get in a hospital are quite content to be there, and a court hearing is unnecessary" (page 156). Is this because the patients like it at Spring Grove Hospital, or because they do not know how to avail themselves of their rights, and no one helps them to do so?

The fact is that the medically committed patient does not know how to make use of his right of a habeas corpus hearing. This contention is borne out by a comparison of the situation at Spring Grove State Hospital with that at St. Elizabeths involving patients committed by the criminal route. In the latter group, each patient has the aid of an attorney, either privately retained or appointed by the courts; hence he is in a better position than his medically committed colleague to know his rights and to implement them. If Guttmacher's opinion—that "most patients when they get in a hospital are quite content to be there, and a court hearing is unnecessary" —is correct, then most of these individuals should *not* sue to get out. What are the facts?

In response to questions about habeas corpus hearings for patients at St. Elizabeths Hospital, Overholser (1961) testified before the Subcommittee as follows:

Most of these petitions, may I say, come from those who are in a criminal category. There are very, very few of them from those who are there under civil commitment, very few, but on the criminal side we are kept very, very busy [page 33].

Approximately 250 petitions for habeas corpus were filed during 1960. The total number of patients admitted by criminal commitment during that year was not given. The testimony revealed, however, that during 1960, 247 patients were admitted by mandatory commitment, having been found not guilty by reason of insanity. Thus, apparently all, or a large proportion, of the patients committed by the criminal route petition for release. This fact supports my contention that the interests of the criminally accused person, whether he be in jail or mental hospital, are better protected than those of the patient confined by civil commitment. The law decrees that the adversaries of the civilly committed patient are, in fact, his friends. From this calamity he can rarely extricate himself.

The adequacy of habeas corpus for protection against improper mental hospitalization was recently affirmed by a court decision in the District of Columbia. In the Ragsdale case (*Ragsdale* v. *Overholser*, 1960), the court of appeals recognized that when a person found not guilty by reason of insanity is automatically confined in a mental hospital—without a specific finding of present insanity—there exists a constitutional problem about the legitimacy of the confinement. To this, the court answered that the writ of habeas corpus is available and should be used to test the legality of the patient's confinement. The court described this habeas corpus hearing as a "*de novo* proceeding to examine petitioner's then existing mental condition; at such hearing he is free to put in evidence, both lay and expert, to demonstrate that he has recovered to the point where he will not be dangerous to himself or others" (page 947).

This sounds easier on paper than it is in practice. How can a lay person effectively rebut the testimony of "prosecuting" psychiatrists? To accomplish this, he would need psychiatrists on his side, at least as prominent and impressive to the court or jury as those who are trying to incriminate him as mentally ill or dangerous. Obviously, this may be extremely difficult—or even impossible—for a patient to secure. (The problem of the litigation between patient and hospital superintendent is discussed in detail in Chapter 14.)

I submit that the psychiatric-legal match between patient-petitioner and psychiatrist-superintendent is very uneven. The odds so strongly favor the latter, that it cannot be fairly argued that the mere availability of the writ of habeas corpus protects the patient from the threat of imprisonment without due process of law.

To me, it is unfair to demand of a psychiatric patient—especially if he is poorly educated and indigent—that he prove his sanity or nondangerousness. We would not ask that he prove his innocence of a criminal charge, and then consider his mere opportunity to do so adequate protection against false or unfair accusations by a district attorney. Yet, this is exactly what we ask the mental patient to do. To make matters worse, such a person must rebut charges of mental illness, charges as amorphous as anything with which K., Kafka's protagonist in *The Trial*, had to contend. It is obvious that such a "defendant" is almost completely helpless and has small chance of winning his battle with an Overholser.

Consider, in this connection, Hugh J. McGee's (1961) testimony at the Senate hearing. Said McGee: "Dr. Overholser could keep any criminal patient, *any patient* committed as a result of a finding of not guilty by reason of insanity, in St. Elizabeths *as long as he wanted to*" (italics added; page 62).

Mr. McGee testified before the Senate Subcommittee as chairman of the Mental Health Committee of the District of Columbia Bar Association. On the whole, his views on mental illness and commitment agree with those of Guttmacher and Overholser. Thus, his opinions about the power of hospital superintendents cannot be said to be biased by a negative attitude toward coercive hospitalization. On the contrary. He referred to good psychiatrists as "good kings," implying that he considered the king-subject relationship the proper model for the psychiatrist-patient relationship. Said McGee (1961) at the hearing:

> The meticulous administration of these laws in the District of Columbia makes the legal safeguards seem at times unnecessary and unduly cumbersome. However, good kings frequently have poor successors. Unfortunately, all jurisdictions cannot be blessed with Overholsers, Schultzs and Guttmachers [page 56].

And yet he described "hospitalization" at St. Elizabeths as follows:

Quite a few people—maybe it is society's desire—feel that a person who commits a crime, a criminal act, should be punished. And *they merely permit that punishment to take place at St. Elizabeths Hospital.* They don't care where it takes place, and many of them, I have heard it expressed, many individuals on the bench and in the bar say *"He will get it just as good and just as hard and maybe even longer at St. Elizabeths Hospital"* and that satisfies them as to the punishment for the criminal act whereas Durham contemplated nothing like that. It contemplated treatment and rehabilitation [italics added; page 60].

But everyone can claim to be well intentioned. In practical matters, affecting the liberty and welfare of individuals, what matters are facts, not "contemplations." And the fact is that mental hospitalization is worse punishment than imprisonment in the penitentiary. This, according to Mc-Gee, is the opinion of those who tried both: "One of my clients who has served in the prison systems of Florida, Georgia, Virginia, and Maryland, and on road gangs too, of those States, told me dead seriously that he would rather serve a year in any one of them than six months at old Howard Hall [at St. Elizabeths Hospital]" (page 659).

Conclusions

The situation at St. Elizabeths Hospital, especially under the Durham rule, gives us a glimpse into what the future might be if psychiatrists were given increasing powers in penalizing offenders. It shows the hospital director as the willing agent of his superiors in general, and of the local courts in particular. His work epitomizes the scuttling of psychiatric and moral considerations in the practice of hospital psychiatry, and their replacement, in quite naked form, by a positivistic legal attitude which equates legality with morality.

I am not concerned here with the allegedly good intentions of legislators and judges responsible for the laws governing mental illness and commitment in the District of Columbia. Nor am I interested in the motives of the psychiatrists who lend their persons and professional prestige to the implementation of these laws. I look only at the facts as I see them. If the laws, and the psychiatric testimony and hospitalization which are such important parts of them, violate the principles of legal fair play—of our basic concepts of constitutional rights and due process—then, I submit, we should frankly recognize the facts and alter our practices to bring them in line with the moral aims and principles of American democracy.

In view of what seem to me glaring shortcomings in such matters as the Durham rule, automatic commitment after acquittal by reason of insanity, and commitment in general, I am impressed by a marked lack of concern among psychiatrists for the liberties, privileges, and rights of men regarded by some as mentally ill. Herein lies the gravest danger. For it clearly suggests that many psychiatrists accord greater importance to the promotion of the self-interests of psychiatry than to the fundamental values of individualism, liberty, and self-government.

CHAPTER 6 » *Testamentary Capacity*

Prosecution of the dead . . . was a mockery in which virtually defence was impossible and confiscation inevitable.
　　　　　　　　　　　—HENRY CHARLES LEA (1887, page 219)

THE LAW recognizes—indeed, decrees—mental incapacity as one of the grounds for contesting the validity of a will. For a will to be declared invalid psychiatrists must testify in court that the testator lacked the capacity to execute a valid will.

In many ways, the psychiatrist's participation in this situation is typical of psychiatric participation in all sorts of legal proceedings. It merits examination not because the problem of testamentary capacity is itself so important, but rather because it offers a striking example of the institutional, as against the scientific, functions of psychiatry.

What Is Testamentary Capacity?

Whether a person is capable of executing a valid will is a problem that the practicing psychotherapist is not likely to encounter. Thus, it is not surprising that psychiatric theorists have neglected this subject. The only psychiatrists to show any interest in this problem have been those who serve interested parties as experts in determining testamentary capacity. Perhaps it is not unrelated to the real-life roles of these psychiatrists how they defined this alleged faculty. Let us look at some of these definitions.

In his textbook, *Forensic Psychiatry,* Davidson (1952) offered the following:

A person's mental ability to make a will is known as testamentary capacity. A psychiatrist is frequently called—usually after the subject has died—to tell the court whether the testator did or did not have the mental capacity to make a valid will. A person making a will must (1) know that he is making a will, (2) know the nature and extent of his property, and (3) know the natural objects of his bounty. These are the three "tests" which, in a sense, the patient must "pass" before he is considered mentally competent to make a will [page 99].

In most medico-legal cases, the doctor examines the patient, and testifies as to his findings. In will litigation, the psychiatrist rarely has the chance to examine the testator who is necessarily quite dead when the case comes to court. The practitioner usually has to depend on a hypothetical question describing the testator's behavior and conclude from the hypothesis whether the subject could have passed the three tests on the day he signed the will [page 104].

Henderson and Gillespie (1950) stated:

The point in this matter is to determine, not whether the testator is sane or insane, but whether his mental capacity is adequate to the testamentary act [page 702].

Finally, in *Psychiatry and the Law,* Guttmacher and Weihofen (1952) provided this tautology: "If a testator was mentally incompetent, the effect can only be to render the will void" (page 344).

These quotations are representative samples from the literature on this subject. They tempt one to dismiss the matter as so much psychiatric double-talk. Many psychiatrists take this position. By so doing, however, they leave the field to the official experts of forensic psychiatry. The social reality of litigations involving psychiatric determinations of testamentary capacity places a moral obligation on all psychiatrists to take this matter seriously.

The definitions of testamentary capacity which forensic psychiatrists have furnished us are purely verbal in character. They only look like definitions: words are strung together so as to give the impression that each one is explained by another. Terms like "mental capacity," "testamentary act," and some others are constructed to conform to the grammatical structure of an assertion. This, however, is not enough to ensure that the result is a logically meaningful proposition.

Such definitions promote neither clear thinking nor scientific work. What, then, is their function? Speaking of his fellow eighteenth century German philosophers, Georg Lichtenberg remarked that "they were running a little business in obscurantism." Forensic psychiatrists are running a large business in it.

The suspicion that promotion of self-interests is an important issue in this matter is borne out by the fact that, although forensic psychiatrists often bewail the difficulties of their work, they never suggest withdrawing from certain activities. On the contrary, they invariably advocate expanding the scope and power of psychiatry. Overholser's (1959) comments, in his authoritative chapter on forensic psychiatry in the *American Handbook of Psychiatry*, are illustrative:

Nevertheless, the law tends to be somewhat too rigid and out of line with psychiatric thought in its definition of delusion. Many are the cases in which the wills of persons, whom the psychiatrist would consider notably out of contact with reality, seriously mentally ill, and deluded, were sustained [page 1890].

Exemplified here is the image of the psychiatrist, busily ferreting out "mental illness," even in persons he never saw and who are dead. He does this, moreover, instead of asking, Who is challenging the validity of the will and why? The next passage is a good illustration of psychiatric self-promotion:

The law relating to testamentary incapacity as a result of mental disease would certainly benefit, from a psychiatric point of view, by the application of modern knowledge regarding mental functioning [page 1890].

But is it the purpose of the law to benefit psychiatry or the testator? To confuse these questions would be bad enough. Overholser, however, does more than this. He treats the whole matter as if the interests of psychiatry were supreme: all the other interests of society ought to be subordinated to them.

Will-Contests and Testamentary Capacity: a Game-Model Analysis

Let us now examine the social situation in which the validity of a will is contested on the ground that the testator was mentally incapable. To do this we shall again look upon the human situation before us as though it were a game: Each participant is a player, following certain rules, in order to win (achieve his particular purposes). To attain an adequate sociopsychological analysis of testamentary capacity, we shall have to account for the following features of this phenomenon.

First, the issue of the validity of a will—and therefore of the testator's mental capacity—arises only if someone contests a will. This implies a struggle between one or more parties, who may have unequal rights and powers.

Second, the rules of the game governing the drawing up of wills, and the rights to inherit money or property, are well established. The laws which define what we could call the *inheritance game* vary from place to place, and from time to time. Obviously, the problem of testamentary capacity cannot arise unless the law recognizes mental incapacity as a valid ground for setting aside a will.

Third, in recognizing the right to make a will, the law permits persons to exercise a measure of control over their properties even after death. Thus, wills express the importance which our society places on the integrity of the self as a psychosocial and legal entity. A person is not just an organism that ceases when it dies. On the contrary, social existence is here radically divorced from biologic functioning—as it is also in creative works of art and science. Through his book, for example, every author achieves a kind of immortality. Through his last testament, so may every person.

The crux of the problem of testamentary capacity is therefore a conflict of interests. As potential testators, we would all like society to insure our right to make a valid and binding will, to be executed as drawn. As potential heirs, we have an interest in enlisting the protection of society to safeguard what we consider our rightful inheritance. Thus, we might wish to have wills unfavorable to us set aside. Between the contestants in this battle of the inheritance game—that is, between testators and inheritors—stands society. Through its legal machinery, it is entrusted to make the inheritance game continue as an active, ongoing enterprise. The interests of society, as a whole, cannot be easily ascertained, because society is composed of a hopelessly complicated mixture of testators and inheritors. However, as in other situations requiring the regulation of social intercourse, the so-called public interest is generally enlisted to support a social game of life that is in harmony with the prevailing sense of justice and reasonableness.

Despite this exquisitely ethical and social character of the subject, psychiatrists tend to deal with the problem of testamentary capacity as if it were a purely psychiatric affair. We are told, for example, that post-mortem examination of the brain, or review of the testator's behavior with members of his family, may be helpful in ascertaining his "capacity" to make a valid will. I would suggest, however, that a will resulting in such a contest is prima facie evidence that the testator had adequate "contact with reality"; after all, it shows that he wished to disinherit his so-called natural heirs, and knew the rules of the game for doing so.

There is reason to doubt, therefore, whether, in a will-contest based on psychiatric grounds, anyone is really interested in the mental state of the testator. Just as in capital cases the function of the insanity plea is to circumvent the death penalty, so questioning the testator's sanity serves to set aside a will which injures the community's sense of fair play in the inheritance game. In such a contest, the issue is not the testator's mental capacity, but who shall inherit his property. This question—and hence also the question of the testator's sanity—is then decided in accordance with whether, and to what extent, the testator's behavior preceding his death, and especially his will, violate the *public sense of decency and right*. If the public sense of right is violated—as when a rich man disinherits his ailing widow and leaves his money to his mistress, or when a rich woman bestows all her property on a home for stray cats and disinherits her poor sisters, who are her only remaining heirs—then it is virtually certain that if the will is contested, the court will find that the testator lacked the capacity to execute a valid will. This, of course, is no more than a reaffirmation of the prevalent social sense of right. No psychiatrist is needed to establish it, since it is, by definition, a matter of common sense. The psychiatrist's participation in this situation obscures the fact that no scientific issue is at stake, and gives the impression that a scientific decision has been reached. Again, a moral conflict has been disguised as a medical-psychiatric problem.

The psychiatrist who testifies in court about testamentary incapacity plays a role similar to that of his colleagues who testify about commitment or criminal responsibility. Each acts as an agent of someone other than the "patient." In each instance, the purpose of the intervention is to impose a measure of social control upon the "patient." The psychiatrist who engages in the inheritance game plays a crucial role in determining the type of social action that will be taken against persons (or their interests) who offend the public sense of decency in relation to the rights of natural heirs.

The Inquisitor, the Psychiatrist, and the Dead

There are striking parallels between the medieval inquisitor and the contemporary institutional psychiatrist (Szasz, 1961, Chapter 12). There are also similarities between the old custom of charging the dead with heresy and the present one of charging him with mental illness.

By the beginning of the thirteenth century, after the Inquisition had gathered momentum, it was common practice to accuse of heresy not only one's friends and neighbors but also the deceased. The dead were prosecuted, tried, and sentenced, much as were the living. The main penalty was confiscation of the dead person's estate. Thus, the consequences of accusing a dead person of heresy were somewhat similar to the consequences of accusing a deceased testator of mental illness. In both instances, there is a change in the beneficiaries of the dead man's estate. In the Middle Ages, the charge of heresy resulted in the confiscation of the property from the natural heirs of the deceased, and its transfer, in general, to the Church and to the sovereign. Today, declaring a testator mentally ill causes his property to be confiscated from the person or persons to whom he bequeathed it, and its transfer, in general, to the natural heirs. If the redistribution of property resulting from the actions of contemporary psychiatrists seems to us more reasonable than that which resulted from the actions of medieval inquisitors, it is only because we live in the twentieth, not the thirteenth, century.

If, however, the practice of psychiatric examination of the testamentary capacity of a dead person still seems reasonable to the reader, I suggest that he consider the following. What exactly is a psychiatrist, as an expert, asked to ascertain in this sort of case? If he is asked to pass upon the testator's so-called mental health, without anyone defining mental health, I hazard that the psychiatrist will find what the highest bidder pays him to find. To be sure, like the Dominican inquisitors, the psychiatrists try to be "sincere." They truly believe it is their duty to assess the dead man's testamentary capacity, just as the priests believed that they were investigating a person's loyalty to the Church. Let us grant them this definition of their task. Should we not conclude, however, that a properly executed will, conforming to the requirements set by law, ought to be considered prima facie evidence of the competency of the testator?

It must be said for the inquisitors, however, that at least they took their work seriously. They did not stop with discrediting a deceased person's right to make a will. If a person was declared a heretic, *all* his business transactions became invalid:

All safeguards were withdrawn from every transaction. No creditor or purchaser could be sure of the orthodoxy of him with whom he was dealing; and, even more than the principle that ownership was forfeited as soon as heresy has been committed by the living, the practice of proceeding against the memory of the dead after an interval virtually unlimited, rendered it impossible for any man to feel secure in the possession of property, whether it had descended in his family for generations, or had been acquired within an ordinary lifetime [Lea, 1887, page 218].

In the thirteenth century, when this spirit prevailed in the north of Italy and the south of France, it had a ruinous effect on both commerce and industry, and hence on the entire fabric of daily life. Indeed, Lea attributed the cultural ascendancy of England and the Netherlands to the fact that the Inquisition was minimal or nonexistent in those countries.

Thus, if a testator is declared incompetent to have executed a valid will, why is this not extended to contracts of other types as well? A testament drawn up a year or more before a person's death may be set aside on psychiatric grounds. However, subsequent to making the will, our hypothetical testator might have invested successfully in the stock market. As a result, his estate, when he died, was much larger than when his will was drawn up. Should his stock transaction also be declared invalid?

Clearly, psychiatrists could not declare all contracts invalid without wrecking the conduct of society's business as we know it. I submit that psychiatrists have avoided doing this because they have been more cynical about their belief in mental illness or incompetency than were the medieval Dominicans in their belief in Christianity. The inquisitors pushed the thesis about heresy to its logical limits, to the destruction of their society, and almost to the ruin of their own religious institutions. It remains uncertain just how destructive these psychiatric activities are for the rational conduct of society. Perhaps this will become fully apparent only after institutional psychiatry has wreaked irreparable damage on the free society.

In sum, comparing the invalidation of wills on psychiatric and heretical grounds shows us psychiatry as an institution of social control, but one whose scope is restricted to the family. When a psychiatrist declares a deceased testator incompetent, he disqualifies him as a contracting individual with members of his family, but not with the community at large. Obligations to nonfamily members, even though incurred after a will has been drawn up which was later declared invalid, are considered binding on the estate.

Conclusions

The psychiatrist who testifies in court about a deceased person's testamentary capacity plays a role in the inheritance game. The rules of this game are the laws and mores governing the inheritance of property.

The practice of forensic psychiatry is a form of social control. Unlike that exercised by the police or the courts, it is disguised, first, as medicine, and second, as the humane application of scientific knowledge of behavior. This type of social control is a threat to a free society, because it is based on mysticism and deceit, not rational thought and honesty.

Litigations employing the notion of testamentary capacity exemplify some of the hazards inherent in the practical applications of modern social science. The setting aside of wills which violate the public sense of right illustrate the close association between the open defiance of public opinion and morality and the notion of mental illness or incompetence. Once more, sanity is compliance with the rules—in this case, with the rules of the inheritance game; deviance is branded as insanity.

Psychiatry, as a modern social institution, has been enlisted to support certain ethical opinions and practices, and to condemn others. Moreover, this has been done covertly, under the guise of promoting health and sanity. This kind of application of psychiatry to everyday life seems to be another example of humanity's persistent attempt to take recourse in the ancient doctrine of natural law. Faced with conflicts and uncertainties, scientism—the modern form of mystic-religious doctrines of certainty—offers man surcease from doubt and responsibility. Many are eager to embrace such doctrines, and to delegate responsibilities—and hence powers—to the twentieth century shamans, the experts. Herein lies the threat of institutional psychiatry to human dignity and liberty.

CHAPTER 7 » *Psychiatric Power*
and Social Action

There is a reason for the general deterioration as regards liberty. This reason is the increased power of organizations and the increasing degree to which men's actions are controlled by this or that large body. In every organization there are two purposes: one, the ostensible purpose for which the organization exists; the other, the increase in the power of its officials. This second purpose is very likely to make a stronger appeal to the officials concerned than the general public purpose that they are expected to serve.

—BERTRAND RUSSELL (1956)

ORGANIZED PSYCHIATRY in the United States is an example of a favored social institution. Not only is psychiatry accorded recognition by state and federal governments; it is also provided with privileges and protections that are withheld from other medical specialties. For instance, psychiatrists may own and operate facilities in which they may hold and treat persons against their will. They may do the same in publicly owned psychiatric institutions. No other medical specialist has this power. Neither internists nor obstetricians nor surgeons operate special institutions for involuntary patients, nor are they authorized by law to subject people to treatments they do not want.

Like all social institutions, institutional psychiatry seeks to achieve two purposes: first, to discharge its official duties; second, to extend its own power and rewards.

One of the main functions of organized psychiatry, and historically the oldest, is the segregation of certain members of society. To perform this function, psychiatrists must have power. In this chapter, I shall describe and illustrate the legal basis for the exercise of this power.

The Legal Structure of Hospitals

The same terms are used to describe medical and mental hospitals. In both cases, the word "hospital" is employed to refer to buildings officially dedicated to the care of persons called patients. Both types of institutions are staffed by professional workers called physicians and nurses, and are devoted to the diagnosis and treatment of conditions called diseases. Finally, both may be supported privately, publicly, or by a combination of funds. In sum, the similarities between medical and mental hospitals are institutional rather than instrumental. Likewise, the similarities between medical treatments and psychotherapy are also largely institutional (Szasz, 1959). It is significant that many general hospitals contain psychiatric units. In these instances, the similarities between the two types of institutions are maximal. As a result, many persons lose sight of the crucial differences between medical- and mental-hospital practices.

All hospitals, whether private or public, medical or mental, must be licensed by the state. Medical and mental hospitals, however, are licensed to do different things. I shall consider the situation in New York State (State of New York, 1957, 1959), since currently I am most familiar with it. Essentially similar regulations govern the operations of psychiatric hospitals in most of the United States (Lindman and McIntyre, Jr., 1961).

The Medical Hospital. Medical hospitals are authorized to provide medical and surgical diagnostic procedures and treatments. These must be performed in the hospital and supervised by the professional staff. The hospital is responsible to three groups: the patients, the hospital staff, and the state (as representative of the interests of the general public). I should like to emphasize here that medical hospitals are authorized to care only for those persons who want hospital treatment. The use of diagnostic or treatment measures without the patient's consent constitutes assault and battery and is a criminal offense. Only in serious emergencies, or if the patient is unconscious or a minor, may hospitals and physicians deviate from this rule. In these circumstances, relatives have authority to grant or withhold permission for medical and surgical procedures. There are a few exceptions to this rule in cases that constitute a public health hazard. For people with diseases like tuberculosis or leprosy, involuntary restraint and treatment may be mandatory. Otherwise, voluntary treatment is the goal of democratic patterns of health care.

The Mental Hospital. The method of admission establishes the initial relationship between the patient and the mental hospital. There are several types of admission procedures—for example, judicial, administrative, and emergency hospitalization, admission for observation only, noncontest admission, and so forth. Despite the apparent complexity and the lack of uniformity in these procedures, the mental patient enters the hospital in one of two ways: voluntarily or involuntarily. It must be emphasized that in neither case does he have a *true contractual relationship* with the hospital. Irrespective of the method of entry, the patient finds himself in a committed status. Not only does this mean that he may be held in a hospital against his will, but also that the law no longer recognizes his right to enter into mutually binding contractual obligations. For example, if a patient enters a mental hospital voluntarily, and with the understanding that he may leave at will, the psychiatrists may nevertheless refuse to release him. This occurs frequently in the hospital practice of psychiatry. It illustrates the fact that although the mental hospital patient may be led to believe, and may think, that he is entering into a contractual obligation, the hospital and the psychiatrists with whom he "contracts" are actually free to interpret the agreement as they wish. This fact has recently been incorporated into the laws of the State of Connecticut. On October 1, 1961, a statute was enacted formally "protecting" the psychiatrist-patient privilege. It specified, however, that "There is no privilege . . . under this act when a psychiatrist, in the course of diagnosis and treatment of the patient, determines that the patient is in need of care and treatment in a hospital for mental illness" (Goldstein and Katz, 1962, page 737).

From the patient's point of view this means that the psychiatrist is free to break his contract. To do so, he must only believe, sincerely or otherwise, that the patient "is in need of hospital care and treatment." Why is this provision needed? And why is it considered good by lawyers and psychiatrists alike? Because the law fails to recognize the patient in the mental hospital—and by the same token, also the patient who allegedly ought to be in such a hospital—as a subject fit to enter into binding contracts. Instead, it treats him as a person having the status of an incompetent or a child (see Chapter 12). Like wives or children in primitive societies, mental hospital patients are treated not as individuals, but as the occupants of statuses. The psychiatrist is given a complementary role: like the *paterfamilias* of bygone kinship systems, he becomes "responsible" for the welfare of his patients.

This deprivation of the basic right to contract may be illustrated by statutes governing hospitalization, and by comments of leading psychiatrists on this subject.

Until recently, all mental hospital admissions were involuntary. This was consistent with the view, once widely held, that mental patients were "demented." Hence, one did not seek their cooperation. Since the end of the Second World War, there has been a growing interest in voluntary admission to public mental hospitals. Voluntary—or, more precisely, ostensibly voluntary—admission policies have been adopted in a number of places, partly in an effort to sustain the myth that mental illness is just like any other illness. Indeed, the fact that voluntary mental hospitalization is available is now being interpreted as evidence of the similarity between bodily and psychiatric illness. It is in this spirit that Guttmacher and Weihofen (1952) have advocated voluntary admission laws. They wrote:

> Whereas commitment connotes a legal command by which a person is placed in an institution, *voluntary admission signalizes recognition of the new conception of "insanity" as a form of illness calling for medical care.* Such a conception was, of course, impossible so long as commitment was resorted to only as a means of confining the dangerous insane. But after the view became accepted, legally as well as medically, that *commitment might be proper, not only where it was necessary for the safety of the public or of the patient, but also where it might be conducive to his restoration of health,* it was inevitable that we should come to regard mental illness as not essentially different from physical illness, and to believe that a person able to realize that he is mentally ill should be able to obtain hospital treatment as easily and as informally as he can for physical illness [italics added; pages 305–306].

The logic of this argument is astonishing. Guttmacher and Weihofen assert that by the mere act of treating A and B in the same way, we shall uncover and establish similarities between them. This is nonsense. Whether mental disease is comparable to physical disease, and if so, in what ways, must be investigated by empirical research and epistemological analysis. Instead of undertaking either of these tasks, the authors, and many others, advocate social action to establish empirical facts and logical constructs.

In addition to this peculiar—and, to me, completely false—reasoning, Guttmacher and Weihofen advocated measures which Wertham (1955a) considered typical of the operations of the "psychoauthoritarian" psychiatrist. After considering voluntary admission laws, Guttmacher and Weihofen proceeded to disregard the contract between mental hospital and patient. Having argued that mental hospitalization should be similar to medical hospitalization—since, in their words, "mental illness [is] not essentially different from physical illness" (page 306)—they went to the other extreme and argued against the mental patient's freedom to leave the hospital. This position is widely shared by psychiatrists.

> Refusal to release a voluntary patient on demand would not only be difficult to justify legally but would be highly undesirable because resort to voluntary admission will be discouraged unless it is made quite clear that a patient may change his mind and leave. Most voluntary statutes . . . [provide] that a voluntary patient shall be released within a specified number of days after he gives

written notice of his desire to leave *unless, in the meanwhile, the hospital authorities start proceedings to have his status changed to that of involuntary patient.* It has been held that detention for a reasonable number of days after written demand for release is proper, although a refusal to release without legal proceedings being taken is illegal and may be ground for claiming damages for false imprisonment.

New York has added another sanction to prevent premature demands for release by requiring an applicant for admission to sign an agreement that he will not give notice for at least 60 days. If a patient nevertheless demands release before that time, it seems dubious whether this provision would justify holding him, although it presumably would at least in theory subject him to liability for damages for breach of contract. *The written agreement, however, no doubt has moral if not legal effect in postponing demands for release* [italics added; page 307].

In my opinion, this amounts to luring the patient into the hospital with false promises. If voluntary hospitalization were really voluntary, the mental patient would be free to enter and leave the mental hospital in the same manner as he enters and leaves a medical hospital. But this is not the case. Voluntary admission is in fact voluntary commitment. Or, to put it another way, the voluntary mental patient's role is a cross between the roles of medical patient and prisoner.

The Hospital for the Criminally Insane. The medical characteristics (instrumentally defined) of hospitals for the criminally insane are virtually nil. They, too, have an infinitesimally small physician-patient ratio. Even if it were raised, and ever if this were advisable, the fact would remain that such hospitals are thinly disguised prisons. Commonly called "maximum security institutions," they are more strictly guarded than many prisons. Finally, in New York State, hospitals for the criminally insane are under the legal jurisdiction of the Department of Correction, whereas state hospitals are under the administration of the Department of Mental Hygiene.

The following is the legal definition of the functions of the two hospitals for the criminally insane in New York State. The Dannemora State Hospital is "for male convicts declared mentally ill while serving a sentence for a felony, or certified mentally ill defectives serving a sentence for a misdemeanor or other offenses" (State of New York, 1959, page 104). The Matteawan State Hospital is "for the mentally ill committed by order of courts of criminal jurisdiction and for male persons convicted of petty crimes or misdemeanors—not felons—or female persons from any correctional institution becoming mentally ill while undergoing sentences; also patients in other state hospitals who were previously convicted or confined in Matteawan State Hospital and still exhibit criminal tendencies or who are adjudged 'dangerously insane'" (page 105). Would it not be more accurate to call these institutions prison hospitals rather than state hospitals? The laws pertaining to them support this viewpoint:

> The *commissioner of correction* shall make bylaws and rules and regulations for the government of the hospital and the management of its affairs. . . . The *commissioner of correction* shall, whenever there is a vacancy, appoint a superintendent for the Dannemora State Hospital, who shall be in the competitive class of the civil service and be a well-educated *physician* and a graduate of an incorporated *medical college* of at least five years' actual experience in a hospital for the care and treatment of the insane [italics added; State of New York, 1957, page 151].

Similar regulations apply to the Matteawan State Hospital (pages 157–158).

I submit, therefore, that these two hospitals for the criminally insane, and others similarly regulated, belong to the state's prison system. They are special prisons—for the criminally insane, if one wishes so to designate their inmates. But prisons they are in every sense of the word. It would seem salutary for the psychiatric and medical profession, as well as for the general public, to recognize this fact.

Psychiatric Power in Action

How psychiatry as an institutional force operates may be seen most clearly when psychiatric intervention takes place in a context of political action. The following two examples are illustrative.

On September 27, 1960, *The New York Times* reported that David B. Pratt, the fifty-two-year-old gentleman farmer, who, on the previous April 9th, tried to assassinate South African Prime Minister Hendrik F. Verwoerd, was declared mentally unfit to stand trial on a charge of attempted murder.

> Testifying in Supreme Court in Pretoria, South Africa's administrative capital, a state-appointed psychiatrist said Pratt's mental condition had deteriorated because of epilepsy and that he was a danger to himself and others. The court ruled that Pratt would be detained in prison until Governor General Charles R. Swart formally committed him to a mental institution.

Who remembers today what happened to Mr. Pratt? Was he treated, did he improve, and was he tried? No. He hanged himself in the mental hospital at Bloemfontein, South Africa, on October 1, 1961, his fifty-fourth birthday. *The Syracuse Herald-Journal* (October 2, 1961) reported that Pratt left the following suicide note:

> Under the circumstances this is the best solution for my problem for everyone. If possible, please arrange for a quiet cremation at Johannesburg, the ashes

to be buried with those of my family at Moloney's Eye [the name of his farm in Transvaal Province]. Please avoid all publicity so that my children can simply be told that their father died in hospital. I am sure the press will cooperate.

Does this note suggest that Mr. Pratt was mentally unfit to stand trial for his crime?

To say that Mr. Pratt was a "danger to himself and [especially to some] others" is, in view of his act, a masterpiece of understatement. I submit, therefore, that the state-appointed psychiatrist performed a function similar to that of a priest when he excommunicates a sinner. This case illustrates the sharp distinction between institutional psychiatry and what may be called rational psychiatry. The state was free to appoint a psychiatrist; the defendant was not. Had he been able to, it is conceivable that his psychiatrist would have argued that Mr. Pratt was sane and that he shot the Prime Minister because he did not approve of the latter's apartheid policies. Understandably, psychiatrists are not eager to play such a role.

Another instructive case occurred in Washington, D.C., in 1960. There a psychiatrist smeared one of his former patients with the psychiatric label "homosexual." The patient had been a former employee of the top-secret National Security Agency, and had defected to Russia. To the credit of the American social scene, many colleagues censured the psychiatrist for his conduct. Although this aspect of the case is itself of interest, the example is cited to illustrate the use of psychiatry by society to promote the aims of the national group. If we assume that every American who defects to Russia is mentally ill and perhaps a homosexual too, should we not think the same of Russians who defect to America? That this is not the case is the most telling clue that psychiatry operates here as a social institution. For those who believe in the large body of contemporary psychiatric mythology, and their numbers are legion, the branding of a political defector as homosexual is as effective as the excommunication of heretics. When the police arm of the group can no longer reach the culprit—because he is dead or has left the country—he can still be condemned morally or besmirched psychiatrically.

Two important facts emerge from this discussion. The first is that it is not often recognized that psychiatry functions as a social institution. Thus, an institutional enterprise may be mistaken for a scientific investigation or explanation. Sometimes psychiatric activity consists of a complicated mixture of both. Second, there is a discrepancy between the ostensible and the empirically observable operations of psychiatry as an institution. Its ostensible function pertains to the maintenance of health, in this case, so-called mental health. If we attempt, however, to impart an operational meaning to the concept of mental health, we find that it cannot be separated from three other basic prerequisites of society: the socialization of members, the maintenance of internal order, and the preservation of meaning and motivation.

Psychiatry as an Institutional Force

The term "social institution" has been used to refer to stable patterns of group behavior, usually pertaining to the regulation of one or another of the functional prerequisites of society (Feibleman, 1956). Institutional behavior, with its institutional goals and rules, may be contrasted with individual behavior, with its personal goals and less conventionalized rules. To make these abstractions come to life, one may consider religion as a private belief, in a Jeffersonian sense, in contrast to religion as an organized enterprise, with a body of public religious opinion and political power.

Since no society is possible without social institutions, it would be false to suggest, as is often done, that institutions are bad because they frustrate individual creativity and initiative, and that rational and skilled individual behavior is good because it is a source of cultural progress. Obviously, the reverse may also be true. While individual and group actions differ, each may be as good or bad as people make them. The main thesis of this chapter is to highlight the differences between psychiatry as an individual enterprise and as an institution.

The history of modern psychiatry mirrors, in a brief span of time, the history of political action. In the latter sphere, the relationship of leaders to followers—for example, of chieftains or kings to their subjects—existed long before the rise of more complex governments (for example, constitutional monarchies, parliamentary republics, and so on). Such political structures express attempts by the people to regulate the relationship between the governor and the governed, often with the specific purposes of preventing the development of certain imbalances between these two interacting factions of society. Similarly, modern psychiatry has been an interplay between healers and sufferers. Historically, this would correspond to the early periods of political institutions. At the beginning, social regulations governing the relationship of psychiatrists and patients were either nonexistent or poor. In the next phase, the regulations guaranteed absolute dominance by the psychiatrist over the patient; this has been the character of state hospital psychiatry during the past century. More recently, institutional psychiatry affecting other areas of life—particularly politics, criminology, and civil law—has also been of this type.

I hope that this analysis will stimulate interest in the problems posed by psychiatry as an institutional force in modern society. Our goal should be to establish checks and balances between the antagonistic elements in the psychiatric social system. As a social institution, psychiatry is now in its infancy. Perhaps, like all babies, it is better at dominating than at serving or cooperating with others. Institutions, no less than persons, may need to be socialized. If so, the question is: Which social values should psychiatrists foster, while they are defining their own institutionalized roles and statuses?

Personally, I believe that psychiatry as an institution should aim at striking a balance between serving the interests and needs of groups and of individuals. We should keep in mind, moreover, that the interests of the group and of the individual may not—and perhaps should not—coincide. In the history of the Anglo-American democracies, the principle of liberty *from,* and even *against,* government has been a central issue (Corwin, 1948). If we—whether as psychiatrists, patients, or individuals not involved with psychiatry—wish to enlarge, rather than constrict, the area of political freedom, then our central concern must be to ensure the liberty of the people from, and indeed against, psychiatry as a social institution.

Conclusions

Medical and mental hospitals are legally authorized to do different things. The medical patient is treated, from the legal point of view, as a person in a democratic society. He must contract for the care he wishes to receive, and the physician must obtain his "informed consent" for hospitalization and treatment (Hirsch, 1961). The mental hospital patient, in contrast, is treated not as a person, but as the occupant of a status. He is deprived of the right to contract, and the physician is given wide powers of control over hospitalizing and treating him. While the verbal similarities between medical and mental patients are many, the legal and social similarities between them are few.

In their relations with potential mental patients, our legislators are bestowing more power than ever on psychiatrists. Seven of our states now permit involuntary hospitalization if physicians testify that the "patient is in need of care or treatment." A recent Pennsylvania statute even authorizes the involuntary hospitalization of anyone who suffers from a mental illness which "so lessens the capacity of a person to use his customary self-control, judgment and discretion in the conduct of his affairs and social relations as to make it necessary or advisable for him to be under care" (Lindman and McIntyre, Jr., 1961, page 17).

In the light of this evidence, the claim that mental institutions are essentially medical hospitals must be rejected as false. Despite the impressive evidence of the actual differences between bodily and mental illness, and the legal differences between medical and mental hospitals, authoritative medical and legal organizations continue to support the medical concept of mental illness and hospitalization. The American Bar Foundation's recent study, for example, although cautioning against the dangers of improper hospitalization and other harms that may be inflicted on mental patients, justifies and rationalizes our problems by stating:

Just as it is entirely possible for two reputable physicians to differ on whether a low back pain is the result of an automobile accident, they may also have a difference of opinion concerning an individual's mental health [Lindman and McIntyre, Jr., 1961, page 37].

But, as I have tried to show, if two psychiatrists disagree in this way, it is because each has a different concept of mental disease.

Mental patients are persons. Hence, their legal right to be treated as persons must be restored. This, it seems to me, is a prerequisite for dealing rationally with the admittedly complex problem of institutionalized mental illness. A detailed discussion of proposals for reform in mental health practices is presented in Chapter 19.

PART THREE » *Psychiatry and the Criminal Law*

CHAPTER 8

Crime and Mental Illness:
A Critical Survey of the Literature

In former days, when it was proposed to burn atheists, charitable people used to suggest putting them in the madhouse instead; it would be nothing surprising now-a-days were we to see this done, and the doers applauding themselves, because, instead of persecuting for religion, they had adopted so humane and Christian a mode of treating these unfortunates, not without a silent satisfaction at their having thereby obtained their deserts.
——JOHN STUART MILL (1859, page 100)

IT IS a traditional function of psychiatry to participate in the administration of the criminal law. Before the end of the nineteenth century, the juristic and penal aspects of psychiatry were hardly distinguishable from its medical and therapeutic aspects. Illustrative is Isaac Ray's *Treatise on the Medical Jurisprudence of Insanity* (1838), which was the most influential pre-Kraepelinian psychiatric text in America.

Since the turn of the century, three different types of psychiatric activities have developed: private office practice, work in state and federal institutions, and forensic psychiatry. Their boundaries, however, have not been clearly demarcated. On the contrary, authoritative psychiatric opinion, especially in recent decades, has sought to obscure the differences not only among the various types of psychiatric pursuits, but even between psychiatry and medicine. In some quarters, psychiatry has thus become an infinitely broad, bio-psycho-social study of man—an enterprise of such all-encompassing character that virtually nothing affecting man falls outside its scope.

A vast amount of psychiatric effort has been, and continues to be, devoted to legal and quasi-legal activities. In my opinion, the only certain result has been the economic enrichment of psychiatrists and the professional aggrandizement of psychiatry. The value to the legal profession and to society as a whole of psychiatric help in administering the criminal law, is, to say the least, uncertain. Perhaps society has been injured, rather than helped, by the *furor psychodiagnosticus* and *psychotherapeuticus* in criminology which it invited, fostered, and tolerated.

In this chapter, I shall present an introductory orientation to the typical problems we encounter when psychiatric concepts and actions are used in administration of the criminal law. I shall describe and analyze the representative views of jurists, psychiatrists, and sociologists on the relation between crime and mental illness.

A Critical Survey of the Literature on Crime and Mental Illness

Many contemporary specialists, in jurisprudence as well as in psychiatry, believe that psychiatric knowledge may be useful in the trial and disposition of offenders. According to this view, most people who break the law are sick. They need psychiatric treatment and rehabilitation, not punishment.

This is the gist of the contributions of such outstanding men as Alexander and Staub (1929), Bazelon (1960), Guttmacher and Weihofen (1952), Overholser (1953), Roche (1955), Weihofen (1956), and Zilboorg (1954). In opposition to this trend, Wertham (1955a), and I (Szasz, 1956) have been the only psychiatrists, and Hall (1958) and Wootton (1959) the only jurists, who, while recognizing the value of psychiatry, have also warned of its dangers.

Scientific knowledge does not contain within itself directions for its "proper" humanitarian use. Legal psychiatry has proved impervious to this simple fact. For we are constantly urged to make "better" use of modern psychiatric knowledge in the administration of the criminal law. What does this mean? Modern psychiatric knowledge may tell one psychiatrist that criminals are sick and need indeterminate sentences to be treated effectively, and another that criminals should be treated as responsible human beings, in the firm but libertarian tradition of Anglo-American law.

Like other problems in which facts and values intermingle, the question of how to use, and perhaps of how not to use, psychiatry is not an easy one.

We must resist efforts at false simplification, for they all seem to offer simplicity at the cost of liberty.

The following survey is illustrative, not exhaustive. The interested reader will find in the Bibliography a guide to the vast and rapidly growing literature in this field.

The Psychopathological Concept of Crime. In 1929, Alexander and Staub published *The Criminal, the Judge, and the Public* (original edition in German). This work attracted immediate attention, and was translated into English by Zilboorg (1931). A revised edition, with new chapters by Alexander, appeared in 1956. This book has become a classic in its field. Much of what others have said since is little more than an expansion of Alexander and Staub's original thesis.

Alexander and Staub (1956) based their argument on the proposition that traditional penology is a failure. They suggested using psychoanalysis as a "rational" basis for criminology and penology. Not only would psychoanalytic criminology be better for the criminal, but also for the public. The authors declared that they hoped "to prove . . . that a psychological understanding of the criminal does not primarily help the criminal but, on the contrary, serves the interests of society" (page xviii). Indeed, they emphasized repeatedly that helping the criminal was not their chief aim. What, then, was it? It was "to understand the criminal in order to be able to judge him correctly, *so that our judgment may be just beyond question*" (italics added; page xix).

According to Alexander and Staub, there are two types of criminals: normal and neurotic. They claimed that psychoanalytically trained physicians know how to distinguish between them. For the normal criminal, traditional "retaliative" penology is acceptable. For the neurotic criminal, in whom Alexander and Staub were mainly interested, they recommended ". . . something new and definite, namely, . . . *the abolition of all forms of punishment,* and suggest that he be turned over to a special agency for psychoanalytically minded reeducation, or to a psychoanalyst for *treatment*" (italics in the original; page 210).

The principles underlying Alexander and Staub's views and recommendations are clearly stated in the Preface to the revised edition. These premises are crucial, for if we agree with them, we shall probably approve of the conclusions. However, if we find the premises unacceptable—as I do—the conclusions will seem preposterous. Here are the premises:

> We propose a more consistent application of the principle that *not the deed but the doer should be punished,* a principle first promulgated by Liszt, the great German criminologist of the nineteenth century. The implementation of this principle requires *expert diagnostic judgment* which can be expected only from specially trained *psychiatric experts.* Before any sentence is imposed, a medical-legal diagnosis should be required. This would amount to an official recognition

of unconscious motivations in all human behavior. *The neurotic criminal obviously has a limited sense of responsibility. Primarily he is a sick person*, and his delinquency is the outcome of his emotional disturbances. This fact, however, should not exempt him from the consequences of his action. If he is curable, he should be incarcerated for the duration of psychiatric treatment so long as he still represents a menace to society. *If he is incurable, he belongs in a hospital for incurables for life* [italics added; page xiii].

These sentences contain the significant premises not only for Alexander's arguments but also for many of those who have since dealt with these problems.

First, the offender is a "sick person." As such, he has a "limited sense of responsibility."

Second, coercive psychiatric "treatment" is advocated in preference to penal rehabilitation.

Third, the "incurable" criminal is to be incarcerated for life.

Fourth, and most important, the ideal criminal law is defined as that which deals with criminals, not crimes.

A detailed criticism of these arguments need not be presented here, for this entire volume is devoted to clarifying and refuting these allegedly psychoanalytic-criminologic principles. I should like to emphasize, however, that Alexander and Staub ignored completely all the great libertarian principles that have animated Anglo-Saxon law since the Magna Charta. Individual rights, due process, the protection of the individual against the group, including the government—not one of these ideas is mentioned. Though harsh, I believe this judgment is accurate: Alexander and Staub's book is of a piece with the rising totalitarian spirit in Europe after the First World War. The principle that the deed is unimportant, that the law should punish the doer—which Alexander proudly proclaimed—fitted into the political-legal schemes of Fascist Italy, Nazi Germany, and Communist Russia. We see here the beginning of an era: psychiatrists rush to serve omnipotent governments by coercing deviant citizens to behave properly —or else!

From the vantage point of psychoanalytic psychology, whether or not the M'Naghten Rules are meaningful is not the issue. To argue that they are not has been a favorite maneuver by forensic psychiatrists who wish to place psychiatry above the law. The issue is more basic. It is whether the paternalistic-personalistic approach advocated by Alexander is compatible with the principles of Anglo-American law, which is based on contract (see Chapter 12).

We should be clear about the fundamental issue: Should the deed or the doer be punished? We must choose between regulating persons *indirectly*, by prescribing rules of conduct and penalties for violations, and controlling them *directly*, through compulsory therapy. Virtually all the problems of forensic psychiatry center around this alternative.

If we leave this issue unclarified, we cannot discuss practical problems, such as whether or not an allegedly incurable criminal who has committed only a relatively minor offense—like forging a check—should be involuntarily hospitalized for life. If the therapeutic premise is acceptable, the conclusion must also be. If, however, government power and therapeutic needs are not absolute—but are expressly limited, as I think they ought to be—then it is meaningless to recommend such alleged reforms. As I see it, coercive therapy of the kind favored by Alexander is no more compatible with the Constitution than the hospitalization for life of the unemployed. Yet, to make the latter practice appear reasonable, we have only to define as sick everyone who cannot secure employment.

In Judge David Bazelon, Alexander's views have found a powerful judicial advocate. Through his influence, many of the ideas of Alexander and Staub have become reality, at least in the District of Columbia. Bazelon has had a strong influence on contemporary developments in forensic psychiatry. His views, therefore, deserve detailed exposition and critical evaluation.

In *Durham* v. *United States* (1954), the United States Court of Appeals for the District of Columbia, under Bazelon's leadership, argued the thesis that "existing tests of criminal responsbility are obsolete and should be superseded . . . [and] a broader test should be adopted" (page 864). What should this test be? "Simply that an accused is not criminally responsible if his unlawful act was the product of mental disease or mental defect" (pages 874–875). To avoid releasing defendants so acquitted, further statutes were enacted to legalize the automatic commitment of such persons to St. Elizabeths Hospital.

To understand this decision, we must turn to Bazelon's (1960) writings in which he has tried to explain the merits of the Durham ruling and of many subsequent decisions. The "underlying purpose" of the Durham decision was

. . . to unfreeze the expanding knowledge of psychiatry, as it could be applied to the law, in order to free the psychiatrist from having to make the moral and legal determinations, required by the right-wrong test for which he has no special qualifications, and to allow him to address himself to the problems of *mental disease and defect* [italics added; page 54].

Bazelon thus claimed that his aim was essentially scientific. He wanted to increase the "knowledge" available to judge and jury. However, Bazelon also professed humanitarian motives: he wished to improve the condition of prisoners.

Bazelon's intention to make the legal decision more rational is suspect. If knowledge is wanted, why speak of mental illness instead of human behavior? The suspicion that the Durham decision has not aided the dissemination or use of psychiatric knowledge, in or outside the courtroom, is borne out by all subsequent events. But let us proceed with Bazelon's own views of the advantages of the Durham formula. He asserted that "since punishment so often fails of its purpose, something else is needed. And this something else is treatment" (page 56).

This is not true. The ostensible aim of modern penal institutions is rehabilitation, not merely punishment. There is no justification for equating incarceration in prison with punishment—as if the prison regime could have no redeeming features. Conversely, Bazelon speaks of involuntary mental hospitalization as treatment—as if such hospitalization were inherently good and therapeutic. But he knows better. The most brutal and inhumane punishments in our day are meted out not in prisons, but in mental hospitals.

Of course, Bazelon is not completely unaware of the shortcomings of mental hospitals. Confronted with this unpleasant fact, he resorts to another justification for mental hospitalization—namely, that as jails, state hospitals are more effective than penitentiaries:

> Punishment as such, remember, is supposed to fit the crime, not the criminal. When the sentence has been served, the warden of the penitentiary signs a certificate to that effect, and the prisoner rejoins society—*even though it may be obvious that the punishment has worked no cure* and indeed may have intensified the prisoner's criminal impulses. On the other hand, an inmate of a mental hospital is released only when certified by the staff as cured, or at least not dangerous to himself or others. No psychiatrist, to be sure, is infallible. He may err in his prognosis and recommend release prematurely, with disastrous results to the community. Many state hospitals, moreover, are too over-crowded and understaffed to provide optimum care. But at least the effort is made to exercise responsible medical judgment, whereas the prison warden is called upon to enter no judgment at all except as to parole. *Is it not evident that treatment rather than punitive incarceration offers society better protection?* [italics added; page 56].

This, the reader will recall, was Alexander's argument. If the offender is not cured, the psychiatrists should keep him under lock and key indefinitely.

In his Isaac Ray Award Lectures, Bazelon (1961) set forth more fully his philosophy of law. He labeled it liberal, but I consider it authoritarian and antiliberal. He wrote, for example:

> The most distressing thing about M'Naghten is that it sets a standard of rationality which all but the most extreme psychotics and drooling idiots can meet. Many of the very persons we readily classify as not equipped to cope with society, and make subject to civil commitment, are held to be responsible for their actions on the criminal side of the court [page 8].

It is easy to see why this seemed inconsistent to Bazelon. He concluded, therefore, that M'Naghten must go. Apparently it did not occur to him to question our system of civil commitment. Indeed, he spoke glibly of mentally sick people whom "we readily classify [as committable]." But who is "we"? This is important, for obviously when Bazelon speaks of psychiatrists he has in mind state hospital psychiatrists. For him, the paradigm of desirable psychiatric action is coercive mental hospitalization. The compulsory psychiatric treatment of offenders can easily be incorporated into this kind of psychiatry.

But what kind of psychiatry is this? Many psychiatrists would rather not practice their profession than practice it in this way. Let us recall that Freud, Jung, and Adler treated only consenting patients. They refused to inflict therapy on people who did not want it. This is true also for most of the best known contemporary psychotherapists. It seems to me that Bazelon has not grasped the fundamental distinction between psychiatric treatments freely undertaken, and psychiatric manipulations inflicted upon people against their will. His model is always the coercive, authoritarian psychiatrist—as typified by the state hospital superintendent. It is never the autonomous psychotherapist, as exemplified by the psychoanalyst (Szasz, 1961, 1962).

Bazelon offered another reason for not wishing to punish offenders. He dislikes blaming people, and does not wish to pass moral judgments on their conduct. As I understand the judge's job, however, this is precisely what he is expected to do. Instead, Bazelon would like to change judges into therapists:

> However much we may tell each other that it doesn't really matter whether we class a man as criminal or sick, as deserving punishment in a prison rather than treatment in a hospital—perhaps because there is so little difference between the custodial care afforded by overcrowded mental institutions and by prisons—there is, at heart, a tremendous difference. Assignment to a mental hospital represents an act in a social affirmation that this man is not to be blamed. Classing the offender as "ill" is one step along the path towards community acceptance of some small share of the responsibility, with all this may imply for the commitment of resources in the future. In contrast, the sentence to prison with its assessment of "fault" or "blame" results only in dealing with him in a manner assuring that he will repeat again and again the acts which bring him to blame and to prison [page 8].

I find this difficult to understand. If the purpose of trial and sentencing is not to blame the accused, what is their purpose? And what is the difference between being blamed for lawbreaking and for mental illness, if both result in similar penalties? We are back in *Erewhon* it seems.

In the passage just quoted, Bazelon made an assumption which was never explicitly stated, but from which his exaggerated psychiatric orientation follows logically. Bazelon claims that prisons are hopelessly bad, and serve only to make confirmed criminals of the convicts. And he insists that prisons cannot be improved, but mental hospitals can. Again, the facts contradict him. In many prisons there are effective programs of rehabilitation: prisoners are taught to read and write, a trade, and so forth. In Sweden and the Soviet Union, for example, penal reforms have wrought far-reaching changes in traditional prison procedures. Obviously, it is possible to transform prisons into humane, rehabilitative institutions. Nor is psychiatric assistance necessary to accomplish this. Bazelon ignores all this. He thinks like Charcot: to treat hysterics decently, we must first call them sick. Similarly, Bazelon: to treat criminals decently, we must first call them sick. So runs the argument. But surely this is humanitarianism under false pretenses. Though the motives behind the acts may be good, the means are not, and this vitiates the effort.

The impression that Bazelon seeks to discard the judicial function altogether, and adopt in its place a therapeutic one, is borne out by his strange denial of the moral function of the law (Bazelon, 1960): "The legal process differs from religion in that, being concerned with factual decisions, it cannot utter moral imperatives" (page 56).

This is an astounding statement. First, it denies the moral function of the law and of the judge. Second, it claims that factual decisions and moral judgments are incompatible. Although science and ethics are different enterprises, we expect a rational jurisprudence to combine fact-finding with moral evaluations. Bazelon's ostensibly amoral view of the law is reminiscent of the views of the legal positivists before the Second World War. Interestingly enough, the introduction to the article quoted was written by Karl Menninger (1960), who described the Durham decision as "more revolutionary in its total effect than the Supreme Court decision regarding desegregation" (page 32). Are we asked to believe that this too was *not* a "moral imperative"?

Let us take one more look at the kind of psychiatry Bazelon (1961) has in mind when he advocates penal reforms along psychiatric lines:

Again, we have been assisted in the District of Columbia by the fact that we have a notable mental hospital, Saint Elizabeths, directed by Dr. Overholser, a leading figure in forensic psychiatry. Persons acquitted by reason of insanity are committed to that institution until recovered or until it is safe to return them to the community. The existence of such an institution, and of an automatic commitment procedure, has done a great deal to make the public feel more secure [page 12].

Evidently, Bazelon looks to the psychiatrist-warden to assist him in his social engineering. Without such assistance—without psychiatrists willing to play the role of jailer—the Durham rule would promptly fail.

And throughout, Bazelon maintains that he is helping not only offenders but psychiatry and psychiatrists as well:

I really cannot say it too strongly—psychiatrists have a great opportunity under a *liberal rule like Durham, an opportunity to help reform the criminal law* and also *to humanize their own work* and increase its relevance. —It is not enough for psychiatrists to point out the obvious defects of M'Naghten—if they then act casually or with studied lack of imagination with respect to an *opportunity* such as Durham has offered them [italics added; page 4].

Echoing Bazelon's sentiments, Fortas (1957) referred to the Durham decision as "a bill of rights for psychiatry." But do we need a bill of rights *for psychiatry?* It is not being accused of anything. But the defendant is. We should be concerned about *his* Bill of Rights.

Eight years have passed since the Durham decision. The champions of psychiatry, at least in the District of Columbia, may feel proud. They have won. As a result, Hugh J. McGee (1961), Chairman of the Mental Health Committee of the District of Columbia Bar Association, could say:

I personally feel the present mandatory commitment possibly for life on the basis of the jury's passive finding of not guilty by reason of insanity is not only a violation of the individual's constitutional rights but also amounts to cruel and inhuman punishment [page 60].

The issues are clear. If every procedure labeled therapeutic is accepted as good—no matter how much it violates a person's liberty, privacy, and self-determination—we shall tend to agree with Bazelon. If, however, we reject as bad, practices such as coercive psychiatric interrogation of persons accused of crimes, or the indeterminate sentence, we shall oppose him.

Many forensic psychiatrists are unaware of, or ignore, the complex ethical and social issues involved in introducing psychiatric procedures into the criminal law. Their attitude is narrow and technical.

Guttmacher's (1954) approach to psychiatry and law exemplifies this trend. He has tried to find "objective" criteria for criminal responsibility:

It seems to me that all that should be expected of the psychiatrist in the courtroom is the following:
1. A statement as to whether the defendant is suffering from *a definite and generally recognized mental disorder* and why and how this conclusion was reached.
2. If it has been asserted that the defendant suffered from a mental disorder, *its name* and its chief characteristics and symptoms, with particular emphasis on its *effect on* the individual's judgment, social behavior, and self control, should be given.
3. There should then follow a statement of the way and degree in which the *malady* has affected the particular defendant's social behavior and self control.
4. He should then be asked whether the alleged criminal act was, in his opinion, a product of *mental disorder* [italics added; page 432].

Whether these suggestions would lead to socially desirable consequences is an open question. But surely, it cannot be claimed that psychiatry, as a science of human behavior, supports such actions.

The concept of a "generally recognized mental disorder" ignores the fact that people of different life experiences have different ideas of mental illness. Such a notion implies that the observers share a large number of significant life experiences. This is best achieved by members of the same profession. Thus, in 1665 Sir Thomas Browne, a distinguished surgeon of the time, testified in court that witches did indeed exist, "as everyone knew." Similarly, today, every well-educated physician "knows" that there are "diseases of the mind," just as there are diseases of the body.

Roche (1958) repeats, with minor variations, the psychopathological view of offenders sketched above. For him, "criminals differ from mentally ill people only in the manner we choose to deal with them" (page 29). This is a remarkable application of operational philosophy to social engineering. By the same token, if we want to slaughter members of a minority group, we need only declare them cattle. If we *treat* them as cattle, that proves that they *are* cattle!

Repeatedly, Roche joins his colleagues in reiterating the proposition that criminals are mentally ill:

If the law should find a way to abandon its untenable concept of criminal responsibility as it pertains to the subjective element in crime and come to the view that *all felons are mental cases,* there should be a reformation in penology. —As matters now stand, the law conjoins with the criminal in a resistance to the idea that a *crime is a disturbance of communication, hence a form of mental illness* [italics added; page 241].

Weihofen (1956), a professor of law, not psychiatry, suffers from a bad case of indigestion caused by an excessively rich diet of so-called enlightened and progressive psychiatry. He is more fanatical on the theme of *illness-über-Alles* than even Alexander or Bazelon. Perhaps this is partly because he accepted as correct a vast amount of psychiatric misinformation. For example, he believes that "in mental illness no less than in physical illness, when a person is ill, he is ill all over" (page 16). Hence, "We would understand mental illness better if we thought of it as similar to physical illness" (page 18).

Weihofen believes that mental illness is really physical. His confusion on this score could not be more complete:

Insulin can relieve perhaps 70 percent of the victims of schizophrenia, the most common and most tragic form of psychosis, *if they are treated within the first three months of an attack* (page 79).

Electric shock therapy can remedy a severe mental depression and help people suffering from certain types of schizophrenia. Interesting experiments are also under way to determine whether chemical agents in the body, such as lysergic acid diethylamide, nicknamed "LSD25," may be a cause of clinical schizophrenia.

In recent years we have learned that there is a close relationship between the amount of sugar present in a person's blood and his social behavior. A fairly long list of aggressive crimes may be committed either under the influence of insulin or in a state of spontaneous hypoglycemia (the medical term for a decrease in the normal amount of sugar in the blood). *The lower the sugar level falls the greater is the tendency to commit crime. Lack of calcium also seems to produce antisocial attitudes and actions* [italics added, pages 80–81].

What is one to say? If this is what a prominent professor of law, and a winner of the American Psychiatric Association's Isaac Ray Award believes, what should doctors, lawyers, and the public believe?

The Conflict Between Civil Liberties and Psychiatric Therapies. Opposition to the psychopathological view of crime has centered on the thesis that civil liberties deserve protection even if a person is considered mentally ill. The advocates of this point of view have resisted the psychotherapeutic frenzy of the self-styled liberal psychiatrists. They have refused to sacrifice the constitutional and moral safeguards that protect the dignity of the individual on the altar of "mental health."

While favoring psychiatric participation in the criminal trial, Wertham has cautioned against the possible dangers to civil liberties from psychiatric domination of the law. Apropos of the Durham case, he wrote (Wertham, 1955a): "Only if we overcome this psychoauthoritarianism will psychiatry find its proper place in the courtroom and play, as it should, a strong but subordinate role" (page 338). In opposition to the prevalent psychiatric and psychoanalytic approach focusing on the personality of the offender, Wertham (1955b) tried to achieve a balance between the psychological and the social: "The whole emphasis on psychology as the basic consideration is misleading, and serves to divert attention from the social environment in which all psychological forces operate" (page 569).

This is a powerful criticism, not of any specific phrase in the Durham decision, but of its entire spirit. To this may be added another trenchant observation by Wertham (1957):

> In a democratic society the function of the judge is not to imbue himself with an extremist point of view within a specialty, . . . ; it is to see that the law is upheld and that civil liberties are not interfered with by psychoauthoritarian points of view [page 101].

Hall, a jurist, not a psychiatrist, has successfully resisted the standard psychiatric slogans of the day. He has repeatedly warned of the dangers to civil liberties inherent in using psychiatric diagnoses as grounds for incarcerating persons. Like Wertham, Hall (1960) considers the M'Naghten rules workable, and believes that the psychiatrist can contribute constructively to the conduct of the criminal trial. He has clearly recognized, moreover, that mental diseases are unlike physical diseases. And he urged that we be careful about the potential conflicts between psychiatric practices and civil liberties: "There is also a very insidious aspect of this expansion of 'disease,' resulting from the fact that persons who are found to have a 'mental disease' on the basis of a psychiatrist's opinion can be incarcerated indefinitely" (page 453).

Despite his excellent grasp of the nature of psychiatric concepts and operations, Hall believes that mental illness should be considered an excusing condition to crime. He suggested the following modification of the M'Naghten rules to solve our present difficulties:

In sum, a sound rule of criminal responsibility must (1) retain irrationality as a criterion of insanity; (2) be consistent with the theory of the integration of all the principal functions of personality; (3) be stated in terms that are understandable to laymen; and (4) facilitate psychiatric testimony. Accordingly, the following is suggested:

A crime is not committed by anyone who, because of a mental *disease,* is unable to understand what he is doing and to control his conduct at the time he commits a harm forbidden by criminal law. In deciding this question with reference to the criminal conduct with which a defendant is charged, the trier of the facts should decide (1) whether, because of mental *disease,* the defendant lacked the capacity to understand the nature and consequences of his conduct; and (2) whether, *because of such disease,* the defendant lacked the capacity to *realize* that it was morally wrong to commit the harm in question [italics added; page 521].

Thus, Hall also succumbs to the view that so-called mental illness is "disease" and may "cause" criminal conduct, much as the Durham decision holds. Hence, hard as Hall strains to avoid the pitfalls of the Durham rule, in practice his recommendations would lead to the same difficulties.

Lady Wootton (1959, 1960), a jurist and social scientist, contends that contemporary psychiatry and social work are repressive welfare agencies. Her views and mine have much in common. Wootton noted the gross neglect of social considerations in the standard psychiatric approaches to crime, and decried that forensic psychiatrists perform moral functions in the guise of medical action. Her book, *Social Science and Social Pathology,* also contains an excellent review of the relation between mental disorder and crime.

In her discussion of the problem of criminal responsibility (see Chapter 10), Wootton (1959) emphasized the frequent psychiatric confusion between explanation and exculpation. She wrote:

Undoubtedly people who suffer from disturbances of mental part-functions have to carry the burden of those disturbances on top of whatever happens to be their share of the ordinary troubles and difficulties of human life. But so also do those who suffer from migraine or weak digestions. How can we be sure that it is legitimate in the one case, but not in the other, to leap to the conclusion that, for those who suffer from these disabilities, the standards of social expectation ought to be lowered? Why is dishonesty excused as well as explained by depression, but not by indigestion? Why should we accept a plea of diminished responsibility for the unlawful revenges of the deluded against their imaginary persecutors, but not for similar actions perpetrated against real enemies by rational persons, if both parties alike recognize what they do is wrong? At what point do the jealousies of the suspicious spouse cross the line that separates the inconsiderate from the crazy? [pages 239–240].

The advocates of the psychopathological view of crime prefer to avoid these questions.

I agree with Lady Wootton (Szasz, 1956, 1961). However, in addition to stressing the need to protect the civil liberties of offenders, my thesis has included the fundamental proposition that so-called mental illnesses are unlike ordinary diseases. As a corollary to this, I have also argued that so-called psychiatric treatments, especially if applied to involuntary patients, are more often punishments than treatments.

Early Psychoanalytic Views on Crime and Mental Illness. At this point it seems appropriate to refer to the views of some of the early psycho-analysts on this subject. Currently, most of those who favor more extensive psychiatric participation in the criminal law claim that their opinions are based on psychoanalytic insights. The material that follows suggests, at the very least, that psychoanalysis may serve as the basis for several mutually incompatible points of view about criminology.

Neither Freud nor the other early psychoanalysts paid much attention to the question of criminal responsibility. They wrote as if they believed that everyone was responsible for his actions.

Freud made only a few references to the possible connections between psychoanalysis and jurisprudence. In an early paper entitled "Psycho-Analysis and the Establishment of the Facts in Legal Proceedings" (1906), he suggested the following analogy between the criminal and the hysteric:

> In both we are concerned with a secret, with something hidden. But in order not to be paradoxical I must at once point out the difference. In the case of the criminal it is a secret which he knows and hides from you, whereas in the case of the hysteric it is a secret which he himself does not know either, which is hidden even from himself [page 108].

Today, we are familiar with this idea. Were we to take it seriously, however, we should have to conclude not only that the criminal is mentally sick but also that the hysteric is a criminal!

Freud then offered the following parallel between the work of the psychotherapist and the judge:

> The task of the therapist, however, is the same as that of the examining magistrate. We have to uncover the hidden psychical material; and in order to do this we have invented a number of detective devices, some of which it seems that you gentlemen of the law are now about to copy from us [page 108].

Today, few psychiatrists or jurists would agree with this statement. Nor is it likely that Freud would have written this later in his life. To explain his work to jurists, he chose to stress the similarities rather than the differences between psychoanalysis and certain purposes of the law.

In the same paper Freud revealed that he was either unaware of, or indifferent to, the fact that in Anglo-American law the accused is protected from incriminating himself. Referring to Jung's experiments with the word-association test, he stated that jurists and psychiatrists shared an interest "in a new method of investigation, the aim of which is *to compel the accused person to establish his own guilt* or innocence by objective signs" (italics added; page 103). After commenting on the method, he stated again that "I know . . . you are at the moment concerned with the potentialities and difficulties of this procedure, *whose aim is to lead the accused into an objective self-betrayal*" (italics added; page 107). Freud thus seemed to think that the psychiatrist's task in this sort of situation was to help the legal authorities to decide whether or not a person had committed a crime. Implicitly, Freud treated the criminal in a paternalistic fashion. The authorities will discover the "truth"; hence, the criminal does not need safeguards to protect himself from them.

Yet, it would be inaccurate to conclude that Freud favored the application of psychoanalytic insights to criminology. On the contrary. In the article cited, he said that his work was "far removed from the practical administration of justice" (page 114). His only concrete suggestion was to undertake an intensive psychological investigation of defendants in criminal cases, but he emphatically opposed *"their results being allowed to influence the verdict of the Court"* (italics in the original; page 114).

Freud's subsequent contacts with jurisprudence were rare. On two occasions he reported on criminal cases. In one, he gave an opinion on a murder case. In the other, a case of assault, he wrote a memorandum for the defense. The latter, written in 1922, is not extant. According to Strachey (1959), "in both these instances he [Freud] wrote to deprecate any half-baked applications of psycho-analytic theories in legal proceedings" (page 102). If this is so, it is clear what Freud would have thought of the contemporary uses of psychoanalysis in legal proceedings.

Freud's (1931) opinion on the murder case deserves a brief comment. In 1929, a young student, Philipp Halsmann, was brought before an Innsbruck court, charged with the murder of his father. The court asked for an expert opinion from the Innsbruck Faculty of Medicine. The opinion introduced the subject of the Oedipus complex, and by means of it tended to incriminate the defendant. Halsmann was found guilty, but was subsequently pardoned. Dr. Josef Kupka, a Professor of Law at the University of Vienna, felt that Halsmann was "left with an undeserved slur on his character and began an active campaign for upsetting the original court decision" (page 251). In preparing his case, Professor Kupka asked for Freud's views on the question, and Freud's memorandum, "The Expert Opinion in the Halsmann Case," was the result. In it, Freud argued:

If it had been objectively demonstrated that Philipp Halsmann murdered his father, there would at all events be some ground for introducing the Oedipus complex to provide a motive for an otherwise unexplained deed. Since no such proof has been adduced, mention of the Oedipus complex has a misleading effect; it is at the least idle. Such disagreements as have been uncovered by the investigation in the Halsmann family between the father and son are altogether inadequate to provide a foundation for assuming in the son a bad relationship towards his father. Even if it were otherwise, we should be obliged to say that it is a far cry from there to the causation of such a deed. Precisely because it is always present, the Oedipus complex is not suited to provide a decision on the question of guilt. The situation envisaged in a well-known anecdote might easily be brought about. There was a burglary. A man who had a jemmy in his possession was found guilty of the crime. After the verdict had been given and he had been asked if he had anything to say, he begged to be sentenced for adultery at the same time—since he was carrying the tool for that on him as well [page 252].

The decision of the Innsbruck court and Freud's protest against it are, in a way, prophetic of what was to come. This was probably the first time in the history of law that psychoanalytic concepts were used to incriminate and harm a defendant. Freud protested against such misuse of his work. His plea resembles that of the nuclear scientists beseeching the American government not to use the atomic bomb against the Japanese. Both protests were to no avail.

Ferenczi (1913, 1919) wrote several articles to acquaint lawyers with the discoveries of psychoanalysis. Neither he nor Freud believed that a person should be exempted from legal punishment—or worse, that he should be punished by compulsory psychiatric "treatments"—because of psychoanalytic information about him. In the light of current thought, this is a startling and sobering fact.

That Ferenczi (1919) did not advocate modifications in our concepts of criminal responsibility is borne out by this statement:

A condemned person has no further reason for concealing anything of the thoughts and associations by means of which the unconscious motives for his actions and tendencies may be brought to light. Once the treatment has been begun, then the so-called "transference," the emotional bond with the person of the analyst, will even render him desirous of and pleased with being dealt with in this way. The comparative investigation of similar offenses will then render it possible to fill in the gaping lacunae of criminological determinism with solid scientific material [page 436].

Note again, first, the application of psychoanalytic knowledge after conviction—not before, to modify the sentence—and second, the emphasis on scientific inquiry. There is a striking contrast between this view and the present emphasis on treating the offender as a mentally sick person.

The Sociological View: Crime and Mental Illness as Social Deviation. The emphatic claim of psychiatrists that criminality is a form of mental illness has struck a responsive chord in the legal profession and in the general public. The dissenting voices of a succession of sociologists have generally fallen on deaf ears. Perhaps the critical impact of their views was weakened by their seeming acceptance of mental illness as a disease-like phenomenon.

Approximately a decade ago, Lemert (1951) published a text on *Social Pathology*, in which he analyzed several types of social deviation, among them blindness, speech defects, crime, and mental illness. Lemert regards both criminality and mental illness as examples of "sociopathic behavior."

An important original concept of Lemert's is the distinction between primary and secondary deviation. Deviation is said to be primary before it becomes a stable social role. Thus, many people steal, drink to excess, and hallucinate, but not all are criminals, alcoholics, and mental patients. A great deal of deviant behavior is occasional or situational; some of it is accepted as normal; only a small portion of it is an early phase of a subsequent, full-fledged deviant role.

Primary and secondary deviation are alike in that both involve deviant social action. They differ in that only in the latter does society cast the actor in a deviant role, and does the deviant accept and live that role. This distinction is not one that psychiatrists tend to make. In the case of criminality, this has resulted in placing the occasional or situational criminal and the permanent or professional criminal in the same class; the criminality of both is then attributed to mental illness. The language and the application of the Durham rule bears out this contention.

The absurdity of ascribing all, or even most, types of criminal activity to mental illness becomes apparent if one considers the frequency of minor or transient types of offenses. According to Lemert "it has been estimated that the 'average' law-abiding citizen in one day unwittingly commits enough crime to call for five years of imprisonment and fines running close to three thousand dollars" (page 317). Clearly, the facts suggest that we ought not subscribe to the hypothesis that crime is mental illness unless we are prepared to convert our society from a political democracy to a psychiatric autocracy.

Lemert summarized his criticism of the psychiatric approach to crime as follows:

> Many writers outside the field of sociology are disposed to regard a large number, if not the majority, of criminals as psychiatric problems. . . . In contrast to this, sociologists are inclined to discount such claims, preferring to emphasize the "psychological" normality of criminals. This is traceable to the scarcity of empirically valid demonstrations that the incidence of neurotic and psychotic cases is any greater in the criminal than in the general population. Especially dubious are concepts like that of the "psychopathic criminal" whose diagnosis is based upon the fact that he or she has no "moral sense," which is simply a way of saying that such persons show no remorse over their crimes [pages 295–296].

Goffman's (1961a) views on mental hospitalization were mentioned in Chapter 4. Although he did not address himself specifically to the problem of the relation between crime and mental illness, his sensitive analyses of mental hospitalization as a form of social control and punishment are relevant. They show that mental hospitalization and imprisonment in jail are more alike than otherwise.

Indeed, there is evidence to suggest that psychiatrists may be more punitive toward persons defined as mental patients (especially if they are labeled "dangerous" as well), than prison personnel toward persons defined as criminals. This opinion is shared, among others, by Lemert (1951), who wrote:

> It comes as no surprise that prisoners so often hate or fear the psychiatrist. Therapies based upon such role definitions are usually roughly rejected by the tough-fibered prisoners; or on the other hand if they are accepted, they may become the conscious aspect of a process of demoralization in which independence and self-resolution of the prisoner decay. It has been argued that constructive clinical work can be carried on within such an authoritative environment, but empirical evidence of the truth of such contentions has yet to be furnished. No matter how social workers or clinicians in the prison may construe their rehabilitative efforts, they must always be pursued within a framework of oppressive security regulations. Social communication is blocked by the tendency of the prisoners to symbolize clinical efforts or research either as espionage or as disciplinary measures at work behind a facade of humanitarianism or of little-understood science [page 315].

A similar criticism of the concept of criminality as mental illness was advanced by Pitts (1961):

> Rather than granting the criminal the "legitimacy" of a rational interest contradictory to the requirements of morality and of social order, American society tends to undercut any such claim by granting his deviance the legitimacy of mental illness. By declaring the criminal mentally ill, the society declares it unthinkable for any sane individual to be alienated from the wider community of Americans and uncommitted to its Puritan values. Far from representing a dissolution of the value base from which deviancy is assessed, the American conception of deviance as illness becomes a way to reassert the Puritan tradition that there can be no human behavior that is not an active search for secularized salvation and in the service of the commonwealth of true believers.
>
> This society asks, about someone who is physically or mentally ill and/or has committed "irrational" crimes: "Is he motivated to get well?" If the answer is positive and the deviant "confesses" to his illness, much energy will be expended to permit him to recover control over his physical and mental capacities. If the answer is negative, he will be isolated from the community of the loyal and well-meaning, under a "sentence" that will probably be much longer and more immune to "fixing" than a prison sentence [page 705].

Comparing the views of Bazelon, Fortas, and Guttmacher, with those of Wertham, Goffman, and Pitts, one is faced with a paradox. To each set of observers, the same social scene presents an entirely different picture. To the first group, contemporary American institutional psychiatry is a great humanitarian enterprise, not yet perfect, to be sure, but steadily improving. It is full of promise for the future. To the second, the same institution is a repressive social agency, whose aim is to control certain types of social deviations.

Perhaps the time is ripe for a change. Social scientists are displaying increasing interest in psychiatry and are growing restless with its institutional practices. At long last, psychiatric attitudes toward criminality are receiving more cogent criticism than ever before (for example, Hakeem, 1958).

Conclusions

The popular view, which regards crime as either a form of mental illness or a result of it, was reviewed and criticized. Logically, such a proposition is absurd. Morally, it is an inversion of an earlier belief—namely, that mental illness was a form of crime or sin. The thesis that the criminal is a sick individual in need of treatment—which is promoted today as if it were a recent psychiatric discovery—is false. Indeed, it is hardly more than a refurbishing, with new terms, of the main ideas and techniques of the inquisitorial process. Instead of recognizing the deviant as an individual different from those who judge him, but nevertheless worthy of their respect, he is first discredited as a self-responsible human being, and then subjected to humiliating punishment defined and disguised as treatment.

CHAPTER 9 » *Crime and Punishment:*
A Game-Model Analysis of Forensic Psychiatry

> *They [Judge Learned Hand and Justice Oliver Wendell Holmes]*
> *jogged down to the Capitol together—it was before the justice had*
> *a car, and he was bound for the Court. To tease him into a response,*
> *as they parted, Hand said: "Well, sir, goodbye. Do Justice!" The other*
> *turned sharply: "That is not my job. My job is to play the game*
> *according to the rules."*
>
> —Quoted by Francis Biddle (1960)

Game, Metagame, and the Behavioral Scientist

It is customary nowadays to consider the psychiatrist a behavioral scientist, whose interests and work are similar to those of the anthropologist, the psychologist, and the sociologist. In his relationship to the law, however, the psychiatrist's position is radically different from that of his nonmedical colleagues.

In practice, psychiatrists relate to jurists in two different ways. First, the psychiatrist may participate in a *game of law*—for example, as expert witness in the courtroom. Second, he may participate in a *metagame of law* —for example, as social scientist analyzing and commenting on the game (see Szasz, 1961, Chapter 13). The nonmedical behavioral scientist is limited to the metagame.

This distinction is important. Although it is impossible to practice the metagame of forensic psychiatry without familiarity with the game proper

109

(technically, the object game), the reverse does not hold true. It is possible to practice forensic psychiatry—indeed, to be an expert—without having any knowledge of the metagame implications of the object game or of one's actions in it. Actually, the psychiatrist who fulfills the social role of expert in determining a person's fitness to stand trial, his criminal responsibility, and so forth, may not only be unaware of the metagame implications of his actions, but may claim that his work has no such implications. Frequently, he believes that the game he plays is not social engineering but pure science.

Although in previous chapters the game-playing model of behavior was used, this chapter will be devoted to a more general and more formal presentation of this model, as exemplified in the practice of forensic psychiatry.

The Law as a System of Game Rules

Of all the social institutions, the judicial system is most readily interpreted in terms of a game model of behavior. The game is social living, and its rules are the laws of the particular society. In a changing social order new legislation continuously modifies the game by creating new rules and abolishing old ones. Other components of the game are judges, who act as umpires; criminal sanctions, chiefly in the form of fines and prison sentences, which serve as penalties; and freedom under the law, which functions as the reward for law-abiding behavior.

The Psychosocial Functions of Law. Psychiatrists generally agree that, as a social phenomenon, the law represents the equivalent of the individual conscience or superego. The three chief aims of the criminal law—deterrence, correction, and punishment—are consistent with this interpretation.

One of the important ideas which has been drawn from this interpretation is that crime is essentially due to the hatred which the criminal feels for society. Similarly, criminal law has been held to be inspired by the counter-hatred of criminals, by legislators, as representatives of the people. This is a convenient oversimplification of a complex social, psychological, and ethical problem. Perhaps for that reason, it is popular today. However, to speak of criminal motivation in terms of "aggression," "hostility," "pregenitality," "lack of sublimation," and so forth—as psychoanalysts tend to—does not carry us beyond the ancient moral view of the problem, which attributed crime to man's evil nature.

I prefer a broader, sociopsychological perspective on crime, which accords psychological factors their proper place, but which holds that criminality, as well as society's methods of combating it, reflect the socioethical style of the community. The organized lawlessness connected with bootlegging liquor was an American type of criminality. Likewise, relatively punctilious compliance with income-tax laws is also typically American. In brief, the evidence strongly suggests that criminal behavior is learned, as is noncriminal, law-abiding behavior.

Crime is a phenomenon that is ethical, legal, and social-psychological, not instinctual-biological and medical. This view is not novel. It requires emphasis only to counteract the medical-psychoanalytic view that tends to attribute criminal behavior either to genetic and neurological factors, or to early human influences over which the individual has little or no control in later life.

The functions of the law for society are comparable to those of the ego and superego for the personality. The law provides a stable framework of rules by which man may order his conduct. Often such rules have been considered limitations or restrictions, just as in psychology parental attitudes used to be regarded as ways of thwarting the child's instinctual needs. This view expressed the classic confusion of license with liberty.

Although it is true that some parental restrictions impose instinctual deprivations on the child, without the control of certain human potentialities men could not congregate in groups and form societies. Instead, they would perish in the evolutionary struggle for survival. Man's superiority to other animals lies mainly in his greater skill to organize social relationships. Thus, on the one hand, controls on behavior are necessary to ensure human survival. On the other, whether imposed by parents or society, the controls help the child organize an otherwise chaotic, and hence cognitively unmanageable, world. Children need a well-ordered world. It is desirable therefore for parents to provide consistent rules for them. Why is this good? Because it simplifies matters, and thus enables an immature personality to acquire techniques of adapting to various situations in a gradual, stepwise fashion.

Our concept of good and just laws is, in many ways, comparable to our idea of a good parental atmosphere for children. We do not consider the law just if it does not apply equally to everyone—that is, to all the children; or if its application depends on external circumstances, for example, on the attitude of the parent at any particular moment.

Closely related to the function of law as an agency for ordering human conduct is its role of protecting people from feelings of unconscious or unexplained guilt. We know—and need not here consider either the evidence or the reasons for it—that everyone is prone to experience guilt feelings. We employ various measures to avoid or combat them. Further, man's survival as a psychosocial animal depends upon the more or less correct performance of a host of social tasks. Thus, performance failure, or the fear of such failure, are constant sources of feelings of guilt, shame, and inadequacy. In this sort of psychosocial situation, one of the most important functions of the law is to protect people from an excessive burden of guilt.

How does the law fulfill this function? It does so by allowing those who are innocent to reassure themselves. They can say something like this: "We are God-fearing and law-abiding citizens. If we were guilty, we would be apprehended, prosecuted, and punished. Since this has not happened, we need not feel guilty." This aspect of the law highlights its psychologically defensive, ego-protective functions.

This guilt-relieving function of the law is especially important when psychiatric testimony is sought about criminal responsibility. The criminal law contains a set of rules which govern the behavior of judges, juries, prison officials, and, indirectly, the public as well. If a person is tried, found guilty, convicted, and sentenced in accordance with these rules, the judge, the jury, and the public will not feel unduly guilty about the fate of the defendant. However, since the rules of criminal procedure specify that an insane defendant should not be punished, the court must, especially if there is doubt, have adequate assurance of the offender's sanity. The responsibility for this judgment has been placed on the shoulders of the psychiatrist. In effect, then, the psychiatrist is asked by the court to give it assurance that it can proceed with punishment without feeling guilty. This may account for the fact that whether psychiatrists testify for the defense or for the prosecution, they almost always find the defendant mentally ill and irresponsible.

In the past, the need to avoid and master the experience of guilt was satisfied mainly by religious symbolism and action. Nowadays it is satisfied by psychiatric action. I submit, however, that if we wish to achieve a more humane and more rational jurisprudence, we must experience, contain, and tame guilt, not deflect and vent it in substitute action.

Psychiatric Expert Testimony. There are four basic questions which a psychiatric expert in a criminal trial is expected to answer. They are:

1. Is the defendant mentally capable to stand trial?
2. Was the defendant mentally ill when he committed the offense with which he is charged?
3. If he was mentally ill at the time of the alleged crime, was his antisocial conduct caused by his mental illness?
4. Is the defendant responsible for his actions?

There is, of course, an element of artificiality in separating these issues. But the questions are in fact often posed. For our present purposes, the second question is the crucial one. The answers to the third and fourth questions usually follow from it. Rarely do psychiatrists claim that a defendant was mentally ill when he committed a crime, but, despite this, his criminal conduct was not caused by his illness. (For a discussion of the problem posed by the first question, see Chapter 13.)

On the surface, the task of the psychiatric witness is to share with the court his supposedly expert knowledge on mental illness and its relation to social conduct. I tried to show previously (Chapters 1–3) that questions like these cannot be answered in a scientific fashion. The main reason for this is that in the courtroom the psychiatrist is expected to help the judge, the jury, and the public to dispose of an offender, not merely explain psychiatric matters. However, the sort of question the psychiatrist is asked makes his answer appear as if it were an expression of learned opinion about observable facts. This is why the work of the psychiatric expert in the courtroom seems to resemble that of other experts. What he in fact does differs basically, however, from what the experts in ballistics, pathology, or toxicology do when they testify (see Chapter 10).

In effect, the law recognizes a psychiatric plea, a psychiatric verdict, and a psychiatric sentence. The defendant may plead "not guilty by reason of insanity." The jury may issue the verdict of "not guilty by reason of insanity." Finally, the judge may sentence the defendant to be incarcerated in a mental hospital. In contrast, the testimony of other experts cannot prevent the trial of the defendant; nor can it serve as the basis for a special plea of innocence; nor can it justify a special method of acquittal; nor, finally, do nonpsychiatric experts furnish society with a system of paralegal penitentiaries in which socially deviant persons may be confined, for life if necessary.

If, then, the psychiatrist does not function as other experts, what role does he play in the criminal trial?

Ostensibly, his role is to be an expert: the psychiatrist informs the court of his opinions on the questions listed above. This is the part which the producer of the play, the legal profession, assigns to the psychiatrist. For the psychiatrist, who usually feels insecure as a scientist, this is a powerful temptation. Psychiatrists have long struggled to be accepted as equals by their medical colleagues. Perhaps because of this, they have been overzealous in accepting this official sign of social recognition, and have failed to scrutinize their own actions.

Behind the officially defined role of the psychiatric expert lies another. In this covert role, the psychiatrist is one of the *dramatis personae* in the real-life drama of crime and punishment. What is this drama, this game, in which the forensic psychiatrist plays a part? It is the criminal trial. The current American style of playing this game is characterized, among other things, by the ethical premise that only healthy persons should be punished, tortured, or killed. Thus, the psychiatrist's task is to ascertain and declare whether the accused is healthy enough to be punished.

If the psychiatrist testifies that the accused is mentally healthy, the court may feel free to sentence him. If, however, the psychiatrist claims that the defendant is mentally ill, should the court wish to punish the offender, it will have to bear an additional burden of guilt. Not only will it be responsible for hurting a person for misbehaving, but also for hurting one already suffering from a mental *illness.*

Finding a defendant mentally sick implies that he is being punished already: to be sick is to suffer. Thus, a positive psychiatric finding places a barrier before the court, halting its efforts to act in an openly punitive manner against the defendant. However, this maneuver does not eliminate the wish of the court and of society to punish the offender, or at least to control him. It only deflects it. Thus, while psychiatric testimony frequently inhibits overt punishment, it fosters punishment disguised as therapy. This is exemplified by the fate of the defendant acquitted by reason of insanity. He is not punished by imprisonment for a specified period of time, but instead by incarceration in a mental hospital for a term not specified in advance and possibly lasting for life.

This shift from overt to disguised punishment may be paraphrased as follows. It is as if, in response to a psychiatric finding of mental illness, the court were to say: "If the offender is *too sick* to be punished, then surely he is *sick enough* to be treated for his disease." This, however, is a kind of double-talk. For were we dealing with an ordinary illness, and one for which there was effective therapy, the court could provide the treatment and let the "patient" take advantage of it. But we are not dealing with an ordinary illness, nor one for which treatment would necessarily benefit the "patient." In theory, the court acts as if it were dealing with a serious public health hazard. It feels justified not only in offering treatment, but in compelling the patient to submit to it. In practice, this is rarely carried out, but what happens is not much better. The defendant, sentenced to a prison disguised as a hospital, receives no treatment, but is nevertheless expected to remain there until cured.

This is a callous game. The court plays by the rule: heads-I-win, tails-you-lose. If guilty, the defendant is sent to prison; if not guilty but insane, he is sent to a hospital for the criminally insane. Why do I consider this callous? Because were it the intention of the court, or of society, to provide psychiatric treatment for certain offenders, this could be provided in prisons. The psychiatric disposition of offenders seems to me a colossal subterfuge. It provides the "offender-patient" neither absolution from criminal guilt *nor* treatment. It is nothing more than an expedient method for "disposing" of persons displaying certain kinds of antisocial conduct.

Another aspect of psychiatric expert testimony which deserves comment is the inevitable partisanship of the expert. At present, most legal and psychiatric authorities favor the abandonment of psychiatric testimony on an adversary basis, and the substitution of so-called impartial expert testimony. This would mean that the psychiatrist would no longer be retained by the defense or the prosecution or both, but instead would be retained by the court itself. This does not mean, however, that the psychiatrist would be impartial, like the judge. When we say that judges are "impartial," we do not mean that they are necessarily unbiased about the issues or people they try. Their impartiality refers only to their pledge to uphold the law—and especially the Constitution—even if in doing so they must render verdicts personally distasteful to them. Psychiatrists, however, have no professional laws or constitution to uphold. How, then, can they be impartial? Making the psychiatrist the servant of the court, and having him paid by the state, will equip him only with the unimportant, external trappings of judicial impartiality. Instead of making him an unprejudiced arbiter of mental health and illness, it is more likely to make him a hired agent of the court.

Although I doubt it, perhaps the examination of defendants by so-called impartial psychiatrists has some merit. No less authoritative a body than the American Bar Foundation (Lindman and McIntyre, Jr., 1961) has endorsed this practice:

> Any accused raising the defense of irresponsibility should undergo a thorough mental examination by a panel of impartial experts.
> This type of examination performs a dual function. First, it removes the label "rich man's defense" from the insanity plea by providing expensive psychiatric testimony to the accused, who otherwise may lack the necessary funds. Second, it would tend to eliminate the "battle of the experts" by offering to the jury a neutral body of psychiatric testimony. This examination should not, of course, preclude the prosecution and the defense from presenting testimony by independent experts at the trial. To avoid treading upon the defendant's rights, the statute should allow him a role in selecting the panel of experts and should prevent the experts from testifying concerning any self-incriminatory statements the accused might have made during the examination [page 366].

I have several objections to this scheme. In the first place, I find it difficult to understand how a psychiatrist testifying in a criminal trial, and aware of the possible effects of his testimony, could be impartial. What would he be impartial about? The defendant? Society? Mental illness? His own role? To me, this proposition makes sense only as an attempt to remove the psychiatrist from the combatants, and to make him a kind of junior judge.

The judge, to be sure, is supposed to be impartial—meaning that he is expected to uphold the law. In the psychiatrist's role as expert, what would correspond to the judge's obligation toward the law? The answer is not clear. Certainly, the psychiatrist could not be expected to be "true" to psychiatry as a science, as the judge is expected to be "true" to the law as a body of social rules. Science is not that kind of enterprise.

There is another objection to considering psychiatric testimony impartial. There must always be a reason for raising the question of insanity in a criminal trial. Why would anyone broach the issue unless he had something to gain from it? We may thus assume that if the state raises the question, and hires a psychiatrist to prove it, it does so because it does not want to try the defendant (see, for example, Chapters 16 and 17). On the other hand, if the defendant raises the issue, and hires a psychiatrist to prove it, we may assume that he does so because he expects to benefit from this action. This makes sense. Indeed, psychiatric expert testimony makes sense only within an adversary system, each side using it for its own advantage.

If what I say is true, can we still speak of "impartial psychiatric testimony"? This phrase can only mean that officially the psychiatrist's testimony will be defined as something more scientific and impartial than it is. Ostensibly, it is to make him appear as a "pure" scientist, like a chemist, whom we might ask about the boiling point of mercury under a pressure of one atmosphere. But, can anyone honestly maintain that this is the kind of task which the psychiatrist in the courtroom performs?

Making the psychiatrist into an allegedly impartial expert can result only in assimilating his role more closely to that of the judge. This outcome would be desirable only for those who wish to give the psychiatrist even more power than he now has. Since I am opposed to the psychiatrization of the law, I am opposed to this measure. Significantly, this proposal, like all the others that usurp judicial functions, seeks only judicial power, but not judicial restraint. If the psychiatrist is to be impartial—in imitation of the judge—then the defense, as well as the prosecution, ought to be protected against this very impartiality. In jurisprudence this is accomplished by a system of appeals to higher courts. The existence of this system—consisting of a hierarchy of courts, each policing, as it were, the one beneath it—provides some guarantee that the work of the lower courts will be carried out properly. I would consider a panel of impartial psychiatric experts much more attractive if its advocates had also foreseen the need for "higher courts" of panels. In other words, if they had anticipated stupidity or malfeasance on the part of the experts, and had provided for the orderly review, and, if necessary, reversal of their findings.

To my knowledge, no such proposal has ever been made. This lack of foresight—if that is what it is—is disturbing, for it reflects the consistent expectation that, while other people in society need watching to ensure their honesty and correct performance, doctors do not. However, as Lord Acton (1887) has pointed out, innocence of wrongdoing and power seldom go hand in hand. On the contrary. Hence, if psychiatric experts are to wield more power, they should also be supervised more carefully.

To summarize: The forensic-psychiatric game is motivated largely by guilt feelings about sentencing lawbreakers, especially among persons charged with enforcing the law. Everyone learns, in growing up, that actions that cause others pain are wrong and should be avoided. In my estimation, this is the psychological core problem of penology. I shall conclude this chapter, therefore, with a brief analysis of the subject of meting out and receiving punishment.

The Psychology of Meting Out and Receiving Punishment

Passive Punishment. If a man loses his money through unwise market speculation or by playing the horses, he has been punished in a manner which we may call passive. By this I mean that another person has not taken special, socially overt steps to harm the "offender." This phenomenon has not received the attention it deserves.

In situations of passive punishment the penalizing agencies usually remain hidden. Under special circumstances, however, they may be explicitly defined. We then hear complaints, for example, about unscrupulous market operators or greedy bookmakers fleecing the public. Popular indignation may then be directed against persons who, at other times, fulfill social functions considered useful. This provides a clue to our understanding of the psychology of the sentencing authorities.

Some Remarks on Pain. Pain and suffering are unpleasant human experiences. They also signify an inharmonious relationship between the parties in whose relationship these affects have arisen. Thus, a crying infant makes his parents feel uncomfortable; whereas lovers promise to make each other happy (Szasz, 1957b). Without going into detail, it should suffice to recall the efforts of parents, and society generally, to inhibit a child's inclinations to cause others pain. The purpose is to make social living possible. To achieve this, destructiveness must be inhibited and sublimated—that is, transformed.

As a result of this process of socialization, almost everyone raised in our culture feels that it is wrong to hurt others except under special circumstances. One of these is self-defense. Another is the punishing of offenders, which is often considered a kind of collective self-defense. Similar considerations apply to the psychology of receiving punishment. It is hardest to bear punishment when it is unjust, that is, when one has done nothing to deserve it. This view is based on the child's experience in the family. Parents punish badness and reward goodness. The law is usually pictured as a later editon of this childhood version of "family justice."

Pain, Guilt, and Law Enforcement. What is wrong with such a view? Only one thing: it does not fit the facts. The function of law-enforcement agencies in a democratic society should not be equated and confused with the parental function. Likewise, in a free society, citizens should not be thought of as children. Although parents may be interested in goodness and badness, the sole concern of law enforcement—as opposed to lawmaking— should be the apprehension and punishment of those who violate society's rules of conduct. If the law is viewed as a system of rules governing the game of social living, then enforcing the law is the same as penalizing cheating in a game. The role of the umpire is more impersonal than that of the judge. We do not speak of umpires punishing players, but we do speak of judges punishing lawbreakers.

Actually, society's law-enforcement authorities—the police, the prosecutor, the judge, the prison personnel, and so forth—regard their relationship with the lawbreaker as something more personal than the relationship between referee and contestants. In a boxing match, the referee performs for the spectators who watch the bout. It is not up to him to punish, rehabilitate, reform, or treat misbehaving boxers. This is not true of law-enforcement personnel. They are expected to influence social deviants, and, accordingly, they take their roles personally. Thus, sentencing—which, in effect, is the imposition of rule-following behavior on others—is easily confused with and experienced as aggression. This may seem like a subtle difference, but it is an important one.

Lawbreaking Is Not Necessarily Sinful, Nor Punishment Necessarily Reformative. The point of view I have been outlining has been well argued by Mabbott (1939). On the basis of purely logical reasoning, he urged that we distinguish lawbreaking from moral evil. In a secular democracy, a person is supposed to be punished only when he breaks the law; never merely because he is evil. That is, after all, what distinguishes a democracy from a theocracy.

From these premises flow some important consequences. First, "if punishment is associated with lawbreaking and not with moral evil, the punisher is not entitled to consider whether the criminal is penitent any more than he may consider whether the law is good" (page 45). We may add that the punisher is also not entitled to consider whether the offender has been rehabilitated.

Second, it is not quite accurate to say that a judge upholds a bad law so that law in general should not suffer. "He upholds it simply because he has no right to dispense from punishment" (page 44). We have seen already (Chapter 8), and shall see further, that jurists, psychiatrists, and people generally, pay little heed to these ethical principles upon which the laws of a free society must rest. Instead, they try to redefine punishers as therapists.

Yet, it is possible to demonstrate, logically as well as empirically, that judges cannot serve as therapists. The function of legal punishment was crisply stated by Mabbott when he wrote that "no punishment is morally retributive or reformative or deterrent. Any criminal punished for any one of these reasons is certainly unjustly punished. The only justification for punishing any man is that he has broken the law" (pages 45–46).

Accordingly, punishment is neither more nor less than a corollary of lawbreaking. This conception tends to assimilate legal punishment with what I call passive punishment. The judge punishes lawbreakers as a burning house injures its occupants. A person may be burned to death while robbing a home or saving a friend. Similarly, from a moral point of view, the judge's work is good or evil, depending on whether the laws he enforces are good or evil. He has no right, however, to *evade* bad laws. If he wishes to protest against such laws, he must resign as judge, and crusade for better laws.

What is the role of legislators, in this view of the law? Just as judges do not punish, in the psychological sense of the word, neither do legislators. "They hope no punishment will be needed. Their laws would succeed even if no punishment occurred" (page 49). Punishment, we must remember, is a corollary of lawbreaking, not of law.

Who, then, punishes? In a sense, the offender punishes himself. Just as the person who gambles away his money injures himself, so the person who breaks the law may be said to punish himself. Mabbott emphasized this point when he said that there is only one condition that makes legal punishment *just,* and over it neither legislator nor judge has direct control: it is that a law must be broken (page 52). Only the actor, the citizen of a free society, can do this.

Needless to say, this point of view does not oppose penal reform. Even if the punishment for lawbreaking is imprisonment, it need not entail more hardship than the loss of liberty to move freely in society.

The Dilemma of the "Guilty" Judge. Judges shoulder great moral responsibilities. The occupational hazard of the judge is to feel guilty and become depressed. This risk will be particularly heavy under two circumstances: if the judge has to enforce laws morally repugnant to him, or if he tries to be therapist instead of judge.

Let us consider the dilemma of the judge beset by feelings of guilt. Curtis Bok (1959), a famous judge, has convinced himself that all criminals are mentally sick. This has led him to conclude that "punishment, not capital punishment alone, is the enemy. Let us turn our guns on punishment itself" (page 199).

Bok's arguments about penology recapitulate all the hoary platitudes of the permissive child-raising school of psychology. Because punishing children is an unpleasant task, many parents let themselves be persuaded that the ideal way to bring up a child is never to punish him. This is what Bok urges as penal reform: "Facile reformers must realize that it is as hard to convince prisoners that *punishment is a sin* as it is to convince the public" (italics added; page 202).

It is not surprising that a judge who feels this way about punishment would eagerly embrace psychiatry: "Penology is the fertile field in which to plant new ideas about crime and to put psychiatry to work" (page 203). Here we see the judge welcoming the psychiatrist as an ally who will protect him from feeling guilty for punishing men. The psychiatrist will take over, he will mete out punishment disguised as therapy, and everyone—well, almost everyone—will be happy. Bok is so carried away with the image of a psychiatric-penologic utopia that he even presents grossly misleading arguments. Having asserted that "criminals are ill men" (page 205), he compared medical hospitalization with psychiatric-penologic "treatment" as follows:

> Hospital patients are to a degree imprisoned, but they do not feel punished on that account, and the criminal should not feel so if he also received the kind of therapy that fits his case. Since the hospital patient does not think of his period of detention in terms of imprisonment, it is likely that in the penology of the future the patient will not either [page 207].

What is one to say to this? The proponent of this view, let us remember, is neither a politician seeking votes nor a psychiatrist selling his wares; he is a prominent humanitarian and a former Justice of the Supreme Court of Pennsylvania. Yet, Bok misleads the reader about medical hospitalization by emphasizing therapy and disregarding the patient's right to seek or reject it. Even if the medical patient is dying of cancer, he feels free in a hospital—not because he is being effectively treated, but because he *is* free. He may leave the hospital, engage in contracts, sue his physicians, and so forth. The prisoner-patient would have to be crazy indeed not to feel imprisoned when he is deprived of basic freedoms, and when he is compelled to submit to "treatment" against his will. To ignore this, is, to me, the essence of antihumanitarianism.

Bok's attempt to avoid punishing offenders leads him to overthrow all reason. He stated that "the worse a man's behavior, the more must be done for him to set him straight; and the more that is done for him, the more likely he is to respond to it" (page 208). To implement this suggestion would not only make society more inhumane than it now is, it would also make it more irrational than any society known to us. Social behavior is always governed by the principle that conduct deemed "good" will be rewarded, and conduct deemed "bad" punished. Bok, however, suggests that society should bestow its greatest efforts on those who perpetrate the greatest mischief. If this were the game played, why should anyone behave well? And who then would be left to "treat" the criminals?

The mistake that Bok and others make, confusing law enforcement with aggression, is like confusing bodily illness with punishment. Many persons cannot accept illness, especially serious or fatal illness, as a natural occurrence. When such a person develops incurable cancer, he will regard it as punishment for something he did, thought he did, or wished he had done. Why should a person think this way? Because it makes the world manageable for him. He sees himself and everything about him as parts of a (happy) family, perhaps ruled by God. In this system, nothing good or bad can happen unless one has done something to deserve it. Clearly, such a world gives a person the feeling—some may call it illusion—of having a measure of control over his destiny, which in fact he may not have. This world view, perhaps held unconsciously, underlies most of our present-day discussions about the role of psychiatry in criminal law.

Methods of Diluting and Distributing Guilt. It has been suggested that the sole function of many features of the criminal procedure is to protect the sentencing authorities from experiencing excessive feelings of guilt for hurting others. This is in accord with my interpretation of the psychiatrist's role in the criminal trial. Many other examples illustrate this thesis. The medieval executioner was covered by a hood. This gave him anonymity and rendered his act impersonal. However, if the executioner was known, he was ostracized. Later, when the firing squad replaced the individual executioner, a new method for disguising the "murder" was devised. Some of the guns were loaded with blanks, others with live ammunition, by men who did not do the firing. Thus, each man in the group who aimed and shot at the victim could believe, if he wanted to, that it was not he who fired the fatal bullet.

Similar practices persist. A jury of twelve men decides whether or not the accused should be punished. This measure serves not only to reduce the effect of individual prejudice against the accused, but also to distribute the guilt among those who pass sentence. The judge, in turn, is protected from excessive feelings of guilt by several features of his role, most important being the exceptionally high social esteem bestowed on him, symbolized by his high salary. The psychiatrist in this social situation functions as another blame-assigning person. He thus helps the sentencing authorities to dilute, distribute, and obscure their guilt feelings.

If meting out punishment engenders apprehension and guilt in the punishers, this fact should be frankly recognized. Instead, psychiatrists now help the court and the public to avoid confronting this problem by hiding it beneath pseudo-psychiatric considerations of mental illness. In this way, we forfeit our chances of dealing rationally with the problem. This is a serious matter for a democratic society in which each man is responsible not only for his own conduct, but, to an extent, also for the kind of society in which he lives (Cahn, 1961).

As psychotherapists, we know that a person cannot change his behavior unless he acknowledges and assumes responsibility for his participation in relationships that go awry and end in trouble. I believe that similar considerations hold true for society. Society will not change unless it recognizes and accepts responsibility for its role in social processes that lead to undesired ends (for example, hypocritical legislation). In brief, social anxiety and guilt may be necessary incentives for socioethical change.

Conclusions

We must distinguish between two types of psychiatric actions. The first is exemplified by the psychiatrist giving expert testimony in the courtroom. He is one of the actors in the drama of crime and punishment. His function is to play a special role in a legal and social game. The second type of psychiatric action is illustrated by my writing this book. In this case, the psychiatrist serves to analyze the games which other individuals and groups play.

These two forms of psychiatric action roughly parallel the distinction between law and science. Failure to remember this distinction results in confusing the intellectual as well as the social functions of both law and psychiatry.

The principal differences between law and science may be summarized as follows:

1. In the administration of the law, facts are necessary to enable the umpire (jury, judge) to decide whether rules have been broken and, if so, the type of penalty to apply. In science, facts are necessary to form new or better theories, and to develop novel applications (for example, drugs, machines). *Novelty* is not a positive value in law. Instead, the lawyer looks for *precedent*. For the scientist, however, novelty is a value; new facts and theories are sought, whether or not they will prove useful.

2. If we endeavor to *change* objects or persons, the distinction between law (both as lawmaking and law enforcing) and applied science disappears. In applying scientific knowledge, one seeks to change objects, or persons, into new forms. The scientific technologist may thus wish to shape a plastic material into the form of a chair, or a delinquent youth into a law-abiding adult. The aims of the legislator and the judge are often the same. Thus, legislators may wish to change people from drinkers into nondrinkers; or judges may want to change fathers who fail to support their dependent wives and children into fathers who do. This "therapeutic" function of the law will be analyzed in greater detail in Chapter 18.

CHAPTER 10 » *Criminal Responsibility*

> *No scheme of inequality can be defended as corresponding to natural fact. . . . Superior and inferior can be determined only with respect to a single quality for a single purpose. Nor can a man's qualities be added together and averaged to give a final score or merit. In short, men are incommensurable and must be deemed equal.*
> —JACQUES BARZUN (1959)

IN MANY trials—including famous murder trials with which the reader will be familiar—the defense has been based on the proposition that, although the defendant committed the crime, he was nevertheless innocent. This defense tactic rests on the premise that a harmful act is considered a criminal offense only if perpetrated knowingly and willfully— that is, with "criminal intent." It is held that if a man is insane or mentally ill he is not responsible for his actions. Hence, the verdict for an accused person who pleads insanity may be "not guilty by reason of insanity." Such a defense requires the testimony of psychiatrists. This fact implies a close connection between "insanity" on the one hand, and "criminal responsibility" on the other. In this chapter we shall examine the problem of criminal responsibility, and the alleged connections between it and so-called mental illness.

What Is Criminal Responsibility?

In criminology, law, and psychiatry there is a vast literature devoted to the problem of criminal responsibility. Through the constant use of this term, many students of crime, as well as lay persons, have come to believe that there is such a thing as "criminal responsibility." All that is needed is a psychiatrist to ascertain whether or not an offender possesses this trait.

But criminal responsibility is neither an object, like a table, nor a natural phenomenon like the Grand Canyon or a rainbow. Furthermore, the idea is neither synonymous with, nor derived from, the concepts of physical or mental illness. Pneumonia, hypertension, schizophrenia are terms designating such diseases, yet none provides a definitive clue to the criminal responsibility of its bearer.

Despite these difficulties, it is possible to provide an approximate definition of criminal responsibility. Briefly, by criminal responsibility we usually refer to a particular kind of relationship between an offender and the society in which he lives. In other words, "criminal responsibility" is very nearly synonymous with "punishability." Accordingly, it is a mistake to think that criminal responsibility is a trait or quality which may be detected by accurate observation of the offender. The concept refers not only to the offender but also to society's right to punish him. The meaning of the concept must therefore be sought in the offender's *human situation*.

Types of Responsibility. The term "responsibility" is used in everyday language in three different ways—to describe, to prescribe, and to ascribe. First, *in the descriptive mode:* "The avalanche was responsible for the death of three skiers." This is a report. It contains no ethical evaluation of the event, nor suggestion of what should be done. In contrast to this, we may use the word "responsible" in the *prescriptive mode*, referring to what happened in terms of what should be done. Used in this way, "responsible" means disapproval (rarely approval), and carries with it the command to change the situation, or to prevent (or encourage) its recurrence. For example, if we say that cigarette smoking is responsible for a high incidence of lung cancer, the implication is that cigarette smokers should give up this habit. It is important to emphasize that this command is only implied, for it hinges on the tacit premise that smokers value, or should value, longevity more than the pleasure of smoking.

The concept of responsibility in the *ascriptive sense* designates the ethical quality that an observer ascribes to a particular person's act (Stoljar, 1959). Ascriptive responsibility is often confused with descriptive responsibility. It is unfortunate that there are not three different words for the three meanings of responsibility. As matters now stand in jurisprudence and psychiatry, the three meanings are used interchangeably, without specifying the necessary distinctions among them. A brief illustration may clarify this discussion.

Let us take the statement "John killed James." From the point of view of descriptive responsibility, the report is either true or false. To evaluate the statement, the listener must find out if it is correct or incorrect. Thus there are three possible reactions to the assertion that John killed James: agreement, disagreement, or indecision.

Criminology and law, however, do not deal with physical facts as such. That is the province of the physical sciences. The province of criminology and law is social relations and ethics, or, more broadly, human rule-following behavior. Death as a biochemical phenomenon does not interest district attorneys. But as a specific psychosocial and ethical problem it does interest them.

Thus the question becomes: *"How* and *why* did John kill James?" and "Is John guilty or innocent?" To answer this question, it is necessary to seek facts and motives. Did John kill James in cold blood to rob him? Or did James throw himself in front of John's truck? Or, when James jumped in the river to commit suicide did John "kill" him by failing to rescue him? And so forth. The point is that special legal, psychological, and social inquiry is often required to discover how and why John killed James. If, for example, John was a soldier and James an enemy, this would not be a legal matter. However, in civil life, "cold-blooded murder" makes prosecution imperative. Under still other circumstances—for example, when the distinction between suicide and homicide is unclear—it may be a matter of choice for the legal authorities whether or not to take action.

From the prototype in religion, both jurisprudence and psychiatry acquired the idea of *responsibility as guilt.* It is, however, senseless to speak of guilt when responsibility is used in the descriptive mode. Hence our answer to the question, "Did John kill James?" will depend on whether we are asked to respond as observers of Nature (say, like military strategists estimating that, in the event of nuclear war, "only" 60 million Americans would be killed), or as observers of Human Nature (say, as members of a jury, who must decide whether or not a particular person is a lawbreaker).

Responsibility for an act may be attributed to a person correctly or falsely. If attributed correctly, the individual is descriptively responsible; if falsely, he is descriptively innocent. In the actual criminal process, ascriptions of both guilt and innocence may be verified or disproved publicly, as by a jury. Hence, for each charge of responsibility, there are four alternatives. The following example should help to clarify this analysis.

The charge is that John Doe killed James Smith, in Columbus, Ohio, on January 30, 1957. Is Doe responsible for Smith's death? There are four possibilities in such a case. First, John Doe's responsibility for the act is proved to be both true descriptively and ascriptively. This is the case of the guilty criminal who is arrested and convicted. Second, Doe may have committed the act, but may not be judged criminally responsible for it by those empowered to pass on the matter. This is the case in accidental homicide. Third, the description of John Doe's responsibility might have been false—for example, he may not have been in Columbus, Ohio, on that date. Nevertheless, responsibility for the act could be ascribed to him. This is the successful frame-up or the conviction of an innocent man as scapegoat. The Dreyfus case is a classic example. Fourth, and last, Doe's responsibility for killing Smith may prove to be false both descriptively and ascriptively. This is the unsuccessful frame-up, or the case of the innocent man finding justice in the courtroom. A summary of these four contingencies is presented in Table III.

Table III CLASSIFICATION OF ACTS ACCORDING TO TYPES OF RESPONSIBILITY

	I	*II*	*III*	*IV*
Descriptive Responsibility	True	True	False	False
Ascriptive Responsibility	True	False	True	False

I = The apprehended and successfully prosecuted criminal

II = The accident

III = The successful frame-up, or conviction of the innocent person (the scapegoat)

IV = The unsuccessful frame-up, or acquittal of the innocent person

Irresponsibility Because of Insanity. Typically, the defense of insanity is raised only in those criminal cases in which the offender's descriptive responsibility for the antisocial act is accepted as true.

It is important to remember that this is true only if the defendant himself pleads insanity, which, in essence, means: "Yes, I committed the crime, but I am not responsible because I did not know what I was doing."

If the question of insanity is raised by someone else—for example, by the judge or the district attorney, and especially if this is done to avoid trial and, instead, to confine the accused in a hospital for the criminally insane—then there is doubt of the accused person's descriptive responsibility. Perhaps the defendant has been falsely accused. If he is not tried, he cannot establish his innocence—that is, his descriptive (factual) nonresponsibility for the crime (see Chapters 13 and 17).

When the defendant pleads insanity, no one doubts that he committed the offense with which he is charged. Admission of descriptive responsibility is logically inherent in such a plea. Hence, the argument falls in Group II (Table III). Such cases are characterized by true descriptive responsibility, and false ascriptive responsibility. The American verdict "Not guilty by reason of insanity" states precisely this. It could be stated in this form: "Although the death of James Smith was caused by John Doe, he is not guilty (ascriptively) because of X." X may stand for many things, but usually for one of these three: accident, self-defense, or insanity (Hart, 1958). Irresponsibility for a harmful act by reason of insanity is thus logically similar to irresponsibility for such an act due to accident or self-defense. The notion of insanity has been added to other conditions that excuse the commission of otherwise criminal acts.

The handling of the insanity plea in English law is different. In a comparable situation, the verdict is: "Guilty, but insane." In actual practice, both maneuvers are inadequate. American lawyers have advocated adopting the English tactic, while some British jurists have expressed preference for the American version. The British attitude toward the "insane criminal" classifies his behavior in Group I, whereas the American viewpoint places it in Group II. In both cases, the focus is on ascriptive responsibility. The main difference is that the American verdict obscures the factual (descriptive) issue, whereas the English does not. The formula "not guilty by reason of insanity" simultaneously denies and reasserts the antisocial character of "insane" behavior. This is accomplished, first, by claiming that the offender is "not guilty (by reason of insanity)." This places the act in the category of noncriminal behavior. The offender's subsequent commitment, however, belies this assertion, and recodifies the behavior as ground for his involuntary detention (now called "hospitalization" rather than "imprisonment") (Hall and Glueck, 1958, pages 313–314).

Historical and Social Aspects of Criminal Responsibility

The idea that some people are "insane" or "psychotic" and hence not responsible for their actions has been held only during certain periods. It was unknown in ancient Greece. In contemporary America, it is very popular. According to this notion, there are two basic types of human conduct: rational and irrational. When behaving in the latter mode, it is alleged that men do not (fully) understand their own actions and are governed by powerful impulses rather than by reason. The shortcomings of this dualistic concept of behavior are well known and will not be discussed here. Let us only note that if behavior is classified as either rational or irrational, the observer is involved once more in judging rather than describing his observations.

Insanity in Early English Law. According to Glueck (1925), the beginning of the legal treatment of mental unsoundness can be traced to early English law. Insanity was officially admitted as a legal excuse for criminal action during the reign of Edward I (1272–1307). The subsequent history of this subject, until M'Naghten's Case, need not concern us here. I should, however, like to mention a feature of the famous early historical cases of legal insanity that seems to have escaped attention. In each of these, a criminal assault had been made—usually with apparent intent to kill—against a person of high social rank, often the sovereign.

The cases to which I refer are, briefly, the following. First, Arnold's Case: the defendant was tried for shooting at Lord Onslow (1724). Second, Hadfield's Case: the defendant was tried for shooting at King George III (1800). Third, Oxford's Case: the defendant was tried for shooting at Queen Victoria (1840). And finally, M'Naghten's Case (1843): the defendant was tried for having shot and killed Drummond, Sir Robert Peel's private secretary, whom M'Naghten supposedly mistook for Peel (Glueck, 1925; Weihofen, 1933).

Men often have grievances against prominent and powerful persons. Historically, the grievances of the powerless against the powerful have furnished the steam for the engines of revolutions. My point is that in many of the famous medicolegal cases involving the issue of insanity, persons of relatively low social rank openly attacked their superiors. Perhaps their grievances were real and justified, and were vented on the contemporary social symbols of authority, the King and the Queen. Whether or not these men's grievances justified homicide is not our problem here. I merely wish to suggest that the issue of insanity may have been raised in these trials in order to obscure the social problems which the crimes perhaps intended to dramatize (see Chapter 16). Examples of homicidal attacks against persons of low social class are noticeable by their absence in the history of famous forensic psychiatric cases.

From M'Naghten to Durham

The most famous and important forensic-psychiatric case in the annals of Anglo-American law is undoubtedly that of M'Naghten. In 1843, Daniel M'Naghten shot and killed Drummond, private secretary to Sir Robert Peel, the man M'Naghten had really wanted to kill. The defense was insanity. Medical evidence was introduced showing that M'Naghten was "laboring under an insane delusion" of being hounded by enemies, among them Peel. The jury found him "Not guilty, on the ground of insanity."

Following this verdict, the question of unsoundness of mind as an excuse for crime was debated in the House of Lords. The judges of England were asked to present their views on the criteria for such an acquittal. The most important part of the judges' answers was the following:

The jury ought to be told in all cases that . . . to establish a defense on the ground of insanity, it must be clearly proved that, at the time of committing the act, the party accused was labouring under such a defect of reason, from disease of the mind, as not to know the nature and quality of the act he was doing, or if he did know it, that he did not know he was doing what was wrong [Weihofen, 1933, page 28].

The judges' idea was reasonable. The purpose of the criminal laws is, or should be, to punish so-called willfully committed wrongdoing. An act that harms a person cannot be judged by considering only what happened. We must also evaluate *how* it happened. Two hypothetical cases will illustrate this point. In the first, a man has an epileptic seizure while driving; as a result, he loses control of his car, and runs down and kills a woman. In the second, a man loses a large sum of money in a card game he believes was crooked; he waits for the winner to cross the street, then runs over him and kills him. In the first case, the man "did not know the nature or quality of the act he was doing"; in the second, he did. The M'Naghten rule was intended to distinguish accidents such as the one caused by an epileptic attack from deliberate acts of mischief. It would be difficult to quarrel with this intention. However, the implementation of this rule—and especially the means of assessing whether or not an offender knew what he was doing, and that it was wrong—resulted in vast difficulties. Most of them were due to the concept that so-called mental illnesses were similar to neurological defects (Szasz, 1961). Hence, the belief that mental illness causes a lack of appreciation of what one does.

To study this subject, three issues must be kept in mind:

1. M'Naghten's Case codified, as law, the notion that certain acts may result from mental illness and that such illness is similar to bodily disease. It made no distinction among organic defects (for example, congenital idiocy), acute intoxication (for example, drunkenness), or ideationally motivated actions (for example, political crime). This global and undifferentiated conception of mental illness has been accepted even by critics of the M'Naghten rule.

2. The post-acquittal fate of the defendant was not explicitly defined. Actually, M'Naghten's fate became a model. Following his "acquittal," M'Naghten was involuntarily hospitalized: from 1843 until 1864, he was held in the Bethlehem Hospital; when the Broadmoor Institution for the Criminally Insane was opened in 1864, he was transferred there. He died in 1865, having been incarcerated for the last twenty-two years of his life (Diamond, 1956). Since then, it has been accepted practice to impose involuntary mental hospitalization, often for life, on persons acquitted on the ground of insanity.°

3. The socioeconomic, political, and ethical implications of deviant behavior were obscured in favor of its so-called medical causes. This, too, has remained a significant issue to our day, even in the modifications of the M'Naghten rule.

Much has been made of the psychiatric dissatisfaction with so-called

° In 1857, fourteen years after M'Naghten was tried, an Act was passed in England which decreed that persons acquitted on account of insanity "be detained at her Majesty's pleasure." History does repeat itself: In the District of Columbia, Durham's acquittal in 1954 was soon followed by statutes making the commitment of such persons "automatic."

tests of insanity, such as are implicit in the M'Naghten rule. In this connection, Isaac Ray's argument against such tests is usually quoted, to show that so-called enlightened psychiatric knowledge militates against the use of such tests (Overholser, 1959). Isaac Ray's (1838) views had a profound impact on American psychiatry, especially on forensic psychiatry, and hence deserve careful study. For our present purposes, it should suffice to recall that he was strongly opposed to reforms advocating nonrestraint in the treatment of mental patients. In general, he was more interested in the so-called legal applications of psychiatry than in psychiatry as a science. He was frequently sought as an expert in criminal cases. Ray's forensic-psychiatric views found expression in the New Hampshire rule. In two celebrated decisions, handed down by the Supreme Court of New Hampshire in 1869 and 1871, the relation between mental disease and criminal responsibility was defined as a problem for the jury. In the Jones Case (*State* v. *Jones,* 1871), the court expressed itself as follows:

Enough has already been said as to the use of symptoms, phases, or manifestations of mental disease as legal tests of capacity to entertain a criminal intent. They are all clearly matters of evidence to be weighed by the jury upon the question whether the act was the offspring of insanity. If it was, a criminal intent did not produce it. If it was not, a criminal intent did produce it and it was crime.

Under this rule, it suffices for a psychiatrist to testify that the defendant has certain standard symptoms, and may therefore be classified as having a particular mental illness. Further, the psychiatrist must testify that the crime was caused by the defendant's condition. This sounds better than the M'Naghten rule, but the improvement is deceptive. Actually, the change may be an ethical retrogression. This rule retains many of the difficulties of its predecessors. It, too, treats some kinds of deviant behavior as illness, and is silent on the disposition of the acquitted "criminal patient." Perhaps the most deceptive but most significant feature of the New Hampshire rule is the positive valuation it places on the absence of a predetermined test of insanity. I think that those who claim that physical and mental illnesses are basically similar should be required to abide by the rules of the game they themselves chose. The presence of ordinary disease—like pneumonia or syphilis—can be established by publicly demonstrable tests. I would argue that if we are going to talk of mental diseases, then there should be publicly demonstrable tests to establish the presence of such diseases. For legal purposes, it is more important that there should be such tests than that they be accurate. Without the tests, expert opinion ceases to be scientific (in the instrumental sense of this word), and instead becomes oracular.

I hold that it is not enough for a psychiatrist to state his diagnosis and perhaps also his opinion that the defendant was not responsible for his acts because of mental illness. Unless he also explains how he arrived at this conclusion—which means making the tests used explicit—his testimony runs counter to the ethic of a rational, democratic jurisprudence. In the absence of such publicly verifiable criteria for judgment, the testimony of the psychiatric expert will be accepted on the authority of the psychiatrist rather than on the merit of the scientific argument. But the concern of the jury should not be the expert *person*, but the expert *testimony*. When other technical experts, for example, toxicologists or pathologists, testify, this occurs. Why not when psychiatrists testify?

We should be wary of the claims of such men as Isaac Ray and those who followed him, precisely because their high public reputation was necessary to bring about progressive psychiatrization of the law. If their claims had been scientifically sound, men of lesser repute could also have established them. Beginning with the New Hampshire rule and culminating in the Durham decision, the oracular pronouncements of eminent psychiatrists have replaced publicly verifiable facts and scientifically acceptable theories. The change from M'Naghten to Durham is thus a move away from a Rule of Law toward a Rule of Men.

Before discussing the Durham rule, it is necessary to mention the so-called irresistible-impulse test. The moral basis of this test rests on the fundamental proposition that freedom of the will is essential to criminal responsibility. Those who have advocated this test have assumed, further, that there are human conditions or situations in which men are irresistibly driven to act in certain ways. Such actions are then placed in the same category as accidents. Neither is purposefully planned and executed. These statements do not, of course, describe observable human behavior. The idea of an irresistible impulse is an example of a common practice in forensic psychiatry: theories of behavior and prescriptions of conduct are presented as if they were empirical observations. Criticism of this practice is not our concern here. It should suffice to note that the idea of an act resulting from an irresistible impulse presupposes the idea that action is impulse-motivated, and that some impulses can be resisted whereas others cannot. Sanity is then conceived as the ability to resist (antisocial) impulses.

The doctrine of irresistible impulse is of American origin and dates from 1834 (Weihofen, 1933, page 46). It was adopted in several states and received its strongest support in a decision handed down in Alabama in 1886. There is a vast literature about these decisions. Most of it deals with the advantages of this test over the M'Naghten formula. As I see it, to many the M'Naghten rule implied a cognitive or intellectual definition of insanity. Accordingly, there has been a constant agitation, mostly by psychiatrists, for the recognition of the so-called emotional aspects of mental illness. The irresistible-impulse test is probably best viewed as an early expression of opposition to the M'Naghten formula, based on the latter's alleged overemphasis of the cognitive aspects of personality functioning.

The Durham rule is a logical sequel to the irresistible-impulse test. It reveals a persistent preoccupation with the question of "sickness" in some part of the personality, and with a refutation of the significance of the role of cognition in behavior.

The Durham rule (1954) was handed down by the United States Court of Appeals for the District of Columbia in 1954. Its most significant assertion is, ". . . that an accused is not criminally responsible if his unlawful act was the product of mental disease or mental defect." This is a semantic modernization of the New Hampshire rule.

This decision has been widely hailed by both jurists and psychiatrists. It is said to represent a great scientific advance in criminal jurisprudence. A few legal scholars, and an even smaller number of psychiatrists, have vigorously criticized the decision and its implications (see Chapter 9).

Clearly, the Durham decision represents the culmination of what could aptly be called the psychiatrization of the criminal law. It is an attempt to transform into legal reality the preconceived notion that there are two modes of existence—one sane, the other insane. Since this rule has had a powerful impact on contemporary American jurisprudence, the psychiatric, legal, and ethical aspects of it will be examined in detail.

The Durham Rule and Its Implications:
A Critical Analysis

According to the jurists who formulated the Durham decision, it was based on the ethical principle that "our collective conscience does not allow punishment where it cannot impose blame." This seems self-evident and commendable. Actually, it is neither.

The quotation lays claim to a moral principle as a regulatory force in social behavior. However, such an assertion should not be regarded as a description of a "natural law." Rather, it is a prescription of principles that ought to govern social living.

And what is prescribed? That there should be no punishment without blameworthiness. The logical corollary of this is that there should be no reward without praiseworthiness. The fact is, however, that our society is not constructed along these lines. Moreover, acceptance of these principles would change our society into an organization quite unknown to us, and hardly imaginable. It would be a human society that would have dispensed not only with punishment for bad performance but also with reward for good performance.

There is another source of difficulty. In the Anglo-American (and also Roman) philosophy of law, ignorance of the law is no excuse. How can a person ignorant of the law be held responsible for breaking it? How can he be blamed for committing an act that he did not know was prohibited? The answer is that the well-being of a free society is based on the assumption that every adult knows what he may and what he may not do. *Legal responsibility is an expectation:* first, that people will learn the laws of the land; second, that they will try to adhere to them. Thus, if they break the law, we consider them "blameworthy."

If we apply this reasoning to offenders who are alleged to be mentally ill, similar conclusions will be reached. If mental illness resembles bodily illness, it will not excuse them from adherence to the law. If, on the other hand, mental illness is similar to ignorance (as indeed it is)—then again it is not a condition that excuses violation of the law. Just as the recognition of ignorance and its correction are the responsibility of the adult citizen, so also are the recognition of mental illness and its correction. Thus, from a purely logical point of view, there are no good grounds for the rule that there should be two types of laws, one for the mentally healthy and another for the mentally sick.

The Durham decision and the attempts to implement it have resulted in a host of specific difficulties. Perhaps the most fundamental problem is the idea that, to be "punished" as a lawbreaker, a person must be blameworthy. If we accept this, we must determine whether, and in what measure, an offender may be blamed. To complicate matters further, the Durham decision has created a firm but vague connection between blameworthiness and mental health: it insinuated the proposition that only mentally healthy persons can be blamed for what they do. This presumption has created a moral and scientific vacuum, into which the forensic psychiatrist has eagerly projected himself.

According to the Durham decision, if the defense of insanity is raised in a criminal trial, it is a "matter of fact" for the jury to decide whether the offender suffered from a mental illness when he committed the act for which he is charged.

This is unadulterated nonsense. The word "disease" always denotes a theory, not a fact (King, 1954). Thus, if the more complex term "mental disease" means anything at all, it too refers to a theory, not to a fact. For example, that a patient is jaundiced may be a fact: his skin is yellow instead of pinkish white. But being jaundiced is not the same as having a disease. Whether this hypothetical patient has gallstones, infectious hepatitis, or cancer, his disease is the theory we construct to explain why his skin is yellow. Hence, it would be a perversion of our language and thought to refer to a "disease" (or its synonym, "illness") as though it were a "fact."

Mental illness, as we have seen, is a more confusing concept than bodily illness. Yet the jury is supposed to determine—as a "matter of fact"— whether the accused has or has not a mental illness. It is possible for a group of people, such as a jury, to *decide to call* someone crazy or mentally ill. But this is then *their theory* of why he acted as he did. It is no more or less a fact than it would be to assert that the accused is possessed by the devil. That is another theory, now discarded. To mistake one's theories for facts is often regarded as a symptom of schizophrenia. Yet this is what the language of the Durham decision does. It reifies some of the shakiest and most controversial aspects of contemporary psychiatry—that is, the definition of mental disease and the classification of such alleged diseases—and by legal fiat seeks to transform inadequate theory into judicial fact.

Further, the Durham formula takes the notion of mental illness and requires the psychiatrist and the jury to determine whether the criminal act was "a result" of it. This, too, is supposed to be a "fact." Unfortunately, not only cannot this be a fact, it cannot even be a rational theory.

To clarify this, let us consider a hypothetical example. A man suddenly pulls a gun in broad daylight, and shoots several people sightseeing in front of the White House. When arrested and questioned, he explains that he was protecting the President from Communist assassins, who were about to throw an atomic bomb on the White House lawn. Many contemporary psychiatrists would readily testify, first, that the murderer suffers from schizophrenia, and second, that schizophrenia was the cause of his act. But was it?

I submit that what we *call* schizophrenia is a theory to explain how such a thing could happen. After all, people rarely shoot strangers. The occurrence of any crime creates a powerful impetus to construct a theory to explain it. People want to know not only what happened but also why. Indeed, each person tends to form his own theory, in accordance with his educational resources and personal prejudice. The psychiatrist, by virtue of his education, may formulate a more sophisticated theory than the layman.

There is a similar difference in the theories of physicists and laymen on the subject of the flow of electricity in a copper wire. For the physicist, the theory may be a set of mathematical equations. The layman, on the other hand, may visualize electrons as little balls rolling along inside the wire. In either case, does the *theory* of electric flow *cause* a light bulb to glow or a radio to play? The question is improper. It is also improper to ask if a murderer's schizophrenia caused the criminal act. An explanation or theory can never be a cause.

What, then, did cause the killer to commit the crime? Psychiatrists could no doubt contribute to the answer. The "cause" of a "schizophrenic murder" might be arranged in a temporal order, beginning with how the offender was treated as a child, and ending with so-called precipitating events a few moments before the crime. For example, the waitress who served him breakfast may have been gruff. This could have been the proverbial last straw that broke the offender's precariously weak self-concept and precipitated the paranoid-megalomanic crime. This, however, is not the sort of cause that would help a jury to assign blame to either the waitress or to the criminal.

We thus discover what we should have known all along—that genuine scientific (causal) theories make it unnecessary and, in fact, impossible to assign moral blame to a person. If we take physics and its various branches seriously, we would conclude—as have most people in our society—that we cannot blame the gods if our crops fail or our cattle die. Similarly, if psychology and sociology were taken seriously—but this few people seem prepared to do—then we should have to conclude two things: first, that insofar as it is always possible to regard antecedent events as explanations of human behavior, men should never be blamed (or praised) for what they do; second, that insofar as men are human beings, not machines, they always have some choice in how they act—hence, they are *always* responsible for their conduct. There is method in madness, no less than in sanity. The whole thesis of this book flows from my commitment to the latter point of view.

It would be a mistake to think that such considerations are judicially nihilistic. On the contrary. They highlight the differences between two different social enterprises or games. In the game of science, the rule is to understand people. In the game of social control, whether through religion or law, the rule is to blame them. While these two games need not be wholly unrelated, it is futile to expect all problems of blame-assigning to be dispelled by better understanding of human behavior and motivation.

Mental Illness as an Excusing Condition

The concept of an excusing condition was clearly formulated by Hart (1958):

> It is characteristic of our own and all advanced legal systems that the individual's liability to punishment, at any rate for serious crimes carrying severe penalties, is made by law to depend on, among other things, certain mental conditions. These conditions can best be expressed in negative form as excusing conditions; the individual is not liable to punishment if at the time of his doing what would otherwise be a punishable act he is, say unconscious, mistaken about the physical consequences of his bodily movements or the nature or qualities of the thing or persons affected by them, or, in some cases, if he is subjected to threats or other gross forms of coercion or is the victim of certain types of mental disease. This is a list, not meant to be complete, giving broad descriptions of the principal excusing conditions; the exact definition of these and their precise character and scope must be sought in the detailed exposition of our criminal law. If an individual breaks the law when none of the excusing conditions are present, he is ordinarily said to have acted of "his own free will," "of his own accord," "volun-

tarily"; or it might be said, "He could have helped doing what he did" [pages 81–82].

From Hart's subsequent discussion, and from the administration of Anglo-American law, it is clear that the logical prototype of an excusing condition is an accident. In a real accident no responsibility can be ascribed to the offender. It is significant, however, that this principle no longer applies to cases of compensation for industrial accidents. The employer need not be at fault for the worker to be awarded compensation for injuries. In practice, no legal system admits without qualifications that all criminal responsibility is automatically excluded by an excusing condition. Hence, mental illness—like accident, provocation, or duress—may or may not constitute an excuse for a given criminal act.

Why do those who believe that mental illness should be an excusing condition think so? Their view is based on the assumption that just as human beings can be divided into two classes by gender, one male, the other female, so they can be divided into classes by psychiatric criteria, one sane, the other insane. Even outstanding legal authorities—like, for instance, Professor Glanville Williams (1953)—adhere to this point of view: "Mentally deranged persons can be separated from the mass of mankind by scientific tests, and can be given treatment instead of being subjected to punitive sanctions. Being a defined class, their segregation from punishment does not impair the efficacy of the sanction for people generally" (page 347).

I have tried to show earlier that the so-called mentally ill are *not* a "defined class" (Part I); and also that their "segregation from punishment" *is* in fact a form of punishment (Part III). In addition to these arguments, we may consider still another point. It is well known that it is easy to obtain both positive and negative psychiatric testimony in the same case. How do we explain this so-called battle of psychiatric experts? Let us compare psychiatric to toxicological testimony. If the toxicologist for the prosecution testified that a body contained a lethal amount of arsenic, whereas the toxicologist for the defense claimed that it did not, one of the experts could be proved guilty of perjury.

Why can psychiatric experts give conflicting opinions? I believe it is simply because the *criteria* for their opinions are not explicit. Thus, psychiatric testimony is, literally, "expert opinion," not fact. It is as if both toxicologists could be right, because one considered the lethal dose of arsenic to be x milligrams, and the other y milligrams. If we do not ascertain the criteria that the experts use—and demand that they be described in objective terms—we encourage the experts to influence and lead us, rather than to inform us. People should not expect, and will not obtain, a scientifically respectable procedure of psychiatric diagnosis, so long as they remain satisfied with psychiatrists trafficking in passing moral judgments, without, however, committing themselves on moral standards. In other words, the presence or absence of mental illness in an offender cannot be ascertained simply because there are no workable standards of mental health.

In addition to this logical argument against mental illness as an excusing condition, we should also consider that mentally sick behavior is more akin to *action* than to *happening* (Peters, 1958). To be sure, in part, such behavior may also be similar to happenings. To the extent that a person acts involuntarily, he cannot be regarded, in the social sense of the term, as a human being. This, then, leads to the dilemma typical of contemporary forensic psychiatry. Either we regard offenders as sane, and punish them; or we regard them as insane, and, though excusing them of crimes officially, punish them by treating them as beings who are less than human. It seems to me that there is a more promising alternative. Let us not consider mental illness an excusing condition. By treating offenders as responsible human beings, we offer them the only chance, as I see it, to remain human.

CHAPTER 11 » *Acquittal by Reason*
of Insanity

> The invention of a technical term often creates facts for social sci-
> ence. . . . Psychiatry is full of such technical terms; and if a criminal
> is rich enough he generally finds experts to qualify his state of mind
> with a sufficient number of technical terms to overawe those not used
> to scrutinizing authorities.
>
> —MORRIS R. COHEN (1931)

THE CONDUCT of criminal trials is regulated by rules of procedure. In Anglo-American law, the rules contain provisions for psychiatric moves on the part of both the defendant and the court. The defendant
may thus plead nonresponsibility because of insanity, while the court may
issue a verdict of "not guilty by reason of insanity." In Chapter 10, I analyzed the logic and the psychosocial implications of the insanity plea. In
this chapter, I should like to discuss not the insanity plea, but the insanity
verdict. Just what does this verdict mean? What are its legal, psychiatric,
and social consequences?

Disposition of the Defendant Acquitted
by Reason of Insanity

Formerly, when a jury found a defendant not guilty by reason of
temporary insanity, he walked out of the courtroom a free man. In the

novel *Anatomy of a Murder* (Traver, 1958), this is what happened to the husband who killed his wife's lover. While this sort of crime has, in my opinion, nothing to do with insanity, the jury's refusal to convict the defendant makes sense. Such a trial is a kind of modern morality play. Its message is to uphold the sanctity of marriage. The husband who kills his wife's lover is like the soldier who protects the fatherland from the enemy. If society wishes to promote this kind of morality, it will sanction this type of murder. The game is reasonable, although not necessarily one in which we might wish to participate.

Today, however, the verdict of insanity does not lead to freedom. In most jurisdictions the defendant who is acquitted by reason of insanity is automatically committed to a mental hospital (Lindman and McIntyre, Jr., 1961, page 353). This procedure is justified by the assumption that if the defendant was insane when he committed the crime, he is still insane enough after trial to warrant his confinement in a mental hospital.

Such a defendant finds himself in a predicament similar to that of the committed mental patient. Indeed, he *is* a committed mental patient. The only difference is that he is committed by criminal rather than civil procedure.

How and when will such a person be released? Rules vary from state to state, and are constantly being modified. Only one thing is certain: such detention represents serious punishment. Should the psychiatric wardens wish to keep the defendant locked up, it will be impossible for him to regain his freedom. To appreciate how effective this type of psychiatric imprisonment is, consider the North Carolina statute which provides that a person acquitted of a capital crime because of insanity may be discharged *only* by a special act of the legislature. If the crime charged was less than a capital offense, then he may be discharged by the governor. Although such defendants are nominally not guilty of their offenses, they are actually treated as criminals with sentences that vary with their crime.

The use of psychiatric hospitals as penal institutions has peculiar consequences: both the entry and exit of a patient are governed by judicial, not psychiatric, decision. This is illustrated by the following case.

The Case of Miss Edith L. Hough

On May 30, 1957, Miss Hough (*Hough v. United States,* 1959) shot and killed a man who called on her to express his sympathy after her father's death. The next day she was ordered to St. Elizabeths Hospital for determination of her competency to stand trial. She was found incompetent and was committed to the hospital until she would be able to stand trial. In May, 1958—a year after the crime—she was declared competent. She was tried for her offense—first-degree murder—on July 10, 1958, and was acquitted by reason of insanity. The District of Columbia has an automatic commitment statute which provides that "If any person tried . . . for an offense . . . is acquitted solely on the ground that he was insane at the time of its commission, the court shall order such a person to be confined in a hospital for the mentally ill." Accordingly, Miss Hough was returned to St. Elizabeths Hospital.

On October 20, 1958, the superintendent of St. Elizabeths Hospital filed in District Court a certificate, stating in part: "Miss Hough has now recovered sufficiently to be granted her conditional release from St. Elizabeths Hospital pursuant to Section 927 (e) of the Public Law 313" (page 2).

The District Court denied conditional release, whereupon the patient appealed to a higher court seeking reversal of this decision. The United States Court of Appeals for the District of Columbia Circuit heard the case and, on September 14, 1959, affirmed the decision of the lower court.

The court's blocking of Miss Hough's discharge from St. Elizabeths Hospital, surprising as it might seem at first glance, was reasonable, inasmuch as she was committed via the criminal route. Criminal commitment implies that the person confined is neither an ordinary mental patient nor an ordinary criminal, but a peculiar mixture of both. The extraordinary legal status of a person such as Miss Hough has not escaped the participants in this difficult affair. Nevertheless, Judge Bazelon insisted that such a person was a patient, not a prisoner:

> Nothing in the history of the statute—and nothing in its language—indicates that an individual committed to a mental hospital after acquittal of a crime by reason of insanity is other than a patient. The individual is confined in the hospital *for the purpose of treatment not punishment;* and the length of confinement is governed solely by considerations of his condition *and* the public safety. Any preoccupation by the District Court with the need of punishment for crime is out of place in dealing with an individual who has been acquitted of the crime charged.
>
> It does not follow, however, that the hospital authorities are free to allow such a patient to leave the hospital without supervision. We readily grant that periodic freedom may be valuable therapy. So, we suppose, may outright release sometimes be. But the statute makes one in appellant's situation a member of *"an exceptional class of people."* It provides generally, that the District Court have a voice in any termination of her confinement, whether unconditional or conditional [italics added; page 7].

The facts, however, belie Judge Bazelon's words that such a person is a patient, not a prisoner. As I see it, the real legal difficulty of such cases is hinted at in Bazelon's admission that the statute under which Miss Hough was committed made her a member of an "exceptional class of people." What is meant by this? Are these persons legally innocent but *really* guilty? Or are they persons, who, by virtue of their actions, shall henceforth be considered second-class citizens? Does this mean that we shall have two sets of laws, one for ordinary citizens and ordinary criminals, and another for the mentally ill? There is always danger in creating an "exceptional class of people." Doing so has always been the first step in justifying the withdrawal of constitutional protection from the group so designated (Douglas, 1961, page 62).

Another item in this record deserves comment. It is an opinion by Judge Wilbur K. Miller stating: "It is, of course, much easier to believe that a sane person will not in the reasonable future be dangerous to himself or others than to believe that an insane person will not be" (page 13).

Here is a modern version of the ancient view that violence implies insanity. Even though the term "insanity" is often used independently of whether or not a person is "dangerous," we habitually infer insanity from acts of violence. This was true in the present case. Legally, Miss Hough was sane until after she killed a man.

The commonsense formulation of insanity propounded by Judge Miller seems to be intended to help the observer—and this means all of us, and especially juries and judges—to wrestle with the problem of a person's so-called possible future dangerousness. By codifying acts of violence as expressions of mental illness, we neatly rid ourselves of the task of dealing with criminal offenses as more or less rational, goal-directed acts, no different in principle from other forms of conduct.

Soon, however, Miss Hough obtained her release, and it is worth noting how. At the time of the 1959 hearing, Dr. Karpman testified that she was still "potentially dangerous":

Q. In your opinion is Edith L. Hough the aggressive type of paranoid?
A. Yes, she is the aggressive type—as evidenced by the fact that she took measures of her own in killing the man. That is aggressiveness.
Q. In your opinion is an aggressive paranoid potentially dangerous?
A. It is conceded universally an aggressive paranoid is dangerous. I would even say that universally we think that any paranoid schizophrenic is potentially dangerous, because one can never tell when the meekness and submissiveness may suddenly turn around and become aggressive.
Q. Would you say Edith L. Hough at this time is potentially dangerous because she has schizophrenia, paranoid type?
A. I would rather not answer this question directly. Ask me whether a paranoid schizophrenic is potentially dangerous, and I would say yes.
Q. You would say yes?
A. Yes.

Approximately six months later, in March, 1960, the attorneys for Miss Hough made a new move to secure her release. They challenged the reappointment of one of the psychiatrists as her examiner. They argued that:

Because of his lifelong personal relationship with the Hough family and his personal feelings toward her it would be "impossible" for him to conduct an interview with her "in an atmosphere of mutual confidence and respect." On the basis of new diagnostic evaluations by psychiatrists not personally involved with the Hough family, and a more detailed and meaningful presentation of the conditions specified for release, the trial judge, abiding by new standards, granted her application for release [page 234].

I shall refrain from commenting on the fact that Miss Hough remained confined largely on the testimony of a psychiatrist who was a family "friend." Let me note only that for a defendant in this predicament to gain his freedom, he must have social standing and money, to retain psychiatrists to testify on his behalf. Miss Hough (whose father was a physician) had both. Many defendants have neither.

Civil Versus Criminal Commitment

Civil commitment, to which my objections were stated earlier (Chapters 4 and 5), differs from criminal commitment in several respects, the most obvious being the judicial procedure. Despite this formal distinction between them, and many practical, social differences as well, it has been argued that civil and criminal commitment are essentially similar. For example, Goldstein and Katz (1960) stated:

Whether commitments to a mental institution be via a "civil" or "criminal" route their functions are substantially the same: that "mentally ill" persons who evidence *dangerousness* to themselves or others be provided by the state with custody and care even if there is no known effective therapy or therapy is unavailable. *Commitment procedures, however labeled, constitute a sanction,* so far as the person confined is concerned, in the form of deprivation of liberty, at least to the extent that commitment is without regard to his "wishes." And a society free of such sanctions is difficult to visualize [italics added; page 229].

It is at this point that clarification is needed. Goldstein and Katz say that commitment, even civil commitment, is a form of punishment. I agree. But if this is admitted, persons accused of mental illnesses, just as persons accused of crimes, ought to be able to avail themselves of their constitutional rights against self-incrimination and false imprisonment. However, because commitment is defined as therapy, not punishment, mental patients are deprived of these rights (see Chapter 15).

There is another contradiction. On the one hand, Goldstein and Katz assert that commitment, whether civil or criminal, is a form of punishment. On the other, Bazelon claims that neither civil nor criminal commitment is punishment: "The individual is confined in the hospital for the purpose of treatment, not punishment." On these issues, there is no limit to the verbal gymnastics. At times mental hospitals are seen as medical institutions, at other times as prisons. This explains why no one shows surprise when a statement of the following type appears in a newspaper. After reporting on the suicide of the daughter of a prominent Hollywood personality, a recent news dispatch went on to explain that "during the past year, she served two 90-day terms for possessing narcotics, one in jail, the other in a mental hospital." Clearly, there can be no substitute for a clear understanding of what civil and criminal commitment actually entail. I shall summarize the essential features of each.

Civil commitment, as the term implies, is the result of civil action. On the basis of medical certification, a court may commit a person to a private or a public mental hospital, but not to a hospital for the criminally insane. Moreover, in civil commitment, but not in criminal, the hospitalized patient is under the jurisdiction of the hospital authorities. The hospital psychiatrists are free to release the patient whenever they wish.

Because of the loss of freedom which mental hospitalization entails, Anglo-American law provides the mental patient with the right to petition for a writ of habeas corpus, so as to afford him the opportunity to argue, in a court hearing, that he is being detained illegally. The fact that the reverse of this does not obtain—in other words, that the court can only authorize, but cannot compel, civil commitment—is consistent with the legal definition of the mental hospital as a hospital, not a prison. Were hospital physicians to testify that a mental patient was sane and should be discharged, a civil court action could not block the release.

In criminal commitment the penal character of the detention can no longer be covered up by psychiatric makeup. The Hough Case illustrates the court's complete control of the criminally committed patient. It is misleading to call such confinement "hospitalization," and to refer to institutions accepting persons under such circumstances as "hospitals." Since the inmate's departure from this type of institution is determined neither by himself nor by his physician, it seems reasonable to conclude that this type of "hospital" is as much a part of the government's penal system as the prison.

Perhaps all this is obvious. Yet the persistent labeling of mental prisons as "hospitals" has muddled the thinking of both the public and the professions involved in these matters. The confusion of mental patients is augmented because they do not know if they are patients or criminals. Were we to plan deliberately to harm mental patients—whose crucial difficulty often springs from not understanding their position in life—we could not devise a more effective pathogenic influence than the present legal-social definition of their status. Psychiatrists are similarly confused. They act as wardens but think they are doctors. Last but not least, the jurists and legislators are confused. They have lost sight of the distinction between "mental illness" and criminality.

For example, state hospital directors in New York State used to be authorized to transfer patients from state hospitals to hospitals for the criminally insane. In terms of the semantic mischief described above, this statute was reasonable. If certain types of prisons are called "hospitals," then transferring a "patient" from one hospital to another will seem no different in principle than moving him from one ward in a hospital to another.

Not until a federal court recognized the injustice to the patient was this statute declared unconstitutional (American Civil Liberties Union, 1962). The fact that there was such a law—legalizing an arrangement that obviously served only the interests of the psychiatrists—proves, I believe, that jurists, legislators, and psychiatrists have all been more concerned with controlling mental patients than with protecting their liberties.

Dangerousness and Mental Illness

The commitment of mental patients, though often rationalized on therapeutic grounds, is also said to be necessary for the protection of society. Despite the fact that there is no evidence that mental patients are a greater source of danger to society than nonmental patients, the myth of the "dangerous mental patient" dies hard. It lingers partly because of our tendency to ascribe mental illness to individuals who have engaged in aggressive or destructive acts. Calling Miss Hough mentally ill is a typical example. When the question of her release from the hospital arose, her "dangerousness" was widely debated. In this sort of case, it would be simpler to say that we fear the patient's subsequent conduct because she had killed someone, and not because she is mentally ill.

Reward and punishment have always been the basic principles of society. To inflict punishment is a responsibility that society cannot shirk. However, through criminal commitment, and to a lesser degree through civil commitment, society evades its duty to punish the lawbreaker. Instead of explicit punishment and humane rehabilitation in a penal setting, the deviant is punished covertly by restraint and "treatment" in a psychiatric setting. This transfer of the punishment from the legal to the psychiatric arena makes the humane care of the offender more difficult (see Chapter 9). It also contaminates and complicates the psychiatric care of the self-defined mental patient.

The ghost of the "dangerous mental patient" will not be laid to rest until it is recognized that the institution to which the so-called mental patient is committed is not a hospital but a prison. Lawbreakers, irrespective of their mental health, ought to be treated as offenders. This would afford possibilities for "therapy" in a context in which personal liberties could be protected; whereas our present practices, which use civil law to deprive people of their liberties, make both therapy and the protection of civil rights impossible.

Society's ambivalence toward the mental patient has found new expression in the Durham and post-Durham rulings. Once more, mental patient and criminal are placed in the same category. In the past this was done by asserting that mental patients were criminals. Today it is done by claiming that criminals are mental patients. This does not make as much difference as our false psychiatric liberals would have us believe. The results are the same. The moral supremacy of the law is raised to undesirable heights by branding as irrational all those who break it. In the unholy alliance of legal, moral, and medical approaches to antisocial behavior, differences among people become blurred. The feebleminded petty criminal, the political dissident, and the "schizophrenic" who hurts a member of his family are all included in the same category. Each is considered irresponsible for his acts, restrained in a psychiatric hospital, and subjected to involuntary treatment for his alleged illness. Given these "liberal" psychiatric criteria of irresponsibility, one must ask how the experts can maintain that the criminals dealt with in the ordinary, legal-penological fashion are less "sick" than those psychiatrically hospitalized. If, on the other hand, the "ordinary" criminals are also considered sick, then we arrive at that favorite psychiatric position which considers all crime a symptom of mental illness.

Is anyone really prepared to take this position seriously? What is a crime? Speeding? Cheating on one's income-tax return? Selling contraceptives in Massachusetts? Operating a Planned Parenthood Clinic in Connecticut?

Conclusions: Private Versus Public Interests

Our views on how to cope with so-called mental patients who have violated laws, or who are believed to threaten the public safety, will depend on our attitudes toward the fundamental conflict between private and public interests. Balancing these interests is entrusted to our democratic institutions—the Constitution, the Congress, the Supreme Court, and so forth. Psychiatrists, and particularly state hospital psychiatrists, have no special mandate from the people to harmonize the needs of the individual mental patient with those of the public. It would be preposterous to assume such a responsibility, if for no other reason than that it could not be discharged properly. Nevertheless, the lure of omnipotence being what it is, many psychiatrists define their task in terms of precisely such a mandate: It is their duty to protect, simultaneously, the patient from society, and society from the patient. This is regrettable. But it is more than regrettable, indeed catastrophic, that our jurists and legislators, instead of recognizing this psychiatric function as a threat to a free society, have fostered and legitimized it. In doing so, they have forgotten the most important lesson which the history of democratic institutions and popular revolutions has taught us; namely, that the misbehavior of those who govern is no less a danger to society than the misbehavior of those who are governed. In other words, so-called mental patients are not the only persons in society who may be dangerous. Jurists, legislators, and psychiatrists may also be.

PART FOUR » *Psychiatry and Constitutional Rights*

CHAPTER 12 » *The Mental Patient's Position in Society: from Contract to Status*

> *Collectivism curtails as surely as individualism extends the area of contractual freedom. The reason of this difference is obvious. The extension of contractual capacity enlarges the sphere of individual liberty. According as legislators do or do not believe in the wisdom of leaving each man to settle his own affairs for himself, they will try to extend or limit the sphere of contractual freedom. During the latter part of the nineteenth century the tendency to curtail such liberty becomes clearly apparent.*
> —ALBERT V. DICEY (1914)

IN RECENT years, the social position of the institutionalized mental patient has received increasing attention from both psychiatrists and social scientists. In this chapter, I shall analyze this problem from the point of view of the basic sociologic concepts of status and contract.

The Concepts of Status and Contract

In 1861 Sir Henry Maine advanced the thesis, which has since been amply corroborated, that the basic principle underlying the modern state is *contract*. Contract means the power of each to give in proportion as he

149

receives and in return for what he receives. This is the logical and ethical basis not only of most of our civil relations but also of the relations between the individual and the modern democratic state. In contrast, the primitive community is organized not by contract, but by *status*, which means privilege according to social position.

The primordial society, according to Maine (1861a), was a group of persons held together by obedience to a parent. His word was law. The term "parent" denotes here both a biological and a social relation. Adoption was an important phenomenon in early societies. A filial relationship between an adult and a child (usually male) was often established merely by the desire of the former to ascribe to the latter the status of son and heir. Thus, in primitive times, society was not "what it is assumed to be at present, a collection of *individuals*. In fact, and in the view of the men who composed it, it was an *aggregation of families*. The contrast may be most forcibly expressed by saying that the unit of ancient society was the Family, of a modern society the Individual" (page 74).

Our laws—which regulate the conduct of both normal and so-called mentally ill persons—incorporate this fundamental distinction between contract and status. So long as an adult is considered mentally well, the law treats him as an individual. Once he is considered mentally ill, however, the law treats him as the occupant of a family status: as father, mother, son, and so forth. Moreover, the law defines the patient's next of kin as a "responsible relative," who, for all intents and purposes, is given possession of the patient as a person. When family members are unavailable for this role, the state assumes the parental function: henceforth, the patient is regarded not as a citizen, but as a ward of the state. It is evident that there will be the greatest difference, at every point in the encounter between patient and psychiatrist, depending on whether their relation is governed by the principle of status or by that of contract.

As we noted before (Chapter 7), there are powerful forces in society which seek to demote the mental patient from the position of a contracting individual to that of occupant of the status of insanity. This sort of social degradation is one of the ways the group punishes those of its members that fail to fulfill some of their contractual obligations. Thus, one way to become an involuntary mental patient is by defaulting on some of one's duties. This simple fact is the cause of many difficulties in hospital psychiatry. Why? Because failure to fulfill certain contractual obligations does not necessarily mean *inability* to honor *all* of them. There are other possibilities. Perhaps the person is able but unwilling to fulfill his obligations. It could also be that breaking the contract was a means of communicating to his partner the wish to redefine the relationship. People do not break their contracts without wishing to do so, unless they are grossly disabled—for example, by brain injury or senility. It is safe to assume that, as a rule, when a person breaks a contract, he does so because he thinks it is to his advantage.

Accordingly, I submit that, except in cases of gross disability, adults should always be treated as if they were capable of fulfilling the contractual obligations they have assumed. If people are to remain responsible, contracting individuals, it is important to respond to their failure to fulfill obligations by punishing them, not by redefining them as inferior beings, unfit to enter into contracts.

The State as *Parens Patriae*

From Roman law comes the idea that in some circumstances the state should relate to the citizen as the parent to his child. Known as the doctrine of *parens patriae*, this concept is firmly recognized in Anglo-American law. It gives "the sovereign both the right and the duty to protect the persons and property of those who are unable to care for themselves because of minority or mental illness" (Ross, 1959, pages 956–957). Herein lies one of the foundations of such psychiatric-legal practices as commitment, guardianship, and laws to control so-called sexual psychopaths.

Under the doctrine of *parens patriae,* certain types of social relations are excluded from those governed by Anglo-American, democratic principle. Further, it is recognized as legitimate that, in some instances, people may be treated as stupid children, and the government as their wise parent. The exemption of *some* men, and *some* governmental functions, from even minimal standards of competence and responsibility threatens to undermine traditional English and American political institutions. Yet, without them, there can be no open society, and no personal liberty. In brief, to whatever extent we bestow the power of *parens patriae* on the government, to that extent we grant it despotic powers. Nor can we expect that such powers, once granted to specific agencies, will remain localized. On the contrary, the process will spread, and unless halted, will envelop the state.

Some illustrations of the consequences of the mental patient's filial status vis-à-vis those who care for him may highlight the sort of problem I have been alluding to. The state as *parens patriae* must provide care and treatment for mental patients, as parents must for their children. In a sense, the state assumes ownership of the patient (Szasz, 1960b). Thus, in state mental hospitals, the need to obtain permission for procedures deemed necessary for the patient's welfare becomes a mere formality. The patient cannot effectively refuse permission. As a rule, his relatives will be eager to transfer all the responsibility for the patient's care to "his doctors." If not, they can be easily persuaded to do so by the hospital staff. This is why certain psychiatric "treatments"—particularly electric shock therapy and tranquilizers—are such effective punitive techniques for subduing recalcitrant inmates.

Another feature of the mental patient's status as ward of the state is his inability to sue for damages. The courts have refused to hold physicians and technicians in the state hospitals liable for injury resulting from shock treatment, except where "gross negligence" can be proved—and this is almost impossible.

The American Bar Foundation (Lindman and McIntyre, Jr., 1961) looks with disfavor on this legal situation, but fails to recognize it as an integral part of the doctrine of *parens patriae,* of which it otherwise heartily approves:

These cases and the Kansas statute make it difficult for the patient either to protect himself from injury or to recover damages for negligence or gross negligence, inasmuch as he is often forced to submit to the treatment and is unable to testify about what happened to him while he was unconscious. In addition, the patient is not extended the privilege of selecting a physician or technician who he believes will observe the necessary precautions. The law's willingness to hold the attending physician harmless from liability for physical injuries due to electroshock treatment points up the drastic aspect of the therapy and underscores the desirability of a consensual relationship between the patient and the doctor [page 150].

This situation is inherent in the patient's status as government property, and in the state hospital's complementary position as omnicompetent parent. Before entering the hospital, the mental patient is usually treated like any other person. Once in the hospital, however, he is treated as a nonperson. This is absurd.

A recent legal decision highlights this problem. In 1960, the Michigan Supreme Court upheld a workman's compensation award to an automobile company employee, who had contended that he had suffered a mental breakdown as a result of psychological stresses encountered in his job (*Carter* v. *General Motors Corp.,* 1960). This man had a history of previous mental hospitalization, the diagnosis having been paranoid schizophrenia. Counsel for the plaintiff argued successfully that the recurrence of the disability was precipitated by stresses at work and that the employer was therefore responsible. However, should this patient be committed to a mental institution, the hospital personnel might injure him, and he would be unable to sustain a claim against them.

This resembles the situation that prevailed under early Roman law. According to that code, parent and "child under power" (who might have been a person of mature years) could not sue each other. This is true of children and parents today. Legal scholars look upon this as an example of the principle of "unity of person" (Maine, 1861a, page 85). Thus, underage child and father are considered by law as one person. And, to an extent, so are the institutionalized mental patient and the state hospital system.

The Individual, the Family, and Mental Hospitalization

We have seen that the mental patient's movement from contract to status is closely related to, and is often precipitated by, his failure to discharge adequately certain obligations. Examples of this are the alcoholic husband who squanders his money on drink and thus endangers the lives of his wife and children, or the young mother with postpartum depression who endangers the life of her newborn baby.

Since the most intense human interactions usually occur within the family, mental illness is primarily a problem for those "close" to the patient. This is why it is mainly family members who "accuse" their relatives of mental illness and summon the aid of the psychiatrist.

Many situations which eventuate in a person's commitment have this in common: the patient has failed to perform certain necessary social functions *in the family*. The emphasis is on the family as the locus of the performance failure. For should a person fail to do his job, he will probably lose it. Or should he neglect to pay his taxes, he will probably be prosecuted. However, what can a person do with his relatives, his so-called "loved ones," who fall down on their jobs? If the failing member of the family is a child, he can be punished. If he is an adult, the problem is more difficult. There are three basic possibilities:

1. A relative may request the failing member to alter his behavior—by asking, begging, coercing, self-sacrificing, and so forth.

2. He may sever the relationship—by emotional withdrawal, separation or divorce, running away and "disappearing," and so forth.

3. He may enlist medical or psychiatric help and secure involuntary hospitalization of the failing member. This, of course, results in separation. Officially, however, it is regarded as an attempt to improve, not destroy, the relationship with the committed person. Involuntary psychiatric hospitalization thus fulfills important social and psychological functions.*

The Conflict Between the Integrity of the Family and the Autonomy of

---

* A fourth solution to the problem is murder. In our culture there are two main types of homicide. One is committed by the professional criminal whose victims are either competing criminals or professionally chosen victims. The other by the amateur, who usually kills a member of his family or a close friend. For some people it is easier to kill a person to whom they have been closely attached than to leave him. Similarly, some find it easier to commit their "loved ones" than to leave them, whereas others have an inverse order of values.

the Individual. As the social institution of the family becomes progressively less viable, the need increases for mechanisms of relief to keep it going. One of these is psychiatric hospitalization. It has the special advantage of relieving family tensions without disrupting the moral integrity of the family as an institution. Unlike legal separation or divorce, commitment achieves a separation of family members on ostensibly medical grounds. The legal structure of the family thus remains intact.

However, as noted before, mental illness (of the kind we are considering) is merely the name we give to certain failures in fulfilling family obligations. Its treatment, and especially commitment, thus involve us in adjudicating moral conflicts. Ostensibly, the question is one of medical treatment; but tacitly, it is one of choice between competing values. The question really is: Which should we prefer, *the integrity of the family or the autonomy of the individual?* Commitment laws favor the former. I suggest that we favor the latter.

A similar situation exists with respect to marriage and divorce. Some people who consider the family and the marriage contract indissoluble may decide not to marry. Those who do, and then find their marriage intolerable will avail themselves of certain alternatives: annulment, separation without divorce, desertion, involuntary mental hospitalization, and so forth.

Thus, for the individual, involuntary hospitalization ensures the maintenance of the family as a good institution. For society, it ensures the maintenance of family relationships, loyalties, and responsibilities as positive moral values. Our whole social system needs the safety valve that commitment laws provide. Without it, our traditional ideas about the duties and rights of family members would have to be reexamined, reassessed, and changed.

The Refusal to Treat Man as a Contracting Individual: An Illustrative Example

A recent murder case offers a striking example of the refusal, by legal and psychiatric authorities, to treat a person as a contracting individual; and of their attempt, instead, to treat him as an inferior, defective object, in need of repair—that is, as a psychiatric patient (Wiseman, 1961). In this case, the person refused to accept the role assigned to him. He thereby exhibited greater autonomy and moral integrity than the experts in charge of him.

On April 20, 1957, Jim Cooper, a twenty-three-year-old airplane mechanic, went to the apartment of his former fiancée, Connie Gilman. Before ringing the doorbell, he released the safety latch on his pistol. When she came to the door, he fired nine shots into her body, killing her instantly.

He then gave himself up to the police. When asked whether he fired with intent to kill, Cooper said: "I fired to blow her fucking head off. How many times do you want me to tell you?" (page 289).

I shall not retell the story of this crime. What interests us is not the crime itself, but rather the way Cooper was handled by lawyers and psychiatrists.

Before deciding to kill the girl, Cooper debated with himself whether it was worth being electrocuted for it. (The crime occurred in Massachusetts, where electrocution is the penalty for premeditated murder.) He decided that it was. In fact, it appears that Cooper murdered Connie Gilman in order to be executed by the state. He described his thoughts just before the murder as follows:

Do you realize if you do this they will electrocute you? And I said, "Yes." And then I thought of my father. I do not know why, it just shot through my head for a minute. And I came to the conclusion that that was exactly what I deserved, that it fitted in with the idea that I have always had, that I would never live to be 30 years old and that I had adopted the attitude while in the service: live fast, die young, and have a good-looking corpse . . . [page 290].

Why did Cooper want to be killed? Because he felt he had murdered his father. Cooper's father died when Jim was nine years old. He slipped on the ice when running after his son with a warm cap to wear to Hebrew school. The fall proved fatal. Jim Cooper never forgave himself for it. Between the ages of 12 and 23, he committed many self-destructive acts. Perhaps it was an "accident" that he lived long enough to kill Connie Gilman.

In accordance with the Briggs Law of Massachusetts, Cooper was ordered to undergo psychiatric examination "to determine his mental condition and the existence of any mental disease or defect which would affect his criminal responsibility" (page 290). The psychiatrists who examined Cooper for the State found him competent and responsible. Cooper had also admitted the murder and wished to be tried for it. How was the state-appointed defense counsel to defend a man who did not want to be defended?

Cooper's counsel refused to comply with his client's wishes and proceeded to construct a psychiatric defense. "He sought assistance from *senior members* of the Boston psychiatric community but was unable successfully to solicit their interest in the case. After considerable effort defense counsel succeeded in finding a psychologist and two *young* psychiatrists who were willing to serve as defense experts" (italics added; page 291). One of the psychiatrists submitted a report emphasizing Cooper's "pathological drives," and concluded with a diagnosis of "personality disorder." The other expressed his conviction that "Cooper was an emotionally sick human being badly in need of psychiatric treatment and that the murder was a violent expression of his illness" (page 292).

At this point, Wiseman, the author of the report, added his own opinion: "the defense counsel had to proceed with the trial knowing his client to be a *very sick young man* but aware that under existing legal standards Cooper's behavior, the murder, of course, aside, was probably not sufficiently bizarre to qualify him for a M'Naghten acquittal" (italics added; page 292). Thus Wiseman too regarded Cooper as sick, deserving acquittal by reason of insanity—followed, of course, by lifelong incarceration in a mental hospital. But Cooper did not want to be acquitted on the ground that he was insane. He wanted to be electrocuted. Has the defendant not the right to refuse defense? This question was never frankly confronted by the people involved in Cooper's tragedy, and was evaded by Wiseman who assumed that Cooper was insane.

During the trial much conflicting and meaningless psychiatric and psychological testimony was heard. But Cooper would not be outwitted by his own counsel. The whole psychiatric, psychologic, and legal tour-de-force was in vain. For after concluding his charge to the jury, the judge gave Cooper an opportunity to make a final statement. This he did masterfully. "It is my opinion"—said Cooper—"that any decision other than guilt, guilty of murder in the first degree, with no recommendation for leniency, is a miscarriage of justice" (page 297). The jury complied with Cooper's wishes, and brought in the verdict he requested. The judge was obligated to sentence him to be electrocuted. After listening to the sentence, Cooper said, "Thank you" (page 297).

This, however, was not the end. Apparently, too many people could not bear the prospect of Cooper's execution. There now came into play all the motives and strategies that can be used to circumvent the death penalty on psychiatric grounds. Several parties petitioned the Governor to commute the sentence. Did they do this in Cooper's behalf, or did the people of Massachusetts now object to living according to laws they had never bothered to modify?

Aware of these appeals, Cooper wrote the Governor:

Now I do not ask for death in the form of punishment, but as mercy. Mercy in the guise of release from a life which is no longer honorable nor desirable. My wish is that you can put aside your moral regrets and do your duty, even as I have done mine [page 297].

And in another letter, he wrote:

If I could but feel that I honestly regretted my actions, I would welcome the prospect of imprisonment and rehabilitation. However, while I do not lack the qualities of pity or compassion, I do not feel one iota of remorse for the crime I have committed. It is not the enormity of the crime itself, but the ease with which I justify it to myself that precludes any possibility of my ever returning to society again. Under these conditions, execution is the only logical conclusion [page 297].

Are these the letters of a mentally sick man? Of a person unmindful of what he is doing, and what is best for him, and therefore not responsible for his actions? Or are they the letters of a tortured man, grown honest and wise after facing the ultimate meaning of his own existence?

The Commonwealth of Massachusetts and the people involved in this case were playing a game of crime and punishment. But this time they were hopelessly outwitted by a sophisticated and superior adversary. Cooper was asking the law-enforcement personnel—jury, judge, Governor, and so forth—to abide by *their contracts*. Each of these persons had accepted, freely and responsibly, the duty of apprehending and punishing criminals. Now, so Cooper was saying, it was their turn to do the work for which the State was paying them—that is, to kill him! If a state retains the death penalty on its statute books, a person has the opportunity—or, as Cooper argued, the right—to commit suicide indirectly, by committing premeditated murder. In this way, the state will be obligated to kill him.

Despite Cooper's letters, the Governor sought, once more, to define Cooper's problems as psychiatric in nature. He requested the Commissioner of Mental Health to initiate a study to determine if Cooper was "too sick to be executed" (page 297). But did not Cooper's letters to the Governor provide sufficient evidence on this score? How much more coherent or touching could a man be? Cooper's letters were infinitely more lucid and honest than the psychiatric opinions offered during and after his trial. I believe that no one was really interested in Cooper's sanity, and perhaps not even in Cooper as a human being. The purpose of all the maneuvering was to undermine Cooper's position as a responsible, contracting individual, and to demote him to the status of a helpless, defective object, a mental patient.

Five more psychiatrists and a psychologist became involved in the posttrial study of Cooper. One of the psychiatrists observed: *I do not think he should be killed,* but at the moment at least, I cannot say that he is too 'mentally ill' to be killed (whatever that means)" (italics added; page 297). This statement implies that the psychiatrist felt he had a right to make a pronouncement on the question of whether Cooper should or should not be killed. Moreover, the sarcastic "whatever that means" implies that the psychiatrist considered the whole problem a farce. He was hired to make an examination to determine a question he considered absurd. Many psychiatrists face this problem. But if a psychiatrist feels that in his role as court-appointed expert he is placed in an impossible situation, he ought to refuse to play the role. The psychiatrist quoted accepted the assignment, and the fee that went with it, and hoped to clear his conscience by adding that he thought it a stupid farce to be asked to determine if a person is healthy enough mentally to be executed.

The Commonwealth of Massachusetts was, at last, able to buy enough psychiatrists to effect a redefinition of Cooper's human condition from dignified defendant to pitied patient. In their final report, the team of psychiatrists and psychologists wrote what the Commissioner of Mental Health presumably wanted to hear:

We find Mr. Cooper an *interesting* challenge in addition to being *genuinely* interested in him as a human being. Our impression is that he is *quite treatable* and might some day be a *useful* member of society. I hope we have the opportunity to continue working with him [italics added; page 297].

This was 17 months after Cooper killed Connie Gilman. Now both the Commissioner of Mental Health and the Commissioner of Correction recommended that Cooper's sentence be commuted to life imprisonment. When told that the Governor would approve their recommendation, Cooper hanged himself.

When the State broke its contract, Cooper himself undertook to make it good. When, in effect, the government said, "Although we have promised to kill you, we will not do it," Cooper replied, "Then I will do it for you." And he did.

CHAPTER 13 » *The Right to Trial*

It is a rule as old as the law, and never more to be respected than now, that no one shall be personally bound until he has had his day in court.

—STEPHEN J. FIELD (1873)

PSYCHIATRISTS MAY be called upon to participate in every stage of the criminal proceeding: at the time the accused is charged with an offense; before the trial; at the trial; during the period awaiting sentence; after sentencing; and at any time after imprisonment. In this chapter, we shall discuss only the pretrial psychiatric examination. In recent years this has become an accepted method for dealing with persons charged with crimes. In many localities—for example, in the District of Columbia and in New York State—it is employed far more often than the insanity plea. This alone makes it important to understand its workings and dangers. In addition, it is significant because it presents one of the gravest threats to the constitutional rights of the ordinary citizen.

Pretrial Psychiatric Examination

Because of the disposition which pretrial psychiatric examination and incarceration in a so-called psychiatric hospital makes available to the courts, a person may be charged with an offense, prevented from standing trial for it, and jailed in a correctional institution for life. This procedure

159

has thus far been considered constitutional. It is a legitimate gambit in the game of law enforcement. It should be obvious, however, that to this move even the affluent and well-educated defendant will be hard pressed to find an effective countermove. How much more hopeless is the condition of the uneducated and poor defendant!

The right to a public trial and to decent limits on methods permitted the prosecution for incriminating the accused are among the most important features of a free society.

Pretrial psychiatric examination of offenders ordered by the courts against the wishes of the accused nullifies some of our most important constitutional rights—namely, the right to a speedy trial and, in the words of Louis D. Brandeis, "the right to be let alone."

The Sixth Amendment to the Constitution guarantees that

> In all criminal prosecutions, the accused shall enjoy the right to a speedy and public trial, by an impartial jury of the State and district wherein the crime shall have been committed, which district shall have been previously ascertained by law, and to be informed of the nature and cause of the accusation; to be confronted with the witnesses against him; to have compulsory process for obtaining witnesses in his favor, and to have the Assistance of Counsel for his defense.

The Sixth Amendment does not say that this right is contingent on the ability of the accused to prove his sanity to the satisfaction of government psychiatrists.

The right to be let alone—more specifically, the privilege against self-incrimination—has received extensive judicial consideration, for example, in connection with wiretapping as a method of securing evidence for use in criminal trials. The majority of the Supreme Court judges—wrote Justice Douglas (1954)—have found "that wire tapping violated the command of the Fourth Amendment against unreasonable searches and seizures, and infringed on the guaranty of the Fifth Amendment that no person shall be compelled to be a witness against himself" (page 352). Chief Justice Oliver Wendell Holmes called wiretapping a "dirty business." Associate Justice Louis D. Brandeis held that the Fourth and Fifth Amendments conferred on the citizen, as against the government, "the right to be let alone—the most comprehensive of rights and the right most valued by civilized men. Wiretapping was the most oppressive intrusion into the right of privacy that man had yet invented" (Douglas, 1954, page 353). Evidently, Brandeis did not anticipate mind tapping—which is what involuntary pretrial psychiatric examination is. This, I submit, is a more insidious invasion of privacy than wiretapping, and an even greater violation of the privilege against self-incrimination.

Mind Tapping

It is traditional in Anglo-American criminal law to relieve a mentally incompetent person of responsibility for his crime. It is therefore logical for the accused or his counsel to introduce this issue into the criminal proceeding. In other words, just as the defendant has the right to plead innocence or guilt, so he has the right to plead insanity. He may also plead that the state of his physical or mental health prevents him from defending himself effectively and that therefore he ought not be tried. This plea implies that the accused will submit to treatment so that he can be tried as soon as he is restored to health (see Chapter 10).

The increasing influence of psychiatry on American criminal law in recent decades has altered this traditional scheme. In the first place, mental illness is no longer considered merely a defense. Instead, it is thought to be a disease "like any other." As such, it is regarded as a scientific "fact" that can be "objectively verified" by psychiatric experts. Second, psychiatrists have shown great alacrity in meting out life sentences in psychiatric institutions to people they think deserve this fate.

These two developments have made the issue of the defendant's possible insanity of considerable interest and attractiveness not only to his defense counsel, but also to the prosecution and the judge. For the prosecution, establishing the defendant's insanity, instead of his guilt, may become an easy method of securing "conviction" and "imprisonment." The defendant will be incarcerated in a psychiatric institution for an indefinite period. This is a sentence at least as severe and probably more so than would result from conviction and sentencing to a penitentiary. To the judge, too, establishing the defendant's incapacity to stand trial may be tempting. It will save him the effort of conducting a trial that might be filled with distressing emotional and moral problems. If the defendant can be shown to be crazy, both he and the jury will be spared a taxing experience. These are only a few of the motivations for subverting the rights guaranteed by the Constitution and the Bill of Rights. There are others.

Between wiretapping and mind tapping there is an important difference. Wiretapping can be carried out without the suspect's awareness, and hence without his consent and cooperation. In contrast, mind tapping requires a measure of cooperation on the part of the subject. What happens if the defendant refuses to submit to pretrial psychiatric examination?

As a rule, this examination is a consequence of a plea of insanity on the part of the defendant. In some of these cases, the defendant submits willingly to examination by the psychiatrists retained by the defense counsel, but refuses to be examined by the psychiatrists retained by the prosecution. In this dilemma, the courts and legal scholars (Krash, 1961a) have held, first, that a person's unwillingness to participate in a psychiatric interview is itself prima facie evidence of mental illness. The defendant may thus be committed to a mental hospital, where he will stay until he cooperates with the psychiatrists, and perhaps longer. Second, they have suggested that when a defendant pleads insanity, and yet refuses to submit to a pretrial examination by psychiatrists appointed by the court or the prosecution, his refusal ought to mean that he is competent to stand trial.

Suppose, however, that the issue of insanity is raised not by the defendant (or his counsel), but by the court (or the prosecution). Suppose, further, that the defendant refuses to submit to pretrial psychiatric examination, and demands to be tried. What would happen? How would the criminal action against the defendant proceed?

Denial of the Right to Be Tried

In most cases, the defendant who is ordered by the court to undergo pretrial psychiatric examination is an indigent person. Unassisted, he is probably unable to comprehend the complexities of the situation. Usually he is poorly represented by a court-appointed defense counsel, who has nothing to gain, and much time and effort to lose, from insisting that his client be tried. There may be other reasons as well why this dilemma has so far not been more sharply etched.

It would be wise for a defendant to refuse to submit to a court-ordered psychiatric examination, for he has nothing to gain from it, and everything to lose. What usually happens is that the defendant lets himself be examined and then finds himself committed to a hospital for the criminally insane. Only then does he realize his predicament. But it is too late. At this point he can gain his release only by petitioning for a habeas corpus hearing. Such a hearing may not be granted, and even if it is, the defendant—now called "patient"—will have to convince a judge, against the contrary opinions of the hospital psychiatrists, that he is sane, and hence should be either tried or discharged. To say the least, this is not an easy thing for an inmate in a hospital for the criminally insane to do. Just how difficult it may be, I shall illustrate presently.

What would happen if a defendant refused to be examined by psychiatrists and instead demanded that he be tried? Two answers have recently been supplied. The first comes from Stephen S. Chandler, Chief Judge of the United States District Court for the District of Oklahoma. Judge Chandler presented his views on law and psychiatry before the Hearing of the Senate Subcommittee on the *Constitutional Rights of the Mentally Ill* in Washington, D.C., on March 30, 1961. When asked what he would do if he suspected that a defendant was mentally ill, Judge Chandler (1961) stated that he would send him to the medical center for federal prisoners, at Springfield, Missouri, for psychiatric examination. He enlarged on this as follows:

I have sent defendants to Mr. Bennett's [James V. Bennett, Director, U.S. Bureau of Prisons] Springfield Institution, and I find that I do not know where the money comes from to pay these psychiatrists but surely it is provided in 4244, is it—I have not read it in many years—but I just appoint them. The Department of Justice pays the psychiatrist, and they have never raised any question to me and I appoint good ones, and then see to it that the psychiatrist does not get any information—*that the Government does not try to influence him.* I ask him to take the case and study it and give me a report that I can depend on.

I do not appoint a psychiatrist in whom I do not have the utmost confidence as to his ability and integrity.

If there are any others, I do not know. I think it is important that the judge have confidence in any doctor whom he appoints.

I might say this: In this work we have lots of problems. Sometimes Government officials do not cooperate fully. But I want to say this about the witness just before me, Mr. Bennett, if a judge cares enough to go to the trouble to take matters up with Mr. Bennett, he will help you work matters out to the extent of his facilities. He does not have enough doctors, he does not have enough facilities, it is pitiful, and I would say to this committee that he is a great and good man. I have learned that in 18 years of contact with him as an official, and I would consider very seriously any of Mr. Bennett's recommendations, because I think he knows better than anyone.

I think he has no ax to grind with anybody except to do a fine job and he looks at it as some Government officials do not, from the standpoint of the defendant as, of course, the judge should [italics added; page 248].

It should be noted that Judge Chandler implied that this procedure is for the welfare of the defendant.

Miss Elyce H. Zenoff [Counsel for the Subcommittee] then asked: What do you do, Judge Chandler, if the defendant himself insists that he is not mentally ill and you think he is?
Judge Chandler: If there is a question about it, of course, I appoint a psychiatrist, and then if the doctor says there is a question about it, I send him to Springfield to get a report from there, and the only trouble with that is it is as good an institution as Mr. Bennett can make it with the help he has, but he should have a great many more psychologists and psychiatrists there to help him, because at the present time I am informed, *that they can only consult with the man you send there about once a month;* and as to the therapy that he gets and what they know about him, they do not have the staff to make the report that they would like to make and we would like to have. What they do, they do very conscientiously.

Miss Zenoff: What I mean, Judge Chandler, is if they report back to you that the man is mentally ill, and he says, "I want to be tried; in others words, I am not mentally ill," what do you do then?
Judge Chandler: Yes. If they find that he is not able to stand trial because of his

mental illness, why, I look into it and have a hearing, and if that is right, *he is left there until such time as they report that he is able to stand trial.* But at any moment that it came to me that *someone* thought he was able to stand trial, why I would see to it that an immediate hearing was had to determine that question [italics added; page 248].

The defendant's plea to stand trial would thus be overruled by the opinion of government psychiatrists. Note, further, that Judge Chandler went so far as to add that should it come to his attention that "someone thought he [the defendant] was able to stand trial," he would hold a hearing "to determine that question." Evidently, the defendant is not included among the people grouped under the heading "someone," for his protestations of sanity have already been ruled out of court by Judge Chandler.

But it is to the accused—not to his wife, father, friend, or attorney—that the Sixth Amendment guarantees the right to be tried!

Recently, in the prosecution of Mr. Bernard Brous, the question we posed received a different answer. Mr. Brous is one of the men charged with blowing up two telephone microwave relay towers in the Nevada-Utah desert in May, 1961. At the time of his arrest, he was quoted as saying that he committed these acts in protest against certain government policies. Thus, the unusual criminal acts were presumably intended to call attention to himself and his views.

According to an Associated Press news dispatch, dated August 14, 1961, printed in *The New York Times,* August 16, 1961, this is what happened to Mr. Brous:

> The Government asked Federal Judge John Ross Monday to find Bernard Brous in contempt for refusing to undergo court-ordered mental examinations.—Judge Ross ordered psychiatric examinations Aug. 3.
> United States Attorney Howard Babcock presented an affidavit by a psychiatrist, Dr. Otto Gericke, Superintendent of the Patton, Calif., State Hospital, who said Brous twice had refused to submit to tests.

If the pretrial psychiatric examination is really for the defendant's benefit, why should he be punished for refusing it? If, on the other hand, it is not for his benefit, then it must be for the benefit of either the judge or the prosecution. In this case, mind tapping would be a clear violation of constitutional rights. Lastly, the prosecution's demand for finding Brous in contempt of court betrays bad faith and unfairness on the part of either the prosecutor or the judge, or both, for it shows readiness to try the defendant for his behavior in the courtroom at the very moment when the court shows itself reluctant to try him for his behavior in the Nevada desert.

Every reader, of course, is free to draw his own conclusions from Judge Chandler's views and from the action of the government in the Brous case. I should like to reemphasize two points.

In the procedure advocated by Judge Chandler, the mere suspicion of mental illness results in the defendant's loss of the right to be tried. In the Brous case, refusal to submit to court-ordered psychiatric examination is not considered an intelligent defense of one's constitutional rights, but rather a new offense. Thus, the defendant who protests against involuntary mind tapping, like the "Fifth Amendment Communist" of the McCarthy era, is not supported by the court in his efforts to avail himself of his constitutional rights. Instead, he is attacked for his very self-defense.

Two Illustrative Case Histories

According to Section 658 of the New York State Code of Criminal Procedure a pretrial psychiatric examination may be requested by the court, the district attorney, or the defendant. If the defendant is found unable to stand trial, he will be committed to a state hospital for the criminally insane, until such time as he is fit to be tried.

If the defendant is examined against his wishes and found insane, he has virtually no redress against the state's refusal to try him, nor against being committed to a hospital for the criminally insane. The courts in New York State have held that a jury trial is not required to determine the issue of "present insanity" in a criminal case. Thus, the defendant may be sent to a *correctional institution*, without having been tried or found guilty, and despite his desire and readiness to be tried. The cases of Michael L. Chomentowski and of Victor Rosario dramatize the predicament of the person denied trial because of alleged mental incapacity.*

Chomentowski, who ran a filling station in a Syracuse suburb, was arrested on June 5, 1955, for allegedly threatening with a gun two men who wanted to erect signs on property he leased. Before being indicted, an Onondaga County Court judge ordered Chomentowski to undergo psychiatric examination. He was found incapable of standing trial and was committed to Matteawan State Hospital. There he remained for six years, until September 29, 1961.

Chomentowski, aided by his brothers, tried every means, including an appeal to the United States Supreme Court, to secure the right to be tried, which is guaranteed by the Sixth Amendment. Finally, in July, 1961, a writ of habeas corpus was granted in the State Supreme Court in Dutchess County (where Matteawan is located).

Chomentowski was ordered to be tried or discharged. As if all this were not bad enough, here is what happened next: "The wheels of justice moved

---

* The cases of two other persons, who were never tried for their alleged offenses, but instead were hospitalized on the basis of a pretrial psychiatric examination, are presented in this volume. For the case of Mrs. Isola Ware Curry, see Chapter 16, and for that of Mr. Ezra Pound, see Chapter 17.

slowly and only when officials were faced with contempt charges did they send Chomentowski back to Onondaga County" (*Syracuse Post-Standard,* October 1, 1961).

Chomentowski was returned to Syracuse on Friday, September 29th, and held incommunicado. "His relatives," reported the newspaper, "have not been allowed to visit him." Chomentowski was to be arraigned in County Court, Monday, October 2nd. His arraignment was adjourned to the following day. On October 3rd, however, he was neither indicted nor released. Instead, he was ordered to be reexamined by two court-appointed psychiatrists.

A month later, on October 31, 1961, *The Syracuse Herald-Journal* reported that the court issued a new order for "mental tests" on Chomentowski:

For the fourth time since his arrest—and the second in less than a month—Michael L. Chomentowski, 46, former operator of a Fairmount gasoline station, has been ordered to a hospital for mental tests.

Chomentowski, who has been in and out of County Court more than a half dozen times since his arrest in 1955, was in court again yesterday.

And again, County Judge Donald H. Mead ordered mental tests.

But—to avoid another habeas corpus proceeding on a legal technicality—Judge Mead has asked Dr. Newton Bigelow, director of Marcy State Hospital, to notify him in writing whether the tests should be made at Marcy or in Syracuse.

It was the lack of such a written order that returned Chomentowski here yesterday [page 19].

The evidence strongly suggests that the court is not eager to try Chomentowski. By every legal and even some illegal measures, the law-enforcement agencies of the state seem to be seeking the continued incarceration of this man in a hospital for the criminally insane. At the same time, they are trying to prevent him from standing trial for his alleged offense. Why? If Chomentowski is guilty, he could be imprisoned at Matteawan after, not before, being tried. If he is innocent, but considered "dangerously insane," the court could institute civil commitment procedure against him. Hence, the safety of society could be ensured by methods that would also protect Chomentowski's civil rights.

The case of Victor Rosario is also typical, except for the fact that he succeeded in gaining his freedom. The following story is excerpted from *The New York Times,* September 28, 1962:

After four years at the Matteawan State Hospital for the Criminal Insane, 39-year-old Victor Rosario became a free man yesterday, largely because he finally got someone to look into a fantastic story that he had tenaciously insisted was true.

The core of the story was that his wife's love had been stolen by another man who drew blood from his arms and drank it in beer to prove his vigor. Mr.

Rosario told this story to everyone, including at least eleven psychiatrists, but not until a woman lawyer verified it did anyone believe him. Yesterday charges of assault that had been brought against him in 1958 were dismissed in Bronx Criminal Court.

In 1957 Mr. Rosario had been placidly married for almost eight years. He and his wife, Caen, had two children, Martha and Victor, now 9 and 7 years old respectively. Then Mr. Rosario introduced a male boarder into their home at 725 Fox Street, the Bronx. It was this man who won Mrs. Rosario's affection. The wife, from whom Mr. Rosario is separated, signed a sworn affidavit in June stating that this was true.

Mr. Rosario, a waiter and longshoreman, ordered the boarder to leave. He refused and the two men lived in the apartment in considerable tension until Mr. Rosario left.

He returned later, however, in a jealous rage and allegedly struck and kicked his wife and threatened her with a bailing hook. She called the police, who said they arrested him on June 22, 1958.

Mr. Rosario was charged with simple assault, resisting arrest, and illegally using a weapon. *He was sent to Bellevue Hospital for observation and was committed to Matteawan on October 14, 1958, on the testimony of two psychiatrists.* They said that he appeared to be a paranoiac and was incapable of understanding the charges against him.

Matteawan is a large and formidable-looking institution in the Hudson Valley hills at Beacon, about 60 miles north of the city. There Mr. Rosario worked in the kitchen cleaning silverware and paring vegetables, and he began his long campaign to free himself.

He had come to New York in 1946 from Puerto Rico and his English was very limited, but he labored painstakingly with a dictionary and wrote to a great many Government figures, to friends and lawyers. *He also drew up six writs of habeas corpus, all of which were dismissed by State Supreme Court in Dutchess County or were ignored.*

Mr. Rosario told everyone who interviewed him the story of the drawn blood. "The doctors told me that if I forgot that story, they might let me go, but the truth is the truth no matter what anyone says," he said yesterday. So he never changed his story.

Last November he wrote the first of several appeals to Mrs. Sara Halbert of Zapata and Halbert, a New York City law firm. He was told that a relative would have to confer with Mrs. Halbert. At length two cousins flew up from Puerto Rico and prevailed upon the lawyer to visit Mr. Rosario.

After a second visit, Mrs. Halbert went to Mr. Rosario's wife. She confirmed his story and signed the affidavit, asserting that the boarder had taken the blood in beer and had written on a wall in letters of blood.

Mrs. Halbert said she presented the affidavit to Dr. Cecil Johnston, director of the hospital on Aug. 27. She asked that Mr. Rosario be released immediately. *The following day, four psychiatrists interviewed him, and he was shortly declared fit to return to the Bronx to face trial.*

Dr. Johnston said by telephone yesterday that more than the affidavit had entered into the decision, but he acknowledged that the "new information" had caused the staff to "look on the patient in a little different manner." He said Mr.

Rosario had been interviewed on seventeen occasions by nine psychiatrists in four years.

Mrs. Halbert moved in court yesterday that the case be dismissed. The motion was granted by Judge Ambrose J. Haddock, after Assistant District Attorney Joseph Tiger had agreed [italics added; page 25].

It seems that poor Mr. Rosario's "delusions" were true, after all. And yet, according to the account in the *Times,* the psychiatric authorities did not feel that a mistake had been made. On the contrary. They implied that whatever the circumstances surounding Victor Rosario's incarceration might have been, the "fact" of his "mental illness," proved by nine psychiatrists over a period of four years, justified his involuntary "hospitalization."

Conclusions

Reflecting on this problem, we should not forget the values inherent in the right to be tried—in *public* and by one's *peers,* and also the values inherent in the right to go to jail—instead of being subjected to unwanted psychiatric "treatments." In a jail, a person is "let alone"; in a mental hospital he may not be. A prisoner will be released after he completes his sentence, and possibly before. A mental patient may be required to undergo a change in his "inner personality"—a change that may be induced by measures far more intrusive than anything permitted in a jail—before the psychiatric authorities let him go. And they may never let him go. Commitment, unlike a sentence, is for an indefinite period.

How different the world might be today if only a handful of people had been sent away for psychiatric "treatments," instead of being tried and sent to jail! Gandhi, Nehru, Sukarno, Castro, Hitler—and of course many others, for example the "freedom riders" in the South—have been sentenced to terms in prison. Surely, the social *status quo* could have been better preserved by finding each of these men mentally ill and subjecting them to enough electric shock treatments to quell their aspirations.

If this is not the kind of tyranny against which the Constitution was intended to protect us, what is?

CHAPTER 14 » *The Hospitalized Mental*
Patient's Fight for Freedom

> *[It is an] axiom that power is a trust and not an inherent right.*
> *. . . The use of force is only justifiable as a last resort in order to*
> *effect a necessary and proportionate good. . . . Certain uses of force*
> *are never legitimate, no matter what the end in view, because of*
> *their debasing effect on the user, [and] because of their utter cruelty*
> *and essential inhumanity.*
> —MARTIN J. HILLENBRAND (1949)

The Double Role of the Institutional Psychiatrist

ONE OF the major dilemmas of contemporary psychiatry is the dual role of the institutional psychiatrist. He tries to be a therapist to his patient, and, at the same time, tries to protect society from the patient. These two roles are largely incompatible. Hospital psychiatrists have always denied that such a conflict of interests exists, and most of them still deny it. Yet until this conflict is resolved, hospital psychiatry is bound to remain an unsatisfactory enterprise for all concerned.

The fact that a patient seeking release from a hospital is denied his request should be considered prima facie evidence of a conflict of interests between himself and the hospital authorities. The argument that the patient is psychotic or insane will not do, even if, in some theoretical-psychiatric sense, it is true, for it rests on the unwarranted supposition that mentally ill persons are incapable of defining their own interests. However, we must beware of making such an assumption. For the issue here is the adjudication of the *legitimacy* of desires, interests, wishes, and so forth, rather than their acknowledgment or description.

Once the patient brings suit against the hospital superintendent (as representative of the hospital), the two become legal adversaries. It is hard to see how anyone can maintain that they could, nevertheless, work together toward the therapeutic rehabilitation of the patient.

The typical form of the type of litigation involved in this conflict is "John Doe (patient) v. James Smith (superintendent)," when the patient sues for release, and its reverse, when the mental hospital superintendent sues to reverse the decision of a lower court ordering the patient's release. The literature on forensic psychiatry is replete with such cases.

Examples of Quasi-Criminal Patients Seeking Release

If an inmate suing the hospital superintendent for his release has been charged with or been convicted of an offense, the situation is complicated by the quasi-criminal status of the so-called patient. When such a person asks to be discharged from the hospital, the superintendent tends to assume the role of warden, entrusted with keeping the patient safely locked up. These quasi-criminal cases, however, have also served as models for the lawsuits of other mental patients who have not committed unlawful acts. In their suits for release also, the superintendent is apt to take the role of warden. Thus, in the management of the mental patient who is involuntarily hospitalized, the concepts of criminality and mental illness are equated and are persistently confused with each other.

Let us begin with the case of *Barry v. White* (1933).* The patient, Paul duV. Barry, sued William Alanson White, the superintendent of St. Elizabeths Hospital, for his release. Barry had been acquitted of a murder charge on the grounds of insanity and was subsequently committed to St. Elizabeths Hospital. He filed three writs of habeas corpus, and when all were denied, he appealed the last ruling to a higher court. The appeal court ruled:

It seems clear that the natural assumption of fact follows that such condition of insanity has continued to the present time. The effect of such presumption is to cast upon the prisoner here the burden of proving that since the commission of the homicide he has become sane to the degree that it is reasonably certain that his enlargement will now be without menace to the public peace or safety. Where insanity has gone so far as actually to take human life, no sensible person

* The examples that follow, each pertaining to a patient at St. Elizabeths Hospital in Washington, D.C., are drawn from a study by Lebensohn (1955).

will be satisfied with evidence of recovery which does not attain to the degree of reasonable certainty [page 543].

This situation deserves critical scrutiny. I shall limit myself to a few brief remarks.

First, how can the plaintiff-patient prove his so-called sanity, or recovery from an alleged mental illness, if the criteria of mental illness have never been clearly defined? This is an utterly Kafkaesque situation: Although the crime is not specified, the defendant must prove that he is innocent of it.

Second, if, as in Barry's case, insanity is inferred from homicide, sanity could be proved only by guaranteeing the noncommission of future homicide. But how could anyone ever predict with "reasonable certainty" that a future event of this sort will not take place? This is a good example of a requirement that cannot be satisfied.

Third, how could the patient prove that he was mentally healthy without psychiatric assistance, powerful enough to counteract the authority and prestige of the hospital superintendent? Therefore, the patient needs not only legal defense but also psychiatric defense. Without the latter, he cannot hope to rebut the diagnostic and prognostic "charges" of the hospital psychiatrists who oppose him.

The Leopold and Loeb case (White, 1938), though an example of the opposite situation, illustrates this contention. In that case, testifying for the defense, Dr. White found himself in opposition to the prosecution and to public opinion as well: He was unable to make his "diagnosis" of insanity stick. We must remember that psychiatrists who testify *against* feared and disenfranchised mental patients are in a position comparable to that of the prosecution in the Leopold and Loeb case. Backed by the power of the state and by public opinion, they cannot lose their case. Therefore, to go through the formalities of a judicial proceeding is not enough. The ethic of democracy requires equal, or nearly equal, representation for both parties.

There is an interesting postscript to the Barry case. After eleven years of hospitalization, Barry escaped from St. Elizabeths Hospital. Although picked up by the police in St. Louis, he was not returned to the District of Columbia, and no more was heard of him.

This kind of mental hospitalization reminds one of the tales of the Count of Monte Cristo: of indefinite detention in prisons with no possibility of legal reprieve, and of escape, intelligently conceived and skillfully executed, as the only means of regaining freedom. The question is: In such a system of unreasoning and unjust imprisonment, why do psychiatrists consent to play the role of warden? Moreover, if psychiatrists believe that Barry, or men like him, should be segregated from society for unlimited periods of time, what training, skill, or legal status permits them to implement such sentences?

Let us review another celebrated case, that of *Overholser* v. *DeMarcos* (1945). While living in Canada, DeMarcos, a native of Tennessee, was tried for murder, convicted of manslaughter, and sentenced to life imprisonment. In jail, he was found to be of unsound mind, and was sent to a mental hospital. Then, in accordance with the "reciprocal trade agreement," as Lebensohn (1955) called it, between that country and the United States, DeMarcos was transferred to St. Elizabeths Hospital. This was in 1939, when DeMarcos was seventy-one years old. At St. Elizabeths Hospital he was diagnosed "as one of the rare cases of true paranoia" (page 544). Between 1940 and 1944, he filed four writs of habeas corpus, all unsuccessful. In his fifth attempt,

Justice Goldsborough took the case out of the hands of a jury and summarily ordered him discharged. . . . The apprehension of the District Attorney's office at having DeMarcos at large was further evidenced by the unprecedented speed with which the appeal was drawn and filed. . . . This was seen in some legal circles as an effort on the part of the District Attorney's office to "get out from under" should anything untoward happen involving the released man. The appeals court ordered the arrest of DeMarcos, and this was interpreted as a direct rebuke of the presiding judge. The wheels of justice moved much too slowly in this instance, for by the time the order for arrest was issued, DeMarcos was already in Knoxville. After some delay, he was apprehended by the F.B.I. on an assault charge and returned to the District [pages 544–545].

In *Overholser* v. *DeMarcos,* the Court of Appeals announced the following decision:

It is not the function of the Judge in habeas corpus proceedings to determine the mental condition of a person who has been committed for insanity. . . . *It should be remembered that persons committed . . . are presumed to be insane. . . . There is also a presumption that the hospital staff are competent . . . and that their opinion is correct.* Their determination that a petitioner should not be at large should not be lightly disregarded. . . . The issue which must ultimately be decided is whether he has sufficiently recovered from a mental disease, so that he may be *safely* released. Lay judgment on such an issue is of little value. If, despite the judgment of the hospital staff that the petitioner has not recovered, there is a substantial doubt on the question, it becomes the duty of the court to see that a new judgment on the petitioner's sanity is made according to the procedure laid down in the District of Columbia code. This procedure requires an examination and report by the Commission on Mental Health [italics added; page 545].

This, however, was not the end, for DeMarcos was indestructible and forever hopeful.

The Commission [wrote Lebensohn] did indeed examine him on two separate occasions and concurred with the Hospital findings. In spite of this, DeMarcos persisted, and in persisting he finally triumphed. In 1946, at the time of his eighth try, he was 78, and possibly the court was influenced by the mellowing effect of his advancing years. At any rate, the court disregarded the unanimous opinion of all Hospital and Commission psychiatrists and ordered his discharge. This time he went directly to Tennessee where, I am informed, *he is engaged in teaching school.* In this instance, the psychiatrists' dire predictions were happily, but surprisingly, unfulfilled. The DeMarcos case is the exception which proves the rule [italics added; page 545].

This story speaks for itself. Without belaboring some of the points already made, I should like to add a few comments.

Because DeMarcos was able to persevere in efforts to gain his release by appropriate legal methods, one may well be skeptical about the kind of insanity he suffered from. Perhaps his was a "case of true paranoia," as claimed by the psychiatrists who saw him, but that alone cannot explain or justify his interminable hospitalization. It can only be justified as serving the purposes of preventive jailing, that is, imprisonment to prevent a future crime. But it is, or ought to be, self-evident that to use psychiatric hospitalization in this way is morally and legally illegitimate.

The case of DeMarcos also illustrates a characteristic feature of these legal contests: unequal distribution of power and expert knowledge. Even though the patient has the right to file writs of habeas corpus and to have legal representation, he is virtually impotent. These safeguards, necessary to be sure, are insufficient to preserve the rights of involuntarily hospitalized mental patients. The writ was designed to protect persons charged with lawbreaking, not with mental illness. As noted before, the latter need not only legal but psychiatric defense as well.

Finally, I should like to call attention to a remark made by Lebensohn. He described DeMarcos' good conduct following his release from the hospital as the "exception which proves the rule." There is no evidence for this opinion. Nor is there for the contrary opinion, that it is "safe" to release everyone who wants to leave a mental hospital. The future is not easy to predict, and usually psychiatrists do not know what patients will do. But even if they did—even if psychiatric predictions were more accurate than they are—would this fact render preventive psychiatric imprisonment legitimate? Hardly. The real issue is not whether this practice is effective, but whether, in a free society, it is morally tolerable.

Example of a Noncriminal Patient Seeking Release

The following story, except for fictitious names of persons and places, is factual.

The first time I heard from Mrs. Betty Kowalski was when she telephoned. She explained that she had been committed to Oakville State Hospital a year before, and now wanted to be released. The doctors had not only refused her request for release, but had filed a petition to declare her legally incompetent. (This would mean losing her right to receive and dispose of funds and to control her assets.) She asked me to help prevent the declaration of her incompetency, and also secure her discharge from the hospital.

During her last convalescent leave, Mrs. Kowalski retained an attorney. He filed a writ of habeas corpus against the hospital, which was to be heard in court within a fortnight. She had also attempted to get psychiatric aid. I was the twenty-seventh psychiatrist she had called. None of the others had been able or willing to take her case. She besought me to testify for her. I agreed to see her the next day.

In my office, Mrs. Kowalski told her story. She was a middle-aged war widow with one daughter. Until she was severely injured in an automobile accident a few years before, she had worked at the same job for fifteen years. Her own earnings, supplemented by monthly payments from the Veterans Administration, had enabled her to support herself and her daughter. Some time after her injury, her hospital benefits expired. She no longer needed hospitalization for surgical reasons, but was not well enough to return home and care for herself. How was she to live? She could not go to her parents' home, nor could she afford to stay in the hospital. Faced with this socioeconomic dilemma, and at the advice of her physicians, she entered Oakville State Hospital for a period of convalescence. She remained there a few months, had many home leaves, and regained her health.

In the meantime, Mrs. Kowalski became involved with a man. When she wanted to break the relationship, he became unpleasant. A tense period ensued. Mrs. Kowalski sought help from her family, but they were unsympathetic. Soon, they became upset about her problems and set off a chain reaction leading to her commitment to the Oakville State Hospital.

The reader may wonder why Mrs. Kowalski was committed. Was she mentally ill? If so, in what way? Did I omit mentioning her symptoms? Let me say at once that I have reported everything of significance. She was committed because her family wanted it and because she had been in a mental hospital before. Not knowing how to cope with her problems and the resulting emotional tensions, her family concluded that Mrs. Kowalski was "too upset and nervous." After all, she had been a patient in a mental hospital. These two facts were sufficient. When her parents demanded that she return to the hospital for more treatment, she refused.

Because the parents insisted that the problem was medical (that is, mental illness), Mrs. Kowalski consented to see her private physician, with whom she had had a good relationship. He was out of town, but was expected to return in a few days. The family, however, would not wait.

A petition to have Mrs. Kowalski committed was prepared. According to law, such a petition must be signed by a responsible member of the family (or by a health officer). It is revealing that the petition was signed by the patient's father, a man over eighty, who knew no English, and who could only write his name. In the eyes of the law, he and his judgment were considered responsible. After all, *he* had never been in a mental hospital.

The rest followed as night follows day. The family called a physician, unknown to the patient. He listened to their complaint, examined the patient briefly, and provided the necessary endorsement for Mrs. Kowalski's certification. The commitment paper was then delivered to the local judge, who signed it. Why should *he* question the evidence? As is customary in such cases, Mrs. Kowalski was not taken before the judge. According to "enlightened" psychiatric opinion, this procedure is harmful for patients. Thus, they are almost invariably denied the opportunity to prevent their commitment.

In New York State a person threatened with commitment has the right to demand a court hearing. (In fifteen of our states even this ineffective safeguard has been abandoned.) However, few people know this, and psychiatrists do not inform patients of their right to protest compulsory hospitalization and treatment. Thus, in actual practice, petitions for commitment are rarely protested.

I do not know the details of what happened while Mrs. Kowalski was a patient at the Oakville State Hospital. She had many long convalescent leaves. During these, she lived in her own home, took care of herself, and was never in trouble. She told me that more than once she was promised her discharge. She wanted very much to be released, but was afraid that if she asked too often she might antagonize her doctors.

Approximately six months before coming to see me, the hospital "filed papers" to have Mrs. Kowalski declared incompetent. She realized then that not only would she not be discharged but that her legal status would be further debased. At this point she resorted to legal action for release. I was never able to discover why she was to be declared incompetent. Perhaps her family wanted to gain direct access to her checks from the government, and to her other property. Perhaps she had antagonized her doctor. It might have been a combination of both, or even something else. She was never told, nor was this matter clarified by the state hospital authorities at her habeas corpus hearing.

I could see no reason for Mrs. Kowalski to be hospitalized or declared incompetent. I agreed to try to help her. Some might ask: If what I say is true, why was she not released? I cannot answer this question with confidence. The following facts may partly explain this riddle. First, it is likely that no one at the hospital took time to listen to *her story*. Mrs. Kowalski claimed that this was so. Occasionally the doctors talked briefly to her family, but rarely to her. Instead, they ordered tranquilizers and home visits. Second, it must be remembered that all patients in state hospitals must be diagnosed. A label, often with ominous connotations—nowadays most patients are called "schizophrenic"—*must* be attached to every patient.

Then, when there is a question of the patient's discharge, future employment, or of some other decision, the label is produced. It frightens everyone, including the doctors.

Mrs. Kowalski was indeed labeled "schizophrenic." For good measure, she was called a doubly bad name: "catatonic schizophrenic." Why? Because she was "uncooperative"—that is, she failed to assist the state in depriving her of her liberty. In the psychiatric context, this act itself is considered evidence of mental illness.

The habeas corpus hearing took place in a small town near the Oakville State Hospital. It had all the drama and excitement of a criminal trial on a television show. Fortunately, Mrs. Kowalski had engaged a capable lawyer, genuinely interested in gaining her release. (I emphasize this, because I have found that attorneys tend to regard hospitalized mental patients as crazy, and consider them distasteful clients. Hence, they are ambivalent in their efforts. They request rather than demand their client's release.)

Mrs. Kowalski's attorney was hopeful that the writ would be sustained —that is, that the judge would order her to be discharged from the hospital. However, his hopes were tempered by the fact that the judge to hear the case had never before sustained such a writ for a mental patient.

Since psychiatric testimony in favor of Mrs. Kowalski was so crucial, I took the liberty to make some suggestions to her attorney. I thought it wise to avoid all references to mental illness. There is so much confusion and circular logic about this subject that it has become impossible to establish a person's sanity. We place people in mental hospitals because they are mentally ill. And yet we also say that people are mentally ill because they are, or have been, in mental hospitals. To most people— probably judges included—being committed to a state hospital is prima facie evidence of mental illness.

I reasoned that the best strategy would be to bring out how Mrs. Kowalski was originally committed, and to demonstrate how well she seemed to be now. We could thus expose the circumstances of her commitment, including the fact that she had not seen her private physician. It is probable that he would not have committed her. In that case, her right to live as a private citizen would not have depended on proof of her mental health.

The hearing began with Mrs. Kowalski on the witness stand, being sworn in. (Although she had been declared mentally ill, incapable of controlling property, and not responsible for her conduct, it was not considered paradoxical to have her swear to tell the truth and nothing but the truth.) Mrs. Kowalski's attorney asked her to relate the events leading to her present hospitalization, her conduct while on convalescent leaves, and her plans if released. She told her story calmly and well.

She was then cross-examined by Mr. Tooley, an Assistant Attorney General for the State of New York. I shall quote some of his questions, and Mrs. Kowalski's answers, from the transcript of the hearing:

Q. When you are home, do you have your own personal physician see you?

A. Yes.

Q. Is that Dr. Lawrence?

A. Yes.

Q. Now, isn't it a fact, Betty, that during the period when you were troubled and bothered about the title of your home, did you on occasions drink a little too much?

A. I don't know that I drank too much.

Q. If you did, would you say it was due to the fact that you were—

Mrs. Kowalski's attorney objected to this question. The judge sustained the objection. Thereupon, Mr. Tooley replied:

I'm really trying to be fair, your Honor, as to whether she resorted to drink because of her problems.

He then resumed questioning the patient.

Q. Now, let's take the last 3 or 4 months, Mrs. Kowalski. I know you were worried about getting your home—let's forget about that worry—are there any things that bother you and worry you—anything on your mind—as you sit at home or in the hospital—is there anything on your mind at all?

A. I don't have a chance to sit at home.

Q. Is there anything—

A. I have a daughter to take care of; I have to keep house; I have to keep busy doing that; that bothers me a little bit—it bothered me a bit at the hospital, because I'd like to be home and make a home for my child—those are my worries now, and its been a long time that I have been away from home.

Q. Is there anything that worries you or bothers you today?

A. My payments—if they're not made.

Q. You mean payments on the mortgage?

A. That's right.

Q. Is there anything else that bothers you or worries you?

A. I have no other problems.

Q. When you were home the last time, did you drink?

A. No, I did not.

Q. Did you have any desire to?

A. No, I can't afford to drink; I have a terrific mortgage to take care of—I can't afford to drink.

Most of Mr. Tooley's other questions were aimed at showing that Mrs. Kowalski must have been mentally ill because her doctors prescribed tranquilizers, and that since she was still taking them, she must still be mentally ill.

Except for one thing, it was just as if she had been on trial for a crime: Mr. Tooley did not try to incriminate her as guilty, but as "having problems" and "being worried." He also tried to insinuate that she "drank too much," even though there was no evidence that she was an alcoholic. This, then, was the state hospital's legal approach to Mrs. Kowalski. Was it improper? Was it destructive to the patient's best interests? If so, should we not hold the hospital as responsible for its legal handling of a patient as for its medical and psychiatric management of him?

The next witness was Mrs. Kowalski's brother. He told of the family squabble that culminated in the patient's commitment. He ended his testimony by pleading with the judge to release his sister, proclaiming that he had never thought her crazy and that the whole thing had been a terrible mistake.

I was called to testify next. Mrs. Kowalski's attorney asked me to relate my findings. I stated that when I talked to Mrs. Kowalski, about two weeks earlier, she seemed all right. I saw no reason for her to be in a mental hospital or to be declared incompetent. Mr. Tooley then cross-examined me. His main concern was whether it would be safe (he never said safe for what or for whom) to release Mrs. Kowalski from the hospital. I answered that no evidence had been introduced, nor had I obtained any, to indicate that Mrs. Kowalski would not get along just as well as others in her educational and economic circumstances.

The last witness was Dr. Johnson, the assistant director of Oakville State Hospital. Upon questioning by Mr. Tooley, he described Mrs. Kowalski as having been "mixed up," "combative and argumentative," and unwilling to eat or talk. But "with time and treatment," he said, she improved. His diagnosis was "schizophrenia, catatonic type."

Again, the court record speaks more eloquently than any summary could.

Mr. Tooley questioning Dr. Johnson:

Q. Very briefly, Dr. Johnson, Betty Kowalski was admitted to the hospital early in May of 1959, is that correct?

A. Yes.

Q. Did there come a time when the staff at the hospital diagnosed the nature of her difficulties?

A. Yes.

Q. And when was that, doctor?

A. Approximately two months after she had come to the hospital.

Q. What was the diagnosis?

A. Schizophrenia, catatonic type.

Q. Is that your diagnosis, too, doctor?

A. Yes, sir.

Q. Can you tell us whether or not the dementia praecox, or schizophrenia, catatonic type, is more or less of a mental illness?

A. It is.

Q. Now, can you express an opinion with reasonable medical certainty as to whether or not Betty Kowalski was mentally ill at the time she was admitted to the hospital in May of 1959?

A. I can.

Q. What is that opinion?

A. My opinion is that she was ill at that time.

Q. Now, I believe that her medical history—going down to the next year and a half—to the present date—is also included in this record?

A. Yes.

Q. Will you please tell the Court what Betty Kowalski's mental condition was or how it is reflected with particular regard to her being mentally ill?

A. She first came to the hospital in May of 1959. She was mixed up, she wouldn't talk; she was combative, argumentive, wouldn't eat, but with time and treatment, she improved to a point where she was placed on convalescence and went along—that went along for a period of time, and then she was returned to the hospital in September of 1959, in the company of her brother. She then received further treatment. She improved and was permitted to go on frequent visits to her home, and this has continued up to the present. To the best of our knowledge, our social service department has investigated these circumstances and it seems that they are satisfied that adjustment at home at this particular time has been excellent.

The hearing was all but over. The judge paused for a few minutes, then gave his decision:

Under the circumstances, the Court will sustain the writ at this time. The Court also hopes that Mrs. Kowalski will be able to work out her problems and not have any further disturbances. Of course, if they do occur, she can always be readmitted and committed to the hospital.

This story, though simple and common, illustrates dramatically the discrepancy between the therapeutic cant of contemporary organized psychiatry and the actual legal status of the state hospital patient. Thus, to continue to speak of state hospital psychiatrists as people "who labor for the medical and legal welfare of the mentally disabled" (Stason, 1961), is to preclude the very possibility of legal and psychiatric reform in the mental health field.

Escapes from the Mental Hospital

No discussion of the mental hospital patient's efforts to gain his freedom would be complete without some reference to escapes from the mental hospital.

One of the significant differences between mental hospital patients and prisoners is that the former are less prone to escape than the latter. Indeed, escapes from mental hospitals are relatively infrequent, and occur only during the early phases of hospitalization. This is largely because a person's sense of identity—that is, his self-esteem and his confidence in his ability to appraise reality and to plan his actions—is more radically undermined by mental hospitalization than by imprisonment. The convict knows who he is: he is an enemy of society. He is strongly motivated to escape, especially when prison conditions are poor and he has a long sentence to serve. The mental hospital patient, in contrast, is subjected to a more complex and more effective process of social degradation (Goffman, 1959), as a result of which he becomes confused as to why he is hospitalized and what he ought to do about it. In my opinion, the fact that escapes from mental hospitals are rare and relatively ineffective is due partly to the fact that these institutions are generally destructive to the patients' initiative.

In a small-scale study of "elopements" from a 1,500-bed Canadian mental hospital, Dewar (1961) found that, on the average, there were less than one hundred escapes a year. The number of serious escapes was even smaller, for approximately one-third of those counted as escapees either returned voluntarily or were found wandering on the hospital grounds. In general, escaped mental patients returned to their homes. Many of them were then brought back to the hospital by their relatives.

The damaging effects of mental hospitalization on the personality of the inmate are most convincingly demonstrated by the fact that so-called chronic patients rarely try to escape. Persons confined in mental institutions for an appreciable length of time lose whatever social skills they had for getting along on the outside. Hence, not only will they have no desire to escape, but, on the contrary, they will come to dread being discharged. For chronic mental patients the hospital becomes a home which, like small children, they can leave only for visits, but to which they must soon return. "There is a repetitive evidence that once a patient has remained in a large mental hospital for two years or more, he is quite unlikely to leave except by death. He becomes one of the large mass of so-called 'chronic patients'" (Bloomberg, 1960, page 814).

Finally, there is a peculiar ambiguity about the legal status of the escaped mental patient. He is not free, and the hospital may enlist the powers of the police to return the patient into custody. Yet neither is the escaped mental patient a fugitive who must hide, like an escaped convict. If he goes home, those who harbor him do not break the law, as they would if they harbored an escaped convict. Nevertheless, the escaped mental patient remains on the rolls of the hospital. Thus, he retains his legal status as committed mental patient, unless the hospital authorities discharge him. And this may never happen. This ambiguity about the status of the escaped mental patient affects his opportunities for employment, for arranging family affairs, and so forth. It must therefore be a powerful deterrent to escape. For, even if a mental patient should succeed in escaping, what can he do with himself?

In practice, the state hospital superintendent has unlimited discretion over the handling of the escaped mental patient. On the one hand, he may discharge him. On paper, this converts an escape into a regular discharge. In subsequent statistical reports such an outcome may even appear as a "cure." On the other hand, the superintendent may elect to treat the patient as if he were an escaped criminal. The law authorizes him to apprehend and return the escapee to the hospital. Article 3, Section 53, of the New York State Mental Hygiene Law states:

A person who has been committed, certified or admitted to an institution under the jurisdiction of the department and who has been reported as escaped therefrom, or from lawful custody, or who resists or evades lawful custody, may be apprehended, restrained, transported to and returned to such institution by any peace officer, and it shall be the duty of any such officer to assist any representatives of an institution to take into custody any such person upon the request of such representative.

Elsewhere (Section 7, Paragraph 14), the New York State Mental Hygiene Law defines the procedure whereby employees of the department may be designated as "escape officers . . . [who] shall possess all the powers of peace officers in the performance of their official duties."

Thus, even if a patient enters a so-called open hospital voluntarily, legally he is a prisoner. Should he leave the hospital a few days after admission against the wishes of the physicians, he may be treated as an escaped criminal. I consider it misleading to refer to mental institutions, where, during the day, some of the doors may be unlocked, as "open hospitals," if control of the patients is supported by such coercive legislation.

Conclusions

In this chapter, I have sought to present further evidence to support the thesis that the relationship between the involuntarily hospitalized mental patient and his psychiatrist is antagonistic rather than cooperative in nature. This fact has received insufficient psychiatric, social, and legal attention. The conception of a mental illness as something similar to a bodily disease serves to obscure the many significant ethical, legal, and socioeconomic aspects of forced mental hospitalization.

The patient's lawsuit for release, and the hospital superintendent's appeal to be permitted to hold the patient despite a lower court's verdict to set him free, were examined as paradigmatic of many contemporary problems in forensic psychiatry. The relationship between physicians and patients in psychiatric hospitals is often a struggle between adversaries; this fact requires legal recognition. In addition, there is a pressing need for more adequate representation, both legal and psychiatric, for the involuntarily hospitalized mental patient.

> *There is only one . . . principle that can preserve a free society:
> namely, the strict prevention of all coercion, except in the enforce-
> ment of general abstract rules equally applicable to all.*
> —FRIEDRICH A. HAYEK (1960, page 284)

The Distinction Between Civil and Criminal Law

TO APPRECIATE the problems of the constitutional rights of
mentally ill persons, it is necessary to understand the important distinction
between civil and criminal law.

Civil law is the law of persons and property. It is defined by the individual governments to establish the "just conditions" of personal status and
the use of possessions.

Criminal law is the law of public order. It is a code which defines
crime and provides the rules of trial and punishment. Crimes are acts or
omissions forbidden by law which are injurious to public rights or which
constitute a breach of duty to the community.

The basic distinction between these two functions of any modern legal
code was stated succinctly by Sir Henry Maine (1861b): "All civilized
systems of law agree on drawing a distinction between offences against
the State or community (crimes or *crimina*) and offences against the individual (wrongs, torts, or *delicta*)." The boundaries of civil and criminal
law are not sharp. The two often overlap, since some acts are not only

182

"wrongs" against persons, for which the injured parties are entitled to compensation, but also "offenses" for which the offender may be prosecuted and punished in the interests of the community. For example, if a man drives while intoxicated, runs over and kills a pedestrian, he may be held responsible for damages in a civil suit, and for manslaughter in a criminal suit.

Since so-called mentally disturbed behavior presents legal problems falling within the scope of both civil and criminal law, it will be worthwhile to consider the kinds of social acts governed by each of these codes.

Unlike criminal law, civil law is concerned with private rights—for example, with business contracts, claims for personal injury, marriage, adoption, wills, and the like. The community does not regard violations of private rights as infringements of its own integrity. Mental cruelty, for example, may be considered a breach of the marital obligation, and hence a ground for divorce. But it is not considered a violation of the public good or safety. Thus, it is not a criminal offense.

Criminal law, on the other hand, deals with the regulation of those aspects of personal conduct deemed essential for the maintenance of the community. Infractions of criminal statutes harm not only the persons directly offended, but the whole community. A bank robbery, for example, is considered to injure not only the depositors of the particular bank, but the whole business community as well, by undermining the confidence necessary to maintain normal banking operations.

The criminal law, in contrast to the civil law, is concerned with enacting and enforcing minimal rules of conduct considered necessary for the preservation of the integrity of the social body (for example, city, county, state, nation). Violations of these laws are offenses against the governing body. Murder is an offense not against the murdered person, but against the state. Treason is an offense not against one's countrymen, but against the government.

The civil law is thus concerned with regulating the behavior of individuals toward one another. Business, family relations, and personal injury are the main sources of civil litigation. The chief purpose of the civil law is to preserve certain types of business and family relationships. The chief purpose of the criminal law, on the other hand, is to regulate the relationship between individuals and governments (for example, city, county, state, or federal). Evasion of the federal income tax, for example, is a direct violation of the individual's obligation to that government.

Why and how does this distinction between civil and criminal law affect the rights of the mentally ill? The significance of this distinction lies in the simple fact that the guarantees set forth in the Constitution and its Amendments apply only to persons jeopardized by criminal proceedings. To an extent, this is reasonable. The Constitution and Bill of Rights deal with the basic structure of the American Republic as a social organization, and more specifically, with the limitations of its powers vis-à-vis the people. When there is a clash of interests between citizens and government, the adjudication of this conflict is a matter for the criminal law. Hence, the close connection between criminal law and problems of constitutionality.

Conflicts of individual interests, for example between husband and wife or patient and doctor, are usually considered to be problems of the affected parties alone. Presumably, in such matters the government is not directly, or at all, involved. Hence, citizens do not need protection from potential abuses of its power.

However, what constitutes a purely interpersonal transaction, of no concern to the government, has been variously interpreted since this Republic was founded. Until the Civil War, for example, slavery was considered to be a private matter, similar to family relations. Then, until the passage of the Sherman Act in 1890, this was true of business relations. That Act, however, was intended to protect people from the overwhelming power, not of government, but of big business. Similarly, the social relations between families and their so-called mentally ill members, and, more specifically, between the medical profession and the mentally ill, have until now been considered to fall wholly within the scope of civil law, thus requiring no federal regulation. This is reasonable if psychiatric actions, by family members or physicians, toward the "mentally ill" are considered beneficial or therapeutic, rather than exploitative and oppressive.

Nearly all medico-legal authorities, even those who consider the sexual-psychopath laws unconstitutional, believe that "No one questions the power of the state to commit to institutions mentally unbalanced persons who become dangerous to the peace and safety of the community" (Mihm, 1954, page 718). But I question this principle—indeed, I condemn it—and I urge everyone to question it. The author of the above quotation explained that: "One of the purposes of these statutes is to escape the *rigidity* of criminal proceedings. The objectives of the act are *remedial, therapeutic* and *preventive,* said the court in a recent New Hampshire case. It seeks to cure and prevent rather than punish. The protection of society as well as *the benefit of the individual* are the main objectives, all of which spell out *a civil rather than a criminal proceeding*" (italics added; page 719). This reasoning governs all types of involuntary mental hospitalization.

However, the matter is not so simple. According to the law, the purpose of commitment is to help the patient. This view leaves no room for the possibility that commitment may also be a deliberate attempt to harm a person. We thus have an anomalous and unrealistic situation. If, for example, a husband beats his wife—that is considered assault and battery, a criminal offense. This is reasonable. Should the wife retaliate by signing a petition for the husband's commitment to a mental hospital—that is regarded as helpfulness, not as veiled counteraggression. This is unreasonable. It is as if, in a crime syndicate, only the henchmen, who committed brutalities, were considered criminals, whereas the bosses, who hired and directed the thugs, but never injured anyone directly, were deemed non-criminals. Offensive as this analogy may be, I suggest that, quite often, husbands and wives who commit their mates act like the bosses of crime syndicates. They hire henchmen—psychiatrists—to dispose of their adversaries. Thus, those who initiate the action can disclaim responsibility for mischief, and those who carry out the action can define their task as mere work-performance, either devoid of moral implications or positively good.

Let us not forget that every form of social oppression has, at some time during its history, been justified on the ground of helpfulness toward the oppressed. No freedom-loving person can accept this argument. It is no more valid for mental patients today than it was for witches in the Middle Ages or for slaves before the Civil War. I submit that there is a compelling parallel between the Negro slaves unprotected by the American courts, the small businessmen unprotected by antitrust legislation, and our contemporary mental patients. Each was unprotected from its vastly more powerful adversary: the Negro from the white, the small businessman and worker from the corporate giant, and, finally, the mental patient from the medical profession. Only intervention by the federal government can prevent, in these instances, the merciless exploitation of the weak by the strong.

Whether a private relationship is considered a proper subject for congressional regulation is always a matter of viewpoint. The passage and subsequent repeal of the Volstead Act is an example of this. Therefore, I suggest serious consideration of congressional legislation to protect the interests of the mentally ill by curtailing the powers of those who oppress them.

The problem of the rights of the mentally ill is a challenge because the distinction between civil and criminal law does not apply to it. To be sure, many so-called mentally ill persons fail to discharge their obligations to both family and government. Thus, they violate both civil and criminal laws, and may accordingly be penalized both by their families and their government. This is exemplified by the commitment procedure, which is usually set in motion by a member of the patient's family, but is executed by the state government.

In examining the constitutional rights of the mentally ill, we must remember that, until now, the courts have regarded involuntary "hospitalization" and involuntary mental "treatment" as therapeutic, not punitive. Accordingly, legal proceedings authorizing these abominations have been considered civil rather than criminal. Hence, the constitutional guarantees so jealously guarded by the courts in criminal proceedings have failed to apply to the victims of psychiatry precisely because they have been defined as *patients!*

We have traversed a full circle since the days of Charcot and Freud:

To help the hysteric, they promoted him from his quasi-criminal status of malingerer to that of mental patient (Szasz, 1961). In twentieth century America, it is the mental patient's role as patient, rather than as criminal— or, more specifically, as suspect or defendant—that has made possible his dehumanization and maltreatment.

Abridgments of Constitutional Rights Suffered by Mental Patients

I should like to present now, essentially in outline form and with only brief comments, the specific abridgments of constitutional rights that mental patients may suffer. The group most affected is composed of persons who are defined as mentally ill by others. People suspected of or charged with offenses are also frequently subjected to psychiatric violations of their rights. The group least affected is composed of persons who seek psychiatric help voluntarily and who are treated as office patients. However, even voluntary patients, when hospitalized, fall victim to various processes which lead to their human and legal debasement, described elsewhere in this volume.

Violations of the mental patient's rights will be listed in order of the Constitutional Amendment affected. In contrast to prevailing practice, I shall apply these constitutional guarantees to all the procedures imposed on mental patients. Since, in my view, most of these procedures are injurious to the patient's self-interest and freedom, I shall view them not as therapeutic, but as penal. Hence, the rights violated deserve constitutional protection.

At this point, I wish to state that I lay no claim to any professional qualification in the law. The interpretations that follow are my personal judgments and opinions. They are buttressed only by the evidence assembled in this book and by whatever additional evidence the reader may be able to supply. In further defense of my thesis, I should like to mention that although the Articles of the Constitution and the Amendments are legal documents, they were not addressed solely to the legal profession. The intellectual and moral contents of the Constitution belong to the people. It is as a human being and an American, not as a psychiatrist or legal expert, that I offer the following analysis.

The Fourth Amendment (1791) guarantees:

The right of the people to be secure in their persons, houses, papers, and effects, against unreasonable searches and seizures, shall not be violated, and no Warrants shall issue, but upon probable cause, supported by Oath or affirmation and particularly describing the place to be searched, and the persons or things to be seized.

Persons defined as mental patients, or suspected of being mental patients, may be seized in their homes. Their persons and effects may be searched for evidence to incriminate them. No warrant, issued by proper judicial authority, is necessary to empower policemen, health officers, and other physicians to take arbitrary action against suspected mental patients.

The Fifth Amendment (1791) guarantees, among other things, that:

. . . nor shall any person be subject for the same offense to be twice put in jeopardy of life or limb; nor shall be compelled in any criminal case to be a witness against himself, nor be deprived of life, liberty or property, without due process of law; nor shall private property be taken for public use, without just compensation.

The protection against double jeopardy is violated when a person charged with an offense is found unfit to stand trial and is committed to a hospital for the criminally insane, only to be tried some years later and then sentenced to a term of imprisonment. Incarceration in a hospital, under such circumstances, is a punishment directly attributable to the offense with which the defendant is charged. His detention for a period in excess of the prison term he would have had to serve had he been tried and sentenced, not hospitalized, constitutes a clear case of double punishment.

The protection against self-incrimination is violated when, for example, a person is committed on the basis of information which he himself has furnished a psychiatrist; or when a court-appointed psychiatrist examines a defendant without informing the latter that he is an agent of the court (or prosecution); or when psychiatrists in hospitals for the criminally insane use their roles as doctors to obtain confidential information, which may then be used to keep the patient incarcerated; or when the psychiatrist appointed by the defendant's counsel divulges to the court material obtained as the patient's agent.

The protection against self-incrimination is also violated in many situations that have little or no connection with the criminal law. Psychiatric material damaging to the patient may thus be divulged, with or without the patient's permission, to employers, school authorities, military agencies, and so forth (Szasz, 1960a). One might take the position that in such cases, which do not directly involve the public good and safety, the law need not interfere to protect people who choose to harm themselves by trusting psychiatrists known *not* to adhere to the principles of strict confidentiality in their dealings with patients. Or one might argue that the courts ought to hold—depending on their view of the contract between patient and psychiatrist—that the patient has a valid claim for damages from the psychiatrist in a civil action for breach of contract.

The Sixth Amendment (1791) guarantees that:

In all criminal prosecutions, the accused shall enjoy the right to a speedy and public trial, by an impartial jury of the State and district wherein the crime shall have been committed, which district shall have been previously ascertained by law, and to be informed of the nature and cause of the accusation; to be confronted with the witnesses against him; to have compulsory process for obtaining witnesses in his favor, and to have the Assistance of Counsel for his defense.

A person is deprived of the right here set forth when, instead of being tried for an offense, he is incarcerated in a mental hospital. The violation of this constitutional guarantee is especially striking when the defendant demands trial but is not tried because of psychiatric opinion furnished by the court or the prosecution. This procedure violates the protection against self-incrimination guaranteed in the Fifth Amendment, the right to trial guaranteed in the Sixth Amendment, and the due process clause of the Fourteenth Amendment (see Chapter 13).

The Seventh Amendment (1791)
guarantees that:

In suits at common law, where the value in controversy shall exceed twenty dollars, the right of trial by jury shall be preserved, and no fact tried by jury, shall be otherwise reexamined in any Court of the United States, than according to the rules of the common law.

The issue of a person's sanity or competency arises at many points— for example, in relation to mental hospitalization, guardianship, capacity to stand trial, the need for hospitalization if judged incapable to stand trial, testamentary capacity, and so forth. Many of these determinations do not require a jury trial. In some states, a person may be incarcerated in a state hospital without recourse to jury trial. In New York State he may be denied the right to trial and imprisoned in a hospital for the criminally insane, with no recourse to a jury trial to determine the issue of "present insanity." Is the right to stand trial worth twenty dollars? And what is the value of protection against incarceration in a correctional institution, albeit one called a hospital?

The Eighth Amendment (1791)
guarantees that:

Excessive bail shall not be required, nor excessive fines imposed, nor cruel and unusual punishments inflicted.

Defendants ordered to submit to involuntary pretrial psychiatric examination are denied bail; they are detained in a mental institution operated by the state or federal government; and are examined by psychiatrists employed by these public institutions. If the defendant is charged with an offense which entitles him to bail, he should not be denied bail on psychiatric grounds. Nor should he be compelled to stay in a public psychiatric institution for observation when an adequate examination could be conducted without depriving him of his liberty. Lastly, if such examination is for the benefit of the accused, as it is generally alleged to be, he should be allowed to select his own examiners, rather than be compelled to submit to the psychiatric verdict of agents employed by his adversaries.

What constitutes "cruel and unusual punishment" depends on the person rendering judgment on this question and on the age in which he lives. Since 1791, our courts have brought an ever increasing number of things within the scope of this phrase. In my view, mental hospitalization *may be* (it need not always be) a form of cruel and unusual punishment; so *may* psychiatric treatments, like electric shock therapy. Certainly, lobotomy *is*. The sentencing of persons to indeterminate restrictions of liberty, under the sexual-psychopath laws, *is*, to my mind, a form of cruel punishment.

The Thirteenth Amendment (1865)

guarantees, in part, that:

Neither slavery nor involuntary servitude, except as a punishment for crime whereof the party shall have been duly convicted, shall exist within the United States, or any place subject to their jurisdiction.

In general, patients in public mental hospitals do a great deal of work, without compensation, necessary for the operation of the institution. Some psychiatrists claim that this is a part of their therapy. On the other hand, it may be claimed that this is a form of involuntary servitude or peonage (Chasan, 1961). In my opinion, the involuntary servitude of many mental patients is an incontestable fact (Goldman and Ross, 1956).

The Fourteenth Amendment (1868)

guarantees, in part, that:

No state shall make or enforce any law which shall abridge the privileges or immunities of citizens of the United States; nor shall any State deprive any person of life, liberty, or property, without due process of law; nor deny to any person within its jurisdiction the equal protection of the laws.

The due process clause in this Amendment repeats a part of the Fifth Amendment. The reason for this is that the first Ten Amendments, commonly called the Bill of Rights, were held to be restrictions on the power of the federal government, not the States. Except for the rights embodied in the First Amendment, "few other provisions of the Bill of Rights have ever been applied in full force to the States" (Douglas, 1954, page 137). The Fourteenth Amendment, adopted after the Civil War, sought to impose upon the States the same restrictions in its dealing with citizens as governed the Republic as a whole.

The protection against deprivation of liberty and property is, of course, violated when a person is confined in a mental hospital against his will or declared incompetent to manage his affairs. To be sure, the validity of this view will depend on the interpretation of the key expression, "due process of law." If one believes that present psychiatric practices afford sufficient protection for the patient's interests and rights, then my judgment will be held erroneous. My judgment will be considered correct, however, if due process in psychiatric affairs requires, first, that psychiatrists not mislead patients to believe they will help them, when, in fact, they are the agents of another party; and, second, that in each case in which psychiatry is used as a social force against a person, he will have equal access to psychiatric authority to use on his own behalf. Mental patients are never accorded such protection. Thus, virtually all existing practices involving involuntary patients violate the due process clause of the Fourteenth Amendment.

The Fifteenth Amendment (1870) guarantees, in part, that:

> The right of citizens of the United States to vote shall not be denied or abridged by the United States or by any State on account of race, color, or previous condition of servitude.

In most states, the mental hospital patient loses the right to vote. Even when he is not legally deprived of this right, he is usually deprived of the opportunity to exercise it.

Conclusions

I have sought to demonstrate that mental patients in the United States suffer widespread and grievous violations of their constitutional rights. I believe that today these people, more than members of particular racial or religious groups, are the principal scapegoats of our society. Unless we wish to foster this state of affairs, it devolves upon us to mobilize adequate social action to correct it.

PART FIVE

Psychiatry and Public Policy

CHAPTER 16

Ethics and Psychiatry: The Case of Mrs. Isola Ware Curry

Men do not like to be protected, it emasculates them. This is what black men know, it is the reality they have lived with; it is what white men do not want to know.

—JAMES BALDWIN (1959)

The Case of Mrs. Isola Ware Curry

AN ASSOCIATED PRESS news dispatch dated November 18, 1958, reported that Mrs. Isola Ware Curry, the woman who had stabbed the Reverend Martin Luther King in a Harlem department store some six weeks before, had been committed to the Matteawan State Hospital. The dispatch went on to comment: "She never gave a coherent reason for the attack."

Mrs. Curry was indicted on a charge of attempted murder in the first degree. However, she was not brought to trial. Instead, she was sent to Bellevue Hospital (in New York City) for pretrial psychiatric examination. There she was declared incompetent to stand trial. She was then committed for an indefinite term to an institution which, for social purposes, functions just like a jail but is called a hospital—a hospital for the criminally insane.

Probably no one was surprised by this sequence of events. An unprovoked attack on an antisegregationist leader by a Negro woman must have seemed to the proverbial man on the street as "just about as crazy as you can get." Consequently, in the public eye, Mrs. Curry was committable.

Suppose, however, that the attack had been made on a segregationist leader. Would she still have been committable in the public eye, or would her act have been interpreted as a political crime based on revenge? Suppose Mr. King had been assaulted by a member of the Ku Klux Klan. Would the public have labeled the attacker as mentally ill? Or would his act have been regarded as a political crime?

Obviously, it is not my intention to imply that in attacking Mr. King, Mrs. Curry thought brightly or acted rightly. Having stabbed her victim in plain view of many witnesses established the fact that she had committed a crime. Her trial and conviction could be circumvented in one way only— by raising the issue of insanity. Thus, psychiatrists were hired, ostensibly to examine her psychiatrically, but tacitly to find her unfit to stand trial. If psychiatrists declared an offender "unable to understand the charges against him or to assist counsel in his own defense," he may be committed without trial (see Chapter 13). This was done in Mrs. Curry's case. Whether Mrs. Curry wanted to be tried we do not know.

I do not know what the psychiatric findings were in this case. But no matter what they were, they could not, *in themselves*, justify her commitment to a state hospital. Psychiatric findings of schizophrenia or psychosis can be demonstrated in millions of people who are not hospitalized. The point here is that she broke the law, and something had to be done about her. Under the circumstances, putting her away quietly was the socially preferred course of action. Why? What sorts of things are involved in this case which would have made us—and here I refer to that hypothetical entity called "most of us"—uncomfortable had they been exposed to the light of day?

The Moral Problem of Racial Discrimination

The problem which was evaded by the psychiatric short-circuiting of this case is the so-called Negro problem. However, the public is so aware of this problem that it would seem difficult to justify new attempts to hide it.

Mrs. Curry committed a crime which is daily advocated by the segregationist forces of our society. Let us not be hypocritical. Many must have greeted her action with glee. We know perfectly well that when a person who strongly advocates a particular view dies, those who believe otherwise feel triumphant. When Hitler was in power, many Jews wished and prayed for his death. Other examples could easily be cited. If these are the facts, it is irrational to behave as if everyone shared the same values and goals in life. Upholding democratic laws demands political equality for Negroes and whites. It also demands, however, the open condemnation of a person who takes the law into his own hands. The need to condemn Mrs. Curry, by taking her and her act *seriously*, was evaded.

There might be an objection to my argument at this point, which might run as follows: "If the attacker had been white and sane, he would have been tried, and his act would have been condemned." Let us take each of these points separately. First, the question of color. We seem to be especially offended and perplexed by the fact that a Negro person should have attacked a leader in the Negro's fight for equality. But in reacting this way, we close our eyes to some well-known facts about human behavior.

The oppressed tend to adopt the ideals of the oppressor. This phenomenon may be observed in prisoner-of-war camps, concentration camps, mental hospitals, and in slave-master relationships of all kinds (Bettelheim, 1960). There is nothing especially mysterious about this. Indeed, freeman and slave are in a similar position, in that neither is satisfied to be as he is or what he is. Most people admire and envy outstanding personalities who have skills and things which the ordinary person lacks but would like to possess. So it is for the prisoner and his captor, slave and master, Negro and white. Long ago, psychoanalysts recognized this phenomenon and called it "identification with the aggressor." In *The Future of an Illusion*, Freud (1927) spoke of "the identification of the suppressed classes with the class who rules and exploits them" (page 13). How can this be explained?

Stripped of technical complexities, it means that a person who has been attacked, violated, and abused—especially over a long period of time—has, in fact, been *doubly* abused. First, by the act itself. Second, by the changes in his personality, in his inner self, wrought by his submissive position vis-à-vis his exploiters. While the first violation is obvious, the second is not, and often eludes attention. Yet, of the two, it is probably the more important, for its consequences are more lasting. The acute harm and the indignity of abuse can be arrested, and perhaps even undone, by disrupting the relationship responsible for it. Freeing the prisoner, over-throwing the oppressor, liberating the slave—each is intended to serve such a purpose.

The second type of harm is more insidious and more difficult to remedy. Its effect is a modification of the personality: the oppressed adopts the aspirations and values of the oppressor. Illustrative of this is the anti-Semitic Jew, or the Negro who wants to be white.

With these considerations in mind we can return to Mrs. Curry's case and ask this question: What explanation would the majority of the people have accepted as a good reason for her act? Public opinion defines reason-ableness as concurrence with its own standards, much as Disraeli charac-terized an agreeable gentleman as one who agreed with him. Applying this principle to the present case, we must conclude that, in the public mind, all Negroes are in favor of integration. The segregationist Negro thus becomes a theoretical impossibility. This, however, does not make it impossible for him to exist. In the public mind there are only two alterna-tives to the problem of desegregation. One, that all Negroes are for it. The other, that if they are not, they must be crazy. Thus, the very possibility of a Negro espousing the ideals of segregationism is ruled out of existence. But this view negates a host of historical precedents which demonstrate impressively that the oppressed classes are not necessarily steadfast supporters of liberty. The Founding Fathers belonged to the upper strata of society. So did men like Lenin, Gandhi, Nehru, and others who, though they fought for the disenfranchised classes of their nations, or of mankind as a whole, were not themselves members of these classes.

We must therefore consider seriously the purpose of Mrs. Curry's attack on Mr. King. The simplest—although, to be sure, not always the best—way to ascertain the aim or meaning of an act is to take it on its face value. Why could this particular act of violence not be so viewed? Why must we assume that it requires some special interpretation which only psychiatrists are able to make? Taking Mrs. Curry's act at its face value would mean that she opposed Mr. King's stand on the Negro problem. She could have had several reasons for this. Perhaps she believed, as do the Black Muslims, that only complete segregation, and possibly even secession from a white world, can give the Negro dignity and independence. Or perhaps she believed, as do the white supremacists, that slavery or second-class citizenship is the Negro's proper place. If this was the case, should her color cancel her right to share this view? Why could her desire to remain a "happy slave" not be considered a reasonable explanation of her act?

By affixing a psychiatric diagnosis to Mrs. Curry, her act was branded as crazy and therefore incomprehensible, except to experts. Thus, the questions raised here were comfortably settled. That she should have a *choice* about the problem of segregation was expressly disallowed. In other words, disposing of Mrs. Curry's case by means of psychiatric, rather than legal, intervention achieved two major objectives. First, it deprived her, and by implication other Negroes, of the *right* to commit a crime against a *prominent* member of their own race. This evasion is particularly significant in light of the fact that Negroes also cannot commit crimes against *undistinguished* Negroes. (White prosecutors are notoriously lax in prosecuting for such offenses.) Second, it enabled society—the public—to disguise and evade the moral and sociopsychological dilemmas inherent in her act. It thus injured values which a humanistic democracy is expected to foster.

The Psychiatrist As Social Tranquilizer

Among the many tasks that psychiatrists assume in our society, one is to treat people; another is to attempt to harmonize, or tranquilize, interpersonal and social discord. Often these two conflict.

The private psychotherapeutic relationship is the best illustration of the role of the therapist as the patient's agent. The patient hires and pays the psychiatrist to help him clarify his problems in living. The purpose of this sort of therapy is to aid the patient in his efforts to live more effectively, according to *his own* goals, both present and future. This does not mean that the patient's moral conceptions and conduct remain unscrutinized. On the contrary, such scrutiny is an essential part of therapy. The point I wish to emphasize is that the therapist is contractually and morally committed to avoid influencing his patient by any means other than by conversation with him. Thus, the psychiatrist may not speak about the patient to others (not even to colleagues), may not testify for or against him in a court of law, nor may he hospitalize the patient against his will. It is in the psychoanalytic relationship that this role is most clearly defined for the psychiatrist (Szasz, 1962). However, the daily work of many other psychiatrists is based on the same principles.

I have chosen to name the psychiatrist's second job *social tranquilization*. Psychiatrists who perform this task may be called social tranquilizers.

Psychiatrists act as social tranquilizers when their goal is to protect the harmony of deeply rooted institutions, such as marriage, social class, profession, nation, and so forth. Faced with conflicting values and social aspirations, psychiatrists may now intervene in order to obscure and evade the issues. Relief is offered by focusing the attention of the contending parties on a substitute problem and its possible solution. For example, a married couple seeking divorce may be advised to have a child or cultivate a common interest. A therapist making such a recommendation is not an agent of either the man or the wife, but rather of marriage as a social institution.

There are two parts to the psychiatric function of social tranquilization. One is to provide relief from tension by means of distraction. The other is to offer solutions to substitute problems. In the Curry case, the significant issue is the relation between Negroes and whites, and specifically the problem of segregation. Preoccupation with the alleged mental health or illness of those who are for or against segregation may be regarded as a psychiatric contribution to creating a substitute problem. Recommendations for easing this problem constitute substitute solutions.

When psychiatrists act as social tranquilizers, their behavior implies approval of existing interpersonal and social conditions. The social prestige of psychiatry as a science is used to ensure this end. This raises the question of how we decide—in general, or in a specific instance—which goal is more desirable: change or preservation of the *status quo*. In this problem the notion of mental illness plays a crucial and, as we see, an ambiguous part.

Conclusions

Mrs. Curry is still incarcerated at Matteawan. Are the psychiatrists treating the mental illness which allegedly prevented her from standing trial? Will they some day declare her competent to be tried? Will she ever be tried? Or will she have to live out her days at Matteawan? I do not know. But I cannot help having some dark thoughts on the matter.

And what shall we think of the psychiatrists who found Mrs. Curry incompetent to stand trial and who now keep her in a mental hospital? Are they helping the cause of mental health? Are they building better race relations?

Perhaps, at this point, we should listen to what an intelligent, sensitive Negro says about madness and the Negro problem in America:

We would never, never allow Negroes to starve, to grow bitter, and to die in ghettos all over the country if we were not driven by some nameless fear that has nothing to do with Negroes. We would never victimize, as we do, children whose only crime is color and keep them, as we put it, in their place. We wouldn't drive Negroes mad as we do by accepting them in ball parks, and on concert stages, but not in our homes and not in our neighborhoods, and not in our churches. It is only too clear that even with the most malevolent will in the world Negroes can never manage to achieve one-tenth of the harm we fear. No, it has everything to do with ourselves and this is one of the reasons that for all these generations *we have disguised this problem in the most incredible jargon.* One of the reasons we are so fond of sociological reports and investigational committees is *because they hide something.* [Italics added. Baldwin, 1961, pages 134–135.]

Freud created psychoanalysis as a therapeutic instrument to render the unconscious conscious. Where id was, ego shall be—this was his prescription, the aim of analysis. But what is to prevent psychiatrists and psychoanalysts from reversing this process?

CHAPTER 17 » *Politics and Psychiatry:*
The Case of Mr. Ezra Pound

It has been your habit for long to do away with good writers,
You either drive them mad, or else you blink at their suicides,
Or else you condone their drugs, and talk of insanity and genius,
But I will not go mad to please you.

—EZRA POUND (1914)

WHEN PSYCHIATRY became a respectable medical specialty—
approximately at the beginning of this century—it became fashionable
to pin psychiatric diagnoses on well-known personages, both past and
present. Freud's (1909) speculations about the psychopathology of Leonardo da Vinci and others are familiar to the contemporary student. It is
less well known that many nonpsychoanalysts were also deeply involved
in this game of psychiatric name-calling, or in protests against it. In the
little-known work *The Psychiatric Study of Jesus,* Albert Schweitzer
(1913) tried to refute three prominent psychiatrists who claimed that
Jesus suffered from paranoia. More will be said about this essay later.

Since its modest beginning early in this century, the enterprise of calling prominent people crazy has proved vastly popular. Not only has this
activity received the blessing of the psychiatric profession, but also the
endorsement of jurists, politicians, writers, and others. It is hardly surprising, then, that newspapermen, political commentators, and the public at
large accept without question explanations that attribute the conduct of
some political leaders to common sense, expediency, or meanness, but

199

ascribe the behavior of others to mental illness. The distinction between the mentally healthy and mentally sick leader, man of letters, or scientist is one that the psychiatrist, of course, is expected to make, and which others are expected to accept. Thus, many people seem eager to dispose of the problems posed by men like Fidel Castro, Earl Long, or Adolf Hitler by labeling them "psychotic."

In this chapter, I shall present and analyze the case of Ezra Pound. This case highlights the significance of the Rule of Law for a free society. It illustrates that psychiatric, as against judicial, disposition of alleged lawbreakers permits the exercise of discretionary power in dealing with them. By means of psychiatric incarceration, the modern government is spared from committing "injustices" that may inflame public opinion. Instead of judging the accused guilty and liable to punishment, he is declared mentally ill and not responsible for his conduct. Then, with "kindness" he is committed to a mental institution. So long as more people do not ask where involuntary psychiatric hospitalization and treatment end, and retribution and punishment begin, this form of liberticide is bound to flourish.

The Case of Ezra Pound

When the war in Europe ended in 1945, Ezra Pound was taken into custody by American troops in Italy. He was returned to the United States and indicted for treason. The charge was based on allegedly treasonous broadcasts which Pound made during the war from Rome. It is important to emphasize that Pound insisted that patriotism was his motive. According to a statement by Robert Frost, prepared for a motion for Pound's release in 1958, "He [Pound] never admitted that he went over to the enemy any more than the writers at home who have despaired of the Republic" (Norman, 1960, page 454). Whether Pound's broadcasts were or were not treasonous was, however, never decided. That is, the issue and the evidence on it were never presented to a jury. Hence, no judicial decision on his guilt or innocence was ever rendered. Instead, it was decided—jointly by the government and by Pound's defense—that Pound be declared mentally unfit to stand trial and that he be hospitalized in a psychiatric institution. This was speedily accomplished. It took the jury all of three minutes to decide that Pound was of "unsound mind." He spent the next 13 years in St. Elizabeths Hospital.

How could this happen? When Pound was indicted for treason, he was fifty-nine years old. He was one of the outstanding and most influential poets of his time. He had married, raised a family, looked after his affairs, helped his colleagues and friends, and never before had any brushes with either policemen or psychiatrists. Eccentric, peculiar, conceited—yes. But was he insane, in the sense that he did not know what he was doing? And, more specifically, was he so out of his mind that he could not assist in his own defense?

Let us remember that the prosecution (the United States Government) and the defense agreed that Pound was mentally unfit to be tried, and so informed the judge. The judge accordingly impaneled a jury, stating:

In the event the jury finds that his mental state is as has been represented to me, then Mr. Pound will not be brought to trial because, under the law, it would not be proper to prosecute him if his mental condition is as has been stated to me [page 419].

The doctors who had examined Pound in the Gallinger Municipal Hospital (for the prosecution) testified that Pound suffered from a "paranoid state." One of the chief witnesses at Pound's insanity hearing was Dr. Winfred Overholser, Superintendent of St. Elizabeths Hospital, under whose care Pound was to spend the next 13 years of his life. Here are the reasons Overholser gave to support his opinion that Pound should not be tried.

He is thoroughly convinced that if he had been allowed to send his messages to the Axis, which he wished to send, prior to 1940, there would have been no Axis even. In other words, that if given a free hand by those who were engaged in stultifying him, he could have prevented the war.

He lays a great deal of his difficulties at the door of British Secret Service, and other groups, which have opposed him.

He assures me, too, that he served a very useful purpose to the United States by remaining at the Italian prison camp to complete his translation of Confucius, which he regards as the greatest contribution to literature.

He is sure he should not have been brought to this country in the capacity of a prisoner, but in the capacity of someone who was to be of great benefit to the United States in its post-war activities.

I might state that this constitutes a grandiosity of ideas and beliefs that goes far beyond the normal, even in a person who is as distraught in his mind as he is [page 419].

Dr. Overholser was then cross-examined by Mr. Isaiah Matlack, counsel for the Department of Justice.

Q. Now, what part does his background history play in your opinion as to his present sanity?
A. It shows that we are dealing now with the end-product of an individual who throughout his lifetime has been highly antagonistic, highly eccentric, the whole world has revolved around him, he has been a querulous person, he has been less and less able to order his life. This has been a gradual evolution through his life, so that now we are dealing with the end-product, so to speak [page 419].

Notice how general and how vague these observations of Overholser's are. No evidence was introduced to prove that, in spite of his peculiarities, Pound could not be treated as a responsible defendant. Instead, unproved allegations were insinuated, such as his being "less and less able to order his life." This psychiatric accusation was simply untrue. Before the American troops landed in Italy, Pound was able to order his life well enough to stay out of the hands of psychiatrists. Whereas since the end of the European War he had been a prisoner, his life having been "ordered" for him.

To recapture the atmosphere of the jury trial in which Pound's sanity was adjudicated, it is necessary to know the instructions that Judge Bolitha J. Laws, who conducted the proceedings, gave to the jurors. After outlining the case and the problem before the court, Judge Laws addressed the jurors as follows:

It has been testified to before you correctly that we brought him to the point of having him examined by psychiatrists and physicians on mental disease; we brought Dr. Overholser, who is the head of St. Elizabeths Hospital, one of the outstanding institutions of the United States, and run by the United States, and we brought to examine him also Dr. King who, as you have been told on the witness stand, holds a responsible position in the Public Health Service which attends to the mental as well as the physical condition of persons in the penal institutions throughout the United States. We brought into consultation also Dr. Gilbert, who is the head of the Division of Psychiatry at Gallinger Hospital, with which I think you are doubtless familiar. Then there was permitted to examine him at the request of Mr. Cornell, who appeared for Mr. Pound, Dr. Muncie, who is a leading psychiatrist, and I think the head of the department at Johns Hopkins University. You heard his qualifications.

These doctors, after consultation, filed a written certificate with the Court indicating their *unanimous view that Mr. Pound under his then present state of mind was not in a position to stand a trial,* to cooperate with his counsel, and go through with a serious charge of this nature.

Government counsel have cooperated very readily in the investigation and were very fair in the entire situation and they, feeling that the code of law which I have explained to you should be complied with, filed in this court a motion that a jury be impanelled to pass upon this proposition. I agreed with the view of Government counsel that a jury be impanelled to look into it *notwithstanding the unanimous opinion of these psychiatrists,* and that is the reason why you have been impanelled today to hear the whole story, and those physicians have been questioned before you fully with regard to the situation.

It therefore becomes your duty now to advise me whether in your judgment you find that Mr. Pound is in position to cooperate with his counsel, *to stand trial without causing him to crack up or break down;* whether he is able to testify, if he sees fit, at the trial, to stand cross-examination, and in that regard, of course, you have heard the testimony of all these physicians on the subject and there is no testimony to the contrary and, of course, *these are men who have given a large part of their professional careers to the study of matters of this sort,* who have been brought here for your guidance.

Under the state of the law you are not necessarily bound by what they say; you can disregard what they say and bring in a different verdict, *but in a case of this type where the Government and the defense representatives have united in a clear and unequivocal view with regard to the situation, I presume you will have no difficulty in making up your mind.* [Italics added. Norman, 1960, pages 423–424.]

The jury was out three minutes and brought in a verdict of "unsound mind." Pound was remanded to St. Elizabeths Hospital.

Pound remained at St. Elizabeths Hospital from 1945 until 1958, when he was released as "incurably insane, but not dangerous." He was retained all this time despite the fact that barely one year after his commitment, under pressure of Pound's defense attorney, Overholser stated that "in his opinion (1) the defendant has been insane for many years and will never recover his sanity or become mentally fit to stand trial to the indictment, (2) the defendant's mental condition is not benefited by his close confinement at St. Elizabeths Hospital where he is kept in a building with violent patients because of the necessity of keeping him under guard, and it would be desirable from the point of view of the health and welfare of the defendant if he could be removed to a private sanitorium, and (3) the defendant is not violent, etc." (page 424).

Eleven years elapsed after this, until, on April 14, 1958, a motion was filed in the United States District Court for the District of Columbia for dismissal of the original indictment. This motion was supported by statements from Winfred Overholser, Robert Frost, and a number of prominent writers and poets. Frost's eloquent statement was read in court:

I am here to register my admiration for a government that can rouse in conscience to a case like this. Relief seems to be in sight for many of us besides the Ezra Pound in question and his faithful wife. He has countless admirers the world over who will rejoice in the news that he has hopes of freedom. I append a page or so of what they have been saying lately about him and his predicament. I myself speak as much in the general interest as in his. And I feel authorized to speak very specially for my friends, Archibald MacLeish, Ernest Hemingway and T. S. Eliot. None of us can bear the disgrace of our letting Ezra Pound come to his end where he is. It would leave too woeful a story in American literature. He went very wrongheaded in his egotism, but he insists it was from patriotism— love of America. He has never admitted that he went over to the enemy any more than the writers at home who have despaired of the Republic. I hate such nonsense and can only listen to it as an evidence of mental disorder. But mental disorder is what we are considering. I rest the case on Dr. Overholser's pronouncement that Ezra Pound is not too dangerous to go free in his wife's care, and too insane ever to be tried—a very nice discrimination [page 454].

On April 18, 1958, with the consent of the government, the indictment against Pound was dismissed by Judge Laws.

What happened next? Pound resumed his habitual style of living. He was hyperactive, flamboyant, at times bizarre. He visited with friends, and annoyed some congressmen. Soon, he and his wife sailed for Italy. On arrival, he greeted the reporters and photographers with a Fascist salute and announced that "all America is an insane asylum" [page 458]. Since then, he has lived with his daughter and son-in-law. At the time of this writing (November, 1961), Pound is still alive. Nor has he required further psychiatric "help." For a seventy-five-year-old man who was pronounced incurably insane 16 years ago, this is not a bad record.

A Critical Analysis of the Pound Case

What can we learn from the Pound affair? Perhaps the first to criticize the use of psychiatry in this case was Wertham (1949). He thought it virtually self-evident that Pound was sane enough to be tried, and cited evidence to support his view. For example, when taken into custody Pound was quoted as having said: "If a man isn't willing to take some risk for his opinions, either his opinions are no good or he is no good" (page 596). Accordingly, Wertham suggested that Pound's insanity was contrived by those in charge of his case, and, more generally, that "His 'insanity' is an example of how we are trying to explain away profound defects in society by placing them outside society, in the sphere of individual pathology" (page 600). Moreover, Wertham observed, if mercy to a great man was the intent of the insanity defense, it could have been "better accomplished democratically by the proper use of clemency than by the dangerous abuse of psychiatry" (page 594).

George Orwell, who demonstrated his knowledge of psychology in his book *Nineteen Eighty-four* (1949), did not regard Pound as a deluded mental patient, but as a Fascist who was nevertheless a fine artist and a respectable human being:

> When one thinks of all the people who support or have supported fascism, one stands amazed at their diversity. What a crew! Think of a programme which at any rate for a while could bring Hitler, Pétain, Montague Norman, Pavelitch, William Randolph Hearst, Streicher, Buchman, Ezra Pound, Juan March, Cocteau, Thyssen, Father Coughlin, The Mufti of Jerusalem, Arnold Lunn, Antonescu, Spengler, Beverley Nichols, Lady Houston, and Marinetti all into the same boat. But the clue is really very simple. They are all people with something to lose, or people who long for a hierarchical society and dread the prospect of a world of free and equal human beings [Orwell, 1943, page 150].

Is this not a more meaningful appraisal of the problem which Pound presented to his American captors than calling him paranoid? And would it not have been more honest to try him? As it is, Pound, self-confessed Fascist, succeeded in provoking his country to treat him with the Fascist methods he so fervently espoused. He was thus imprisoned without benefit of trial. But, someone may object, this is not so. He was not imprisoned at all; he was hospitalized as a mental patient. How was Pound's hospitalization generally perceived? In a review in *The New York Times* of a biography of Pound by Mullins (1961), Herbert Creekmore (1961) wrote: "It is sad that Pound was imprisoned [*sic*], and I think it was unjust, especially in that he was held for twelve years." Creekmore's review elicited several letters to the Editor, but no one commented on, and I assume therefore that no one objected to, Creekmore's referring to Pound's detention as imprisonment. Psychiatric hospitals are, of course, prisons. One of the principal aims of this book is to impress this fact upon the reader, and to show the maneuvers that legislators, attorneys, and physicians use to deceive the public as well as one another of the facts.

The Pound case affords an example of the type of psychiatric participation in the criminal process which substitutes the Rule of Men for the Rule of Law (Hayek, 1957, 1960). Although there are laws that govern the use of psychiatric action in criminal law, one cannot predict whether or not psychiatric participation will be enlisted in any particular case. The severity of the expected punishment seems to be an important variable. If the penalty is heavy—especially if it is death—the likelihood of psychiatric participation is great.

Not only is the use of psychiatric opinion in criminal cases unregulated by strict rules of law, but also the interpretation of the opinion permits so much latitude that the very possibilities of consistency and predictability are negated. The judicial process is thus allowed to drift from the impartial and predictable enforcement of rules toward an unpredictable decision of each case on what is thought to be its own merits.

Lacking the integrity of a scientific definition, the concept of mental health—and its antonym, mental illness—has succumbed to what Bertrand Russell (1953) called the cult of common usage. In contemporary America it has come to mean conformity to the demands of society. According to the commonsense definition, mental health is the ability to play the game of social living, and to play it well. Conversely, mental illness is the refusal to play, or the inability to play well (see Chapter 1).

Are there differences between social nonconformity or deviation and mental illness? I submit that the difference between saying "He is wrong" and "He is mentally ill" is not factual but psychological. If we take the actor seriously, regard him as having human rights and dignities, and being essentially like us—we speak of disagreement, deviation, crime, perhaps even treason. Should we feel, however, that we cannot communicate with him, that he is different from us—we then speak of insanity, mental illness, emotional immaturity, racial inferiority, and so forth. Once a person is placed in the second category, *what* he says becomes irrelevant, though *why* he says it may be considered interesting.

Thus, a serious disagreement implies a basically dignified human relationship. At least in the context of the conflict, the participants treat each other as equals. In contrast, a situation in which the position of only one of the participants is taken seriously, while that of his opponent is disregarded, bespeaks a relationship between a superior and an inferior, a master and slave. When initiated by the former, it is a means of degrading his partner. When it is invited by the latter, or is placidly accepted by him, it is self-inflicted degradation.

Occasionally both parties benefit from this shift in attitude. Since kindness, or at least pretended kindness, toward the sick is an integral part of our ethic, the offender who is considered mentally ill may be treated more sympathetically than he might otherwise be. The stronger or superior member of the conflicting pair may also benefit from this arrangement. First, he does not have to take seriously the charges of a critic who is his inferior; second, he avoids the guilt feelings which are invariably associated with meting out punishment. These feelings tend to be particularly distressing when someone who is loved or admired is punished. Prominent artists, Ezra Pound among them, fall into the group of the admired, and hence are not expected to adhere completely to the social rules binding for others. The parental obligation to punish children for infraction of rules gave rise to the saying, "It hurts me more than it hurts you!" This saying is as misleading as it is incomplete. Still, it suggests what parents feel when they discipline their children. Enlarged, this phenomenon is analogous to that of a nation judging and punishing one of its revered members.

Still, it may be asked, what can be the objection to showing kindness to Pound, as was allegedly done by not bringing him to trial? Is this not a fair way to treat the so-called mentally ill criminal? The basic objection is that the social sanctions employed in such cases violate the principles of the open society, by substituting for the Rule of Law the Rule of Men. If this violation of the Rule of Law is due to the humanistic wish to be kind to those who break the laws, it is committed unnecessarily, for trial and, in case of guilt, conviction of offenders need not prevent us from treating them with decency and kindness.

I have previously criticized the practice of giving psychiatric testimony in ordinary criminal trials (see Chapter 10). This practice is particularly undesirable in cases of political offense. When psychiatrists participate in the social disposition of such persons, they renounce the ethics of science for the values uppermost in society at any given time.

Let us recall in this connection that many prominent men have served time in jail for political offenses. Castro, Gandhi, Hitler, Nehru, Russell,

Sukarno, to name a few, have all been sentenced to jail for opposing laws. In the past, Galileo, Jesus, and Socrates found themselves in opposition to duly appointed social authority. These men were taken seriously, and were punished in the manner prescribed by law. Surely, the way Pound was treated impugns his stature.

Pound was originally confined in a mental hospital ostensibly because of his alleged mental illness. Was he released because he recovered? Or because there was a change in the political climate? Or because he was punished enough? The psychiatrists in charge of Pound stated that he was still mentally ill, indeed that he would never be sane enough to stand trial. But, they added, he was no longer a danger to himself or to others. Appropriately enough, reporting on these developments, *Time* magazine (April 28, 1958) captioned his picture with the words: "Freedom for the warped." Are we to assume that he was given the precious gift of freedom *because* he was warped? Had he not been warped, but healthy, would he have continued to be deprived of his freedom?

It seems to me, as it did to Wertham (1949), that Pound played the game against the United States, played it well and honorably—but lost! As we have noted, Pound was not alone among artists in his admiration of "strong" men. George Bernard Shaw, for example, also admired the Fascist leaders. The point is, however, that Pound allegedly violated the laws of his country. The Rule of Law demands that the government play the game seriously, according to the rules: that is, that Pound be tried, sentenced if guilty, and later, if it be deemed just, pardoned and released. It may be objected that avoidance of trial on the grounds of insanity is part of the laws of our country. That is true. But as Hayek has shown, a duly constituted law is not the same as the Rule of Law. The latter is characterized by its consistency and inflexibility, in brief, by the fact that it is applied predictably and without exceptions. Since the issue of insanity is raised in some cases but not in others, and when raised is interpreted in an unpredictable manner, it serves as a particularly useful means for individualizing the administration of justice. But we cannot have our cake and eat it too. Exceptions to the Rule of Law on the grounds of mental illness are exceptions nonetheless, and compare with those that favor or penalize a group because of race or religion.

On the Discretion to Invoke Psychiatric Action: An Example of the Rule of Men

As the Rule of Law requires impartial application of rules to all men, so the Rule of Men allows discretion in the choice of rules for each case. The psychiatric disposition of alleged offenders means, first, that the legal and psychiatric authorities are free to seek or avoid psychiatric participation in the criminal process, and second, that they have wide and arbitrary powers to judge a person's sanity.

Until charged with an offense Pound's sanity had never been questioned. In other words, the issue of commitment never arose in his role as private citizen. It is important to keep this in mind, because the subsequent psychiatric picture of him implied that the diagnosis of Pound's paranoia was a purely medical finding, unrelated to his indictment.

What were the grounds for this diagnosis? The main ones were Pound's eccentric and grandiose behavior, and his belief in a "self-appointed mission to 'save the Constitution.'" To be sure, such conduct is sometimes labeled "paranoid," but not always. The labeling also depends on who the person to be diagnosed happens to be. This is where the psychiatric diagnostic and dispositional process can be shown to be crassly arbitrary. In this procedure, men do not apply established rules impartially, but instead follow their own desires.

Men other than Pound have exhibited traits of eccentricity, egocentricity, and grandiosity. Indeed, Jesus was said to have shown these "symptoms," and, accordingly, several psychiatrists diagnosed him as having suffered from paranoia. Schweitzer's study (1913), referred to earlier, was an attempt to refute the works of three psychiatrists, each of whom claimed to have established that Jesus was mentally abnormal.

De Loosten, a German, described Jesus as a "hybrid, tainted from birth by heredity, who even in his early youth as a born degenerate attracted attention by an extremely exaggerated self-consciousness combined with high intelligence and a very slightly developed sense of family and sex. His self-consciousness slowly unfolded until it rose to a fixed delusional system, the peculiarities of which were determined by the intensive religious tendencies of the time and by his one-sided preoccupation with the writings of the Old Testament" (Schweitzer, 1913, page 37).

Hirsch, an American, diagnosed Jesus as paranoid. Said he: "Everything that we know about him conforms so perfectly to the clinical picture of paranoia that it is hardly conceivable that people can even question the accuracy of the diagnosis" (page 40). To which Schweitzer added: "At the conclusion of this exposition he goes so far as to assert that no textbook on mental disease could provide a more typical description of a gradually but ceaselessly mounting megalomania than afforded by the life of Jesus" (page 41).

Binet-Sanglé, a Frenchman, also considered Jesus paranoid. Wrote Schweitzer: "Binet-Sanglé wishes to establish the secretiveness of the paranoid. He adduces as evidence of this the fact that the Nazarene regarded his Messiahship and certain points in his teaching as secrets to be veiled, gave evasive answers to questions and was brought to admit his system of delusions only under the stress of emotion, as, for example, in the proceedings at the trial" (page 44).

Schweitzer rallied to the defense. He argued, quite cogently, that it is difficult to know what the behavior of Jesus was really like, and, in any case, it must be evaluated in the context of the society in which he lived. Concluded Schweitzer: "The only symptoms to be accepted as historical and possibly to be discussed from the psychiatric point of view—the high estimate which Jesus has of himself and perhaps also the hallucination at the baptism—fall far short of proving the existence of mental illness" (page 72).

Of greater interest than the efforts of those hostile to Jesus to incriminate him as paranoid, and of those friendly to him to exonerate him, is Schweitzer's quaint protestation of impartiality. In the Preface of his book, he wrote:

That I command the impartiality necessary for this undertaking I believe I have proved by my former studies in the field of the life of Jesus. Should it really turn out that Jesus' object world must be considered by the doctor as in some degree the world of a sick man, still this conclusion, regardless of the consequences that follow from it and the shock to many that would result from it must not remain unuttered, since reverence for truth must be exalted above everything else. With this conviction I began the work, suppressing the unpleasant feeling of having to subject a great personality to psychiatric examination, and pondering the truth that what is great and profound in the ethical teachings of Jesus would retain its significance even if the conceptions in his world outlook and some of his actions had to be called more or less diseased [page 28].

Thus, instead of acknowledging his pro-religious, and especially his pro-Christian, bias, Schweitzer claimed that he was impartial.

It is of particular interest to us, as students of the Pound case, that Overholser (1948), who found Pound to be paranoid, wrote a warmly approving Foreword for the American edition of Schweitzer's book. This is an excellent example of the discretionary attitude toward psychiatric evidence. That Overholser sided with Christ and Schweitzer, rather than with the psychiatrists who called Jesus paranoid, is not surprising. We may well ponder whether, and for how long, the Superintendent of the United States Government's Number One mental hospital could retain his position if he publicly announced that Jesus was a paranoid. However, he could claim with impunity—indeed, with public approbation—that a person indicted for treason by the government was paranoid.

And so, as in Orwell's *Nineteen Eighty-four*, history is made by "bringing facts up to date." The great poet, Robert Frost, applauds as a "very nice discrimination" Overholser's pronouncement that Pound is not too dangerous to be released, but too insane ever to be tried. And so, in 1961, before a Hearing of a United States Senate Subcommittee, the following statements were made about Pound:

Mr. Creech [Counsel for the Subcommittee]. I note that you say with regard to Ezra Pound, or similar-type individuals, they should not be confined without a civil commitment proceeding. What is your feeling with regard to the psychopath?
Mr. Krash [Attorney, testifying]. Well, first, as to Ezra Pound, Ezra Pound was suffering from paranoia. He was not a psychopath. *Paranoia is an extremely severe illness, an extreme form of insanity.*
Senator Keating. He was not what we call a sociopath?
Mr. Krash. No, not at all. He was suffering from paranoid psychosis. He was insane. *There is no question whatever about that.* He was also not dangerous, may I say. [Italics added. Krash, 1961b, page 613.]

These divergent attitudes toward diagnosing Pound and Jesus are instructive. There are, of course, endless inconsistencies in applying psychiatric criteria to contemporary cases as well. If Pound was considered insane because of his extremist views, why not also Robert Welch, leader of the John Birch Society? He claimed that President Eisenhower is a Communist sympathizer, and has asked for the impeachment of Chief Justice Warren. Should Welch be committed as a "dangerous paranoid"? Of course, say some psychiatrists. In response to an article on the "Rampageous Right" in *The New York Times Magazine* (November 26, 1961) Victor Bloom, a Detroit psychiatrist, wrote (December 17, 1961): "If the group in question [that is, the Birchers and other right-wing groups] were instead an individual, and the material presented to a body of psychiatrists intent on formulating a diagnosis, that diagnosis would unquestionably be 'paranoid psychosis'" (page 4). I submit, however, that those who advocate restraining Welch on psychiatric grounds would infringe on his right to free speech just as surely as if he were tried and incarcerated on a trumped-up charge.

There are, finally, many cases of grossly peculiar behavior on the parts of defendants for which psychiatric participation in the criminal process is never sought. When the famous psychiatrist Wilhelm Reich (1954) was accused of violating the provisions of the Federal Food, Drug, and Cosmetic Act, he sent a response to the Federal Judge in Portland, Maine, with statements such as these:

According to natural, and in consequence, American Common Law, no one, no matter who he is, has the power or legal right to enjoin:
. . .
The stir to mate in all living beings, including our maturing adolescents;
The emergence of abstractions and final mathematical formulae concerning the natural life force in the universe and the right to their dissemination among one's fellow men [page 541].

Why was the question of insanity never raised in this case? Surely, these brief quotations alone provide ground enough for raising this issue. (I do not say this, of course, because I advocate psychiatric participation in this type of social problem.) Perhaps the fact that Reich was a famous psychiatrist was a deterrent. For if there are no Rules of Law for mental illness, and if the existence of mental illness can be established only by the testimony of psychiatric experts, can the sanity of the expert be questioned?

CHAPTER 18 » *Toward the Therapeutic*
State

Experience should teach us to be most on our guard to protect liberty
when the government's purposes are beneficent. Men born to freedom
are naturally alert to repel invasion of their liberty by evil-minded
rulers. The greatest dangers to liberty lurk in insidious encroachment
by men of zeal, well-meaning but without understanding.
—LOUIS D. BRANDEIS (1928)

ALTHOUGH WE may not know it, we have, in our day, witnessed
the birth of the Therapeutic State. This is perhaps the major implication
of psychiatry as an institution of social control. Accordingly, in this chapter
I shall discuss the setting up of the state as a therapeutic instrument.

The Indeterminate Sentence

For many years, penologists and psychiatrists have held that although
fixed sentences may be satisfactory for the "ordinary" criminal, they are
unsatisfactory for certain others. It is claimed that these "special" criminals
—particularly persons guilty of so-called sex crimes—should be sentenced
to indefinite prison terms and released only when "cured."

Originally, this sort of handling was advocated only for a small proportion of lawbreakers. However, the widespread acceptance of the idea that
criminals are sick, and hence need treatment, has led to the present official

212

policy of the United States Government: the therapeutic approach to justice. In a recent address, Attorney General Robert Kennedy (1961) stated:

It is encouraging to note that we seem to be turning toward a wider use of the indeterminate sentence principle. The number of defendants committed under this plan nearly doubled in the 12-month period ending June 31. This follows the national trend among the states where more than half of all defendants committed to prison are sentenced under some form of indeterminate sentence. . . . In the long run, a flexible sentencing procedure which works to rehabilitate offenders offers the best hope in the majority of cases in the federal courts [page 5].

Kennedy went on to assert that "immaturity, blind rebellion against some real or fancied social injustice"—and, *mirabile dictu*, "mental illness" —are often the "basic causes" of criminality. Hence, the logical remedy is indeterminate sentencing. It is pointless, so we are told, to release people from captivity until they have "demonstrated a capacity for assuming the responsibilities of citizenship" (page 5).

If mental illness is a cause of criminal activity, the government presumably has adequate judicial power forcibly to "treat" offenders defined as sick. This principle has been approved by the federal courts and the Department of Justice. Only the Supreme Court has not yet recognized it. Nor has it repudiated it.

The Sexual-Psychopath Laws. Those most affected by indeterminate sentence laws are the so-called sexual psychopaths and the habitual criminals. In twenty-seven States and the District of Columbia, special statutes govern the incarceration and "treatment" of sexual psychopaths and certain other persons. In many jurisdictions no conviction is necessary, the decision to incarcerate being medical or psychiatric.

Ostensibly, sexual-psychopath laws aim to eliminate from the community, and possibly "cure," so-called sexual psychopaths. In practice, there are two major difficulties. First, there is no adequate definition of psychopathy, sexual or otherwise. Second, the States have provided no facilities for the treatment of persons incarcerated because of these statutes. Both these problems have been widely discussed in the psychiatric and legal literature (see, for example, Hall, 1960).

What sorts of persons fall within the purview of this type of legislation? In Maryland, a "defective delinquent" is defined as:

An individual who, by the demonstration of persistent aggravated anti-social or criminal behavior, evidences a propensity toward criminal activity and who is found to have either such intellectual deficiency or emotional unbalance, or both, as to clearly demonstrate an actual danger to society so as to require . . . confinement and treatment [Lindman and McIntyre, Jr., 1961, page 299].

Any person convicted of two or more offenses, punishable by imprisonment, qualifies as a "defective delinquent" under the Maryland law. Lord

Russell, who went to jail in 1961 in protest against England's nuclear preparedness, and who had been imprisoned also during the First World War, would therefore have been a well-qualified candidate, in Maryland, for compulsory psychiatric therapy, or possibly for permanent incarceration as a "defective delinquent."

Despite widespread criticism of sexual-psychopath laws (Ploscowe, 1951), their basic rationale has been generally accepted. In the view of the American Bar Foundation (Lindman and McIntyre, Jr., 1961):

> A major premise of these laws is that punishment is not a deterrent to some sex offenders. This assumption has not been challenged and, indeed, is often accepted. Few psychologists or psychiatrists challenged the premise that the treatment of sexual psychopaths is the only basis for ultimate success. . . . On the whole, very few authorities have called for repeal of these laws on the ground that the underlying assumptions are incorrect [page 305].

Not only does the American Bar Foundation approve of special legislation for "sexual psychopaths," it also recommends universal acceptance of "The basic assumption that prison sentences are no deterrent to the sexual psychopath" (page 312). But why should such a fantastic claim be recognized? To do so would imply that there is a medical syndrome called "sexual psychopathy," and further, that although sexual psychopaths are not deterred by prison sentences, others, like professional criminals, are.

Like the antilibertarian psychiatrist, the Foundation maintains that determinate prison sentences are unsuitable for "sexual psychopaths." But if these men are truly sick, why should their sickness "excuse" their conduct when other kinds of sicknesses do not? Why not rather recommend merciful prison sentences for a determinate period, and the establishing of adequate "treatment" facilities in prisons? This would seem to be the logical remedy for two good reasons. First, the clients to be "treated" would be lawbreakers, defined as "patients" against their will. Second, public mental hospitals, where such individuals are supposed to be "treated," cannot, in fact, rehabilitate them. This fact leads directly to our next example of political therapeutism.

The Right to Mental Treatment

Most people in mental hospitals do not receive what one ordinarily considers treatment. With this as his starting point, Birnbaum (1960) advocated "the recognition and enforcement of the legal right of a mentally ill inmate of a public mental institution to adequate medical treatment for his mental illness" (page 499).

Although it defined neither mental illness nor "adequate medical treatment" for it, this proposal was received with enthusiasm in both legal and medical circles (Gregory, 1960). Why? Because it supported the myth that mental illness is a medical problem that can be solved by medical means.

The idea of a "right" to mental treatment is both naïve and dangerous. It is naïve because it accepts the problem of the publicly hospitalized mental patient as medical rather than educational, economic, religious, and social. It is dangerous because the remedy creates another problem: compulsory mental treatment. For in a context of involuntary confinement, the treatment too shall have to be compulsory.

What Is Psychiatric Treatment? Hailing the right to treatment as "A New Right," the editor of *The American Bar Association Journal* compares psychiatric treatment for patients in public mental hospitals with monetary compensation for the unemployed. In both cases, we are told, the principle is to help "the victims of unfortunate circumstances" (page 516).

But things are not so simple. We know what is unemployment. But we are not so clear about what is mental illness. Moreover, a person without a job does not usually object to receiving money; and if he does, no one compels him to take it. The situation for the so-called mental patient is quite different. Usually he does not want psychiatric treatment, and the more he objects to it, the more firmly society insists that he must have it.

Of course, if we *define* psychiatric treatment as "help" for the "victims of unfortunate circumstances," how can anyone object to it? But the real questions are: What is meant by psychiatric help? and, What will the helpers do should the victims refuse to be helped?

From a legal and sociologic point of view, the only way to define mental illness is to enumerate the types of behavior psychiatrists consider indicative of such illness. Similarly, we may define psychiatric treatment by listing the procedures which psychiatrists regard as instances of such therapy. A brief illustration should suffice.

Levine (1942) listed 35 methods of psychotherapy. Among these, he included "physical treatment as psychotherapy, medicinal treatment as psychotherapy, reassurance, authoritative firmness, hospitalization, ignoring of certain symptoms and attitudes, satisfaction of neurotic needs, and bibliotherapy" (pages 17–18). In addition, there are physical methods of psychiatric therapy, such as prescription of sedatives and tranquilizers, induction of convulsions by drugs or electricity, and brain surgery. Obviously, the term "psychiatric treatment" covers everything that may be done to a person under medical auspices.

The Implications of the Right to Psychiatric Treatment. If mental treatment is all the things Levine and others tell us it is, how are we to determine whether or not patients in mental hospitals receive adequate amounts of it? Surely, many of them are already being treated with large doses of "authoritative firmness," with "ignoring of symptoms," and certainly with "satisfaction of neurotic needs" (page 18). This last therapeutic agent has particularly sinister possibilities for offenders. Psychoanalysts have long maintained that many criminals commit antisocial acts out of a sense of guilt. What they "neurotically" crave is punishment. By this logic, indefinite incarceration itself might be regarded as psychiatric treatment.

At present, our publicly operated psychiatric institutions perform their services on the premise that it is morally legitimate to "treat" so-called mentally sick persons against their will. But if psychiatric treatment is compulsory, how can it be a right? I believe we ought to reformulate the problem posed by the neglect and mistreatment of the mentally ill by asking: What do involuntarily hospitalized mental patients need more—a legal right to receive treatments they do not want, or a legal right to *refuse* them?

The Therapeutic State

Although the control of sexual psychopaths and the governmental guarantee of the right to mental treatment may easily be made to appear as psychiatric problems, they are fundamentally political problems. Both programs reflect a paternalistic conception of the state. They illustrate, in the field of psychiatry, the operations of the collectivistic welfare state.

Psychiatry as a Form of Administrative Law. I have argued that psychiatric action often deprives people of their liberties. Few would dispute this. The disagreement between my views and those of certain other authorities centers on two other points. First, the defenders of institutional psychiatry claim that the mental patient is deprived of his freedom legally, in accordance with due process of law. Second, that this loss of freedom is in his own best interests. I have already dealt with the second point, and shall therefore confine myself here to the first. I shall argue that deprivations of rights by means of psychiatry are illegal and improper in exactly the same way as are deprivations of rights by means of administrative law.

What is administrative law? This expression refers to a system of settling social problems by means that have little to do with law in the Anglo-American sense of this term. In such a system, public officials, called administrators, bureaucrats, or civil servants, settle certain disputes in accordance with rules made, not by legislators, but by the administrators themselves. No less a person than the Right Honourable Hewart of Bury, Lord Chief Justice of England (1929), asserted that this was not a system of law, but of lawlessness.

Why? Lord Hewart gave several reasons. One was that it exempts public officials—acting in performance or in purported performance of their official duties—from the jurisdiction of ordinary legal tribunals. Another was that "under this system, the ordinary Courts of Justice are regarded as having no jurisdiction to deal with any dispute affecting the Government or its servants, all such disputes being within the exclusive cognizance of the Administrative Courts" (page 36).

Administrative law thus differs from the Rule of Law in that the former system lacks a body of general rules or principles that must be applied impartially in all cases. On the contrary, there is an *ad hoc* quality to each decision.

Last but not least, administrative law violates the basic Anglo-Saxon notion that a person may not be both a party to a controversy and its judge. Yet when bureaucratic agencies deal with matters like censorship or public health, they play precisely such a double role. Lord Hewart was not thinking of social control through psychiatry when he wrote this, but he might as well have been:

The official charged with the final and unimpeachable right of giving the decision is to all intents and purposes the other party to the controversy. The scheme is really ludicrous. *One of the parties is absent; there is no hearing; the decision is given by the opposite party and there is no appeal.* It is certainly a simple and expeditious way of disposing of controversial questions. But it is hardly likely to bring into existence a body of case-law that would stand examination. The other consideration—and it is fundamental—is that this invidious task, this almost impossible duty of *doubling the parts of party and judge* in the absence of the other party, is not something which is thrust from outside upon a body of reluctant officials. *No, it is they who seek it, it is they who ask for it, and it is they who contrive it. . . .* That is a sinister fact which should never be forgotten [italics added; pages 162–163].

Each of these criticisms applies with equal force to legal psychiatry (see Chapter 14).

In traditional English law, there are three remedies for a person deprived of his personal liberty: (1) The writ of habeas corpus. (2) Action of damages for false imprisonment. (3) Prosecution of the person inflicting the illegal restraint—that is, prosecution for assault.

The person deprived of his rights on account of mental illness loses all but the first of these protections. He cannot bring action for false imprisonment. For just as the official duties of bureaucrats under administrative law are exempted from judicial scrutiny, so are certain psychiatric actions (for example, certifying a patient for commitment, detaining him in a mental hospital against his will, and so on).

Similarly, the mental patient cannot sue the persons who restrain him, if they do so in accordance with the rules provided by administrative law— that is, in accordance with accepted psychiatric practices. In other words, not only administrative law but forensic psychiatry as well are systems of social control lacking a body of general rules and principles. From this basic parallel stem certain similarities between the bureaucrat and the forensic psychiatrist.

The public official is not independent. He is a civil "servant." "One would have thought it perfectly obvious that no one employed in an administrative capacity ought to be entrusted with judicial duties. The respective duties are incompatible" (Hewart, 1929, page 46). This is equally true for the institutional psychiatrist. The state hospital psychiatrist is expected to treat and help the patient; yet he is also expected to protect the public from potentially dangerous mental patients.

As an official, it is the administrator's duty "to further what he knows to be the policy of his Department. His position makes it inevitable that he should be subject to political influences" (page 46). The psychiatrist employed by a State Department of Mental Hygiene is similarly subject to political influences. The election of a Governor is often followed by great upheavals in state hospital administration. Even when such crudely political influences are absent, the state hospital physician is not independent. To advance in the system he must remain in the good graces of his superiors. It is absurd, therefore, to rely on him for impartial opinion in matters affecting the hospital and its institutionalized values.

Soviet Law as an Instrument of Mental Health

Fully to grasp the nature and significance of psychiatric influences on law and penology in the West, it will be helpful to view our subject in the perspective of Soviet law.

The Soviet state has an explicitly "therapeutic" program: it seeks to provide a better life for its people. In 1936, Stalin stated that the Communists did not build their society to restrict personal liberty but rather to make the human individual "truly free" (Hazard, 1949, page 196). Obviously, it is fruitless to dwell on the declared goal of the Marxist, the Stalinist, the Jeffersonian, and the modern therapeutic penologist, for each seems to want the same thing: "freedom" and a "better world." It will be more profitable to examine their assumptions and their actions.

As I see it, the crux of our problem seems to be this. If we regard the state as the father, and the citizens as children, there are three alternatives. First, the father may be bad and despotic: this, most people will agree, was the case in Czarist Russia. Second, the father may be good, but somewhat tyrannical; this is the way the Communist governments in Russia and China picture themselves. Third, the father may not act as a father at all, for the children have grown up, and there is mutual respect among them. All are now governed by the same rules of behavior (laws): this is the Anglo-American concept of nonpaternalistic humanism and liberty under law.

Soviet law is a deliberate instrument for educating the people. "The

Soviet judge is like a father to those who come before him with their grievances; the complainants and defendants are as youths; the law is the teacher" (Berman, 1949, page 452). What are some of the consequences of this system? In a divorce case, for example, husbands and wives become, in effect, wards of the court. Soviet divorce law is designed to unite the family, to heal its wounds (page 458). In this respect, Soviet law is indistinguishable from contemporary American family therapy (Grotjahn, 1960).

In Anglo-American law, the citizen is treated as a reasonable adult; in Soviet law, as a confused child. This is the crux of the difference between them.

The Soviet litigant or accused is treated less as an independent possessor of rights and duties who knows what he wants and must stand or fall on his own claim or defense than as a dependent member of the collective group, a youth whom the law must not only protect against the consequences of his own ignorance but must also guide and train. The Soviet judge may upbraid or counsel those who come before him, explaining to them what is right and what is wrong. The atmosphere of the trial may approximate that of our juvenile or domestic relations courts [Berman, 1949, page 457].

As a result, the criminal trial in the Soviet Union focuses on establishing whether or not the defendant was a "bad boy," not on whether a crime was committed. Berman called attention to similar tendencies in American law. He observed that, in the name of public policy, our substantive law has been steadily eroded. This is due to a change in attitude. We no longer think of the person before a court as a reasonable man. Instead, we think of him, in Berman's words, as "someone a little more helpless, a little more dependent, a little more like a youth to be protected and guided than a mature and independent man to be held to have intended the natural and probable consequences of his acts" (page 462). Accordingly, there has been a slow but steady drift in American law toward considering not only persons formally discredited by psychiatrists, but everyone, a little bit "insane," hence "irresponsible" and in need of governmental "therapy."

I think that this brief glimpse at the basic ethic of Soviet law explains, better than anything else, why the Communists have no use for psychoanalytic psychiatry and its historicist doctrines and therapies (Popper, 1944–45). The Marxists have their own brand of historicism and social therapy. In a sense, the Soviet system is nothing but a vast attempt to "treat" mankind. For that therapeutic venture, psychoanalysis is an unwanted distraction and competition, just as the formal religions of the West are unwanted distractions and competition for those who want to remake man through psychoanalysis.

Two Systems of Law: Adversary and Parental. On the relation between crime and mental illness, there is virtually no difference between the Soviet view and the American judicial-therapeutic view. The thesis which Alexander and others developed, allegedly on the basis of psychoanalytic discoveries, and which jurists like Bazelon and Bok embraced so eagerly, was familiar to the Soviets as early as 1917. They regarded crime as a "socially dangerous act, which must be met by measures of social defense—the criminal must be rehabilitated as a good citizen" (Berman, 1948, page 260). Soviet therapy aimed to provide the prisoner with useful work rather than with insight into his behavior. Corrective labor camps were organized, and, in some cases, model reformatories, where inmates could come and go freely. The so-called open hospital, recently "discovered" by American mental hospital administrators, and proudly proclaimed as a novel psychiatric approach to patients, is neither novel nor psychiatric. It is an old and sound concept of penal reform. Thus, in the handling of nonpolitical crimes the Soviets have made many innovations similar to those advocated by psychiatrically oriented American penologists.

In general, Soviet law is more subjective than ours. In cases of criminal negligence, for example, the accused is not measured against the standards of the so-called reasonable man, but against "his own standard as determined by his knowledge and intelligence" (page 260). The aim is to try the "whole man" in the context of his social relations. Thus, an ignorant man will be treated more leniently than a well-educated one. Members of the Communist party are apt to be treated more severely than nonmembers.

With all the emphasis on therapy and rehabilitation, this state of affairs should appeal to American judicial therapeutists. But let us not forget that this is a "parental" legal structure, whereas our traditional Anglo-American system is an "adversary" one (Llewellyn, 1950). Typical examples of the parental system are the Inquisition and the laws of the New Mexico Pueblo Indians. The main characteristics of such a system are:

1. The court may dig up evidence for the defendant.
2. The court may make a prior investigation of the facts.
3. The purpose of the trial is to reintegrate the offender into the community.
4. The separation between civil and criminal offenses, and civil and criminal law, tends to be blurred and may cease altogether.
5. It is considered natural and right to draw into the case any past misconduct, even though previously punished. Similarly, in judging the case, not only are the defendant's acts considered, but also his attitudes.

The parental orientation is steadily gaining ground in the American system of jurisprudence. Indeed, our laws for so-called mentally ill persons have shed the last vestiges of the adversary system and are now completely of a parental type.

Although the contrast between parental law and adversary law is clear, its implications might not be. A few examples drawn from Soviet law will suggest the kind of consequences that may result from such a system.

Berman (1949) relates the case of a young man who was treated badly by his stepmother. His father acquiesced to his maltreatment. As a result the boy grew despondent and committed suicide. Although suicide is not a crime in Soviet Russia, treating a child badly and driving him to suicide is. The parents were brought to trial: "The step-mother, a teacher, was sentenced to five years' deprivation of liberty and deprived of the right to teach for five years thereafter. The father, a neuropathologist, was sentenced to two years' deprivation of liberty, for the crime of bringing a minor to suicide" (page 460).

Here is mental health legislation with a vengeance. The example just mentioned may appeal to some because it affixes blame where it frequently belongs. Be that as it may, there is a very serious objection to such laws: they cannot be administered equitably. Where would the blame begin and where would it end? Why try only parents whose children commit suicide? Why not also hospital psychiatrists whose discharged patients commit crime or fall ill again? Or legislators for making bad laws? Indeed, why not the head of the state, for making his people unhappy? These questions are not as absurd as they might seem. Although this kind of "blaming" and "sentencing" are impractical in everyday life, they can be carried out conveniently on the dead. Perhaps Khrushchev's discrediting of Stalin should be viewed in this light. Like the parents of the suicidal youth quoted by Berman, Stalin was tried and convicted, posthumously, to be sure, of the crime of making life unnecessarily hard for his people.

Having surveyed these parallels between American and Soviet law, we may conclude, with Berman, that "the truth seems to be that the Soviets have plunged crudely and violently along a path which we are treading slowly and cautiously" (page 465). To me, our movement toward juristic despotism based on paternalistic therapeutism seems anything but slow. Perhaps this is because I am a psychiatrist. For today, only psychiatrists and mental hospital patients are familiar with the full scope of psychiatry as administrative law—and hence, in Lord Hewart's words, as administrative lawlessness. It is high time for an informed public to know it too.

Conclusions

Individualistic societies will differ from collectivistic ones only so long as they eschew governmental paternalism. The spirit of the welfare state, inflamed by the therapeutic ambitions of the mental health professions, is inimical to individual liberties and the institutions of a free society that make such liberties possible.

Today, people everywhere look to the government, not so much for freedom, as they used to in the past, but for aid in attaining their personal goals. This is as true in China and Russia in the East, as it is in England and the United States in the West. When personal goals include the maintenance of health and the cure of sickness, people expect the state to be their therapist. If, however, the state assumes the roles of parent and therapist, the citizens will be forced to assume the complementary roles of child and patient. This is bound to lead to the parentification of the government, and the infantilization of the governed. Thus, by offering to care for the health of its citizens, the state may succeed in depriving them of certain opportunities to become self-reliant individuals. The resulting political system might resemble the unhappy family: a submissive but greedy people, the spoiled children, faced by an indulgent but irresponsible and despotic government, the spoiling parent.

Legislative prescriptions, no matter how enlightened, will not create a good society. Our best chance for success still lies in a political system that is consistently noncoercive, limiting its power to the prevention and punishment of crime, and deploying its resources to providing relatively equal opportunities for various kinds of personal self-development.

CHAPTER 19 » *Proposals for Reform*
in the Mental Health Field

*The only purpose for which power can be rightfully exercised over
any member of a civilized community, against his will, is to prevent
harm to others. His own good, either physical or moral, is not sufficient warranty.*

—JOHN STUART MILL (1859, p. 13)

IN MANY parts of this book, I criticize our present legal and
psychiatric practices with respect to mental patients. Although the suggestions for improvement are implicit in the criticisms, the reader is entitled
to a systematic exposition of my views on reforms in the mental health field.

My objections to many current practices, as well as my suggestions for
reforms, rest on a fundamental proposition: We should value liberty more
highly than mental health, no matter how defined.

The Presumption of Crime and of Mental Illness

If a society wishes to combat some type of evil, it must have proper
techniques for detecting it. Such things as crime, witchcraft, bodily illness,
and mental illness have been regarded as socially undesirable, and hence
worthy of a community's remedial efforts against them. Each of these
categories denotes a departure from socially approved norms—of law,

religion, medicine, or psychiatry. However, they differ, first, in the specific norms violated; second, in the methods used to establish the violation; and third, in the techniques employed to combat the deviation.

Comparing our practices with legal deviation will prove instructive. In Anglo-American law, a person is considered innocent until proved guilty. We tend to take this rule for granted. It is, however, an arbitrary rule. In past ages, the accused rarely enjoyed such protection. Some contemporary legal codes also do not adhere to this principle. Finally, let us not forget that even in England and the United States, this formula was reversed in witch trials; the accused was considered guilty unless he could prove his innocence. In witch trials, individual liberty mattered not at all. The rule was: better to burn a thousand innocent men at the stake than let a single guilty one escape. With such immoderate emphasis on never missing a diagnosis of witchcraft, it was inevitable that brutal diagnostic methods would not only be used but accepted as legitimate.

Physicians face a similar problem of uncertainty. As judges and juries must decide whether a person is guilty or innocent, so physicians must decide whether a person is sick or well. Unfortunately, the rules governing the medical game are less explicitly formulated than those determining criminality. Physicians are taught always to suspect illness. Thus, they usually follow the rule that once a person is suspected of being ill, he should be considered sick until proved healthy (Szasz, 1961, page 100).

Before the special problems posed by so-called psychiatric diagnoses can be considered, two other issues deserve comment. First, the object of medical investigation is usually a consenting patient. In other words, the patient hires the physician to search for and detect illness, and pays him to use all "reasonable" methods necessary to accomplish this. If a person prefers the risk of undetected sickness to the dangers of certain diagnostic procedures, he is free to so decide. Thus, a person may avoid physicians altogether, or having consulted one, may consent to some procedures but not to others. He can therefore control, to some extent, the dangers of pursuing too aggressively the possibility of his sickness. In contrast, the involuntary patient lacks the authority to refuse diagnostic procedures and is therefore unprotected from its hazards.

The second issue is the social and legal consequences of a medical diagnosis. Sometimes, medical diagnoses remain confidential. Frequently, however, the nature of a person's illness is communicated to other people. When President Eisenhower suffered a coronary occlusion, his illness was public knowledge. However, medical diagnoses of this type, unlike legal judgments of criminality, do not damage the person's reputation and status in life. Hence, from a social point of view, there is no harm in falsely suspecting such illnesses. The mental anguish which a false medical diagnosis might cause may be regarded as a risk the patient assumes for wishing to take advantage of the opportunities that modern medicine offers.

The logical difficulties and social dangers of making so-called psychiatric diagnoses were discussed in detail in Chapters 2 and 3. It should suffice here to summarize the main problems.

1. Inasmuch as there are no clear or generally accepted criteria of mental illness, looking for evidence of such illness is like searching for evidence of heresy: once the investigator gets into the proper frame of mind, anything may seem to him to be a symptom of mental illness.

2. Frequently, the person suspected of mental illness does not consult the psychiatrist voluntarily. In this respect he differs from the ordinary medical patient, and resembles instead the person suspected of witchcraft or crime.

3. A diagnosis of mental illness may not serve the patient's interests, as he sees them.

4. The social and legal consequences of psychiatric diagnoses are unlike those of ordinary medical diagnoses.

What are we to conclude from these characteristics of the psychiatric diagnostic process? The consequences of labeling a person mentally ill may be indistinguishable from the consequences of bringing criminal charges against him and securing his conviction: in both cases the person will be incarcerated against his will. Accordingly, we shall be bound to inflict grave injustices on people if we apply the rules of the medical-diagnostic game to psychiatry: that is, if we readily suspect (mental) illness, and, once having suspected it, assume that it is present unless it is proved absent. If we are to respect human dignity and rights, the model for the rules of the psychiatric-diagnostic game must be our traditional legal maxim: Every person should be considered mentally healthy (innocent) until he is proved mentally sick (guilty).

My proposals for reform are animated by the wish to extend to the so-called mentally ill the traditional safeguards for personal dignity and liberty embodied in the Constitution.

I have divided my suggestions into two groups—long-range and short-range objectives. Practical necessities require this division. It is inadvisable to depart suddenly and radically from habitual methods of handling social problems. For example, one of my suggestions is to eliminate involuntary mental hospitalization. As a short-range goal, this is impractical. However, as a long-range goal it is not. If, then, some of my short-range proposals fall short of the ethical ideal which libertarian thinkers have set for us, and which I support, it is because I agree with Popper (1945), that "piecemeal social engineering" is the most desirable method for effecting social change.

Long-Range Goals

The underlying purpose of these reforms is to restore to the hospitalized mental patient the full range of his constitutional rights.

1. *Involuntary Mental Hospitalization Should Be Abolished.* All provisions for involuntary mental hospitalization should be abolished. Like the institution of slavery, the institution of hospital psychiatry, as we know it, must go.

This is a radical idea. But it is a goal worth attaining. The full import of my recommendations cannot be appreciated unless it is contrasted with other approaches to this problem.

Most important among these is the American Bar Foundation's proposal. This group urged that "The degree of mental illness which justifies involuntary mental hospitalization should be clearly expressed in the statutes" (Lindman and McIntyre, Jr., 1961, page 40). This seems reasonable, but it is not. It disregards the fact that thus far jurists and psychiatrists have been unable to agree on even a qualitative definition of mental illness. It is therefore unreasonable to ask for a quantitative definition of the severity of mental illness precise enough for the purposes of law enforcement.

Despite the good intentions, such a proposal, if enacted into law, would only invite more verbal gymnastics from psychiatrists. The result would be greater psychiatric discretion and less justice.

Legal provisions for so-called psychiatric emergencies are, of course, necessary. I believe that the existing provisions for dealing with medical emergencies and with crimes are adequate. Psychiatric emergencies fall into one of two categories. The passive, stuporous, uncommunicative patient is one type. Legally, he should be treated like the unconscious medical patient. The other is the aggressive, paranoid person, who threatens violence. Legally, he should be treated like a person charged with an offense; psychiatrically, it would be desirable, of course, if he were not incarcerated in an ordinary jail, but in a prison-hospital, where he could receive both medical and psychiatric attention.

True psychiatric emergencies are rare. They constitute only a small proportion of cases of involuntary hospitalization. Moreover, in this group, the patient often suffers from bodily illness or intoxication—for example, brain tumor or diabetic hypoglycemia. Such patients should therefore be hospitalized in medical, not mental, hospitals. Like hospitalization for medical emergencies, this type of confinement should last only until the patient regains his powers.

In the scheme I am proposing, two classes of people could no longer be forced to submit to psychiatric hospitalization. The first is composed of persons threatening to commit suicide; the second, of those considered mentally ill by others, who refuse to submit to psychiatric treatment. Later, I shall discuss the individual who is said to be "dangerous to himself and others."

2. *The Hospitalized Mental Patient Should Not Lose His Human Rights.* Mental hospitals, both private and public, should be restricted to the care of consenting, voluntary, adult patients. Both the hospital and the patient should be treated as independent, contracting parties. Patients should be free to enter or leave the hospital at will. Similarly, psychiatrists and psychiatric hospitals should be free to refuse to accept patients they do not want. In brief, the power of both patients and psychiatrists should be curtailed. Thus, patients should be deprived of the power to coerce psychiatrists, for example, by a threat of suicide; psychiatrists should be deprived of the authority to coerce patients, for example, by a threat of commitment. The power of both parties should be limited by law to persuasion. If persuasion fails, each should be allowed to act autonomously, in its own best interests.°

The therapeutic tasks of such voluntary psychiatric institutions might range from social rehabilitation to intensive individual psychotherapy. However, protection of the public from harm by so-called mental patients would *not* be one of them. There would be no need—indeed, it would be absurd—to copy the penal model. Psychiatric hospitals, like school dormitories, medical hospitals, museums, or personal homes, would be at once "open" and "closed." Like the inhabitants of these places, those in mental hospitals would be fully responsible for their acts. Mental hospital personnel should have no more concern about the antisocial conduct of their patients than should, say, a medical school faculty have of its students.

The mental hospital should be a new kind of institution, resembling neither prison nor medical hospital. Its purpose would be to provide the kind of help rendered today by many psychiatrists, psychologists, and social workers. These services are more comparable to those obtainable in certain schools, hotels, vacation resorts, and aboard ocean liners, than to those furnished by ordinary hospitals. Accordingly, in mental institutions (the term "hospital" would only be distracting) few physicians would be needed, and they would care only for bodily diseases. Until new standards are developed, personnel for this sort of organization should be recruited from those who demonstrate interest and skill in this type of work, not from those who meet the existing, but irrelevant, institutional qualifications.

This type of institution would be unsuitable for many persons who are now confined in mental hospitals. Those who break the law, but are now classified as mental patients, should be held in what I call "prison hospitals."

° So long as hospitalized mental patients are regarded as children, and psychiatrists their parents who are largely responsible not only for their welfare but for their conduct toward society as well, the psychiatrists shall be compelled to exercise autocratic controls over their charges. The basic structure of the bargaining situation (Schelling, 1960) between these two parties is faulty and requires change.

Children regarded as mentally ill would also require another kind of facility. Minors do not have the legal rights of adults. Hence, a "therapeutic" program designed especially to safeguard the legal rights of adults would be inappropriate for them. Finally, the mentally retarded, whether child or adult, would also need a different type of institution.

3. *The Insanity Plea Should Be Abolished.* The reasons for not considering mental illness an excusing condition for crime were set forth in Chapter 10. Not only do I believe that mental illness should never be accepted as a release from criminal responsibility, but also that it should never be the ground for a refusal to try a person charged with an offense. Everyone accused of breaking the law should be tried. This sweeping statement requires clarification.

I believe we should continue to adhere to the principle that a person should not be tried unless he can understand the charges against him and can assist in his own defense. It might be argued that if a person is in a catatonic state—mute, immobile, and perhaps unable even to feed himself—he should not be put on trial. The point of my argument is this: the reason for not trying such a person is that he is unable to assist in his own defense—not that he is schizophrenic.

My thesis is that psychiatric considerations *as such* are irrelevant to the conduct of a trial. The psychiatric expert may be allowed to testify on certain facts or observations, but not on psychiatric disease or criminal responsibility. Because such a modification would, in effect, abolish the special psychiatric plea (the insanity plea), and the special psychiatric disposition (not guilty by reason of insanity), there would be little need for psychiatric testimony. Extreme psychiatric conditions, such as a catatonic stupor, make it obvious that a person is unfit to stand trial; hence no psychiatrist is needed to make that determination. On the other hand, such conditions are usually temporary, and lead either to death or a remission of symptoms. Trial would thus be postponed only until gross behavioral incapacity disappeared. A person with "mental illness" of less than extreme proportions should not be declared unfit to stand trial. No two people are equally capable of defending themselves against criminal charges. Hence, even if some so-called mental illnesses should impair a person's capacity to defend himself—others, however, might improve it—it would be no more logical not to try a person for this reason than for relative lack of education. Surely, a cleaning woman, accused of political subversion, cannot defend herself as well as a professor of political science. This, however, does not prevent us from trying her. Thus, even if so-called mental illnesses were to impair a person's ability to defend himself, we could not, on this basis alone, declare him unfit to be tried, unless we were to limit the privilege of standing trial to the most highly educated members of society.

In sum, then, all persons charged with offenses—except those grossly disabled—should be tried. The emphasis here is on gross disability: it should be readily apparent or easily explicable to a group of lay persons, like a jury. The claim that trial may endanger a defendant's physical or mental health seems to me preposterous. Such a claim can *always* be made, and therefore, except for gross disability, should never be allowed. If found innocent, the defendant should be set free, even though considered mentally ill. If he is found guilty, he should be sentenced, according to the law. Finally, if the accused is declared both guilty and "mentally ill" he could be cared for in institutions suitably equipped and staffed.

Comments. The scheme I have outlined would eliminate the confusion between mental sickness, defined as an illness-like phenomenon—and criminality, defined as lawbreaking. Obviously, these concepts and phenomena are not mutually exclusive. However, we must distinguish between mental illness and crime, not because our theories of human conduct demand it, but because the ethic of a free society requires it. The hybridization of mental hospitals with jails undermines the security of every person's constitutional rights. The undoing of this hybridization, with the consequent separation of institutions for voluntary care from prisons, will guarantee that if a man keeps within the law, he cannot be deprived of his liberty. And it will guarantee, also, that if he does break the law, he will lose his liberty for a limited period only.

Such reforms will be difficult to implement if we maintain our hypocritical attitudes toward the problem of mental illness, and especially toward suicide. The standard contemporary justification for involuntary mental hospitalization is that the person is "dangerous to himself and others." This phrase combines two quite unrelated issues. In a free society, a person must have the right to injure or kill himself. I think Mill was right when he asserted that there is no moral justification for depriving a person of his liberty in order to treat him. If a man wants to kill himself, he can always do so. Thus it is actually impossible to deprive men of their "right" to kill themselves. Some efforts to prohibit suicide, like those of the Roman Catholics, are at least honest. In the United States, however, the attitude toward suicide is hypocritical. If a person kills himself, his suicide tends to be viewed as evidence of mental illness, and as an event that might have been prevented. In the mental hospital, however, the occurrence of suicide is accepted with equanimity, as a risk inherent in "mental illness." To see the problem of suicide only from the medical point of view is to be blind to its moral and psychosocial aspects.

While being "dangerous to oneself" should never be considered a legitimate reason for depriving a person of his liberty, being "dangerous to others"—if it involves breaking the law—is the best reason for doing so. One of the main functions of society is to prevent violence among its members. Thus, if so-called mental patients commit violence, or threaten to do so, they should be treated for what they are—lawbreakers.

Judicial sentencing of lawbreakers does not deprive us of the opportunity of also trying to help them. Even if we accept the argument that many criminals are mentally sick, it does not follow that they should be in mental hospitals rather than in prisons. Mental hospitalization of offenders should not be, and cannot be, a substitute for prison reform.

If we sincerely desire that prisoners be rehabilitated, so that they become useful members of society, instead of hardened criminals, what is to prevent us from doing so? As Bixby (1961) pointed out, this can be achieved by decent and humane treatment of criminals. It need not be done under the guise of quasi-medical psychiatric therapy.

While we go to great lengths to cut off a prisoner's contact with free society, the European nations do everything possible to minimize isolation from the outside world. Visiting and mail regulations are liberal; furloughs to go home are not unusual; and many prisoners are on a status of *semiliberté* which allows them to go out daily to private employment and return at night without escort. These practices, together with shorter sentences, extensive use of open institutions, and a genuine effort to give prisoners as much freedom of choice as possible, serve to reduce the danger of turning men into convicts [page 7].

The desire to treat decently those who break our laws does not require or justify turning prisons into mental hospitals. Mental hospitalization of offenders, however sincerely advocated, can only aggravate an already bad situation in both our penal and psychiatric institutions.

Short-Range Goals

The basic aim of the short-range goals which I suggest is to improve the bargaining power of the mental patient in his dealings with psychiatrists and others.

1. *The Antagonistic Character of the Relationship Between the Involuntary Mental Patient and the Psychiatrist Should Be Frankly Recognized and Publicly Acknowledged.* We must begin by candidly acknowledging the role of the hospital psychiatrist vis-à-vis his patient. Such a psychiatrist, especially if he works in a state hospital, is not the patient's agent. The law, the mental patient, and the public must cease to look on hospital psychiatrists—and perhaps even on current psychiatry as a profession—as the patient's helpers and friends. To be sure, sometimes they *try* to be. But more often they are the patient's adversaries. Perhaps this is a shocking statement. I shall try to explain it.

The relationship between hospital psychiatrist and mental patient is one of oppression disguised as benefaction. The institutional psychiatrist, though not necessarily the patient's enemy, is neither his friend nor his therapist. I believe that there is a conflict between them.

Let us compare this with the struggle between industry and labor at the turn of the century. To solve that problem, American legislation embraced the principle that workers have a right to organize and strike. I believe that mental patients should have a similar opportunity to protect themselves against the psychiatrists who coerce them.

One reason why this has not happened is that mental patients despised their own identities. (Until recently, the American Negro had the same problem.) This has led them to dissociate themselves from their fellows, and to identify with their aggressors. Clifford Beers's (1908) life story, including his founding of the National Committee for Mental Hygiene, is a good example of this. Though ostensibly wishing to help mental patients, Beers actually despised them. When Beers was first hospitalized, only an attendant treated him with decency and kindness. Nevertheless, he despised attendants. He showed interest only in psychiatrists, especially prominent psychiatrists.

Wrote Beers (1908): "Of course, an insane man is an insane man, and while insane, *should be* placed in an institution for treatment, but *when that man comes out* he should be as free from all taint as the man who recovers from a contagious disease and again takes his place in society" (italics added; page 218). Facts are said to be stubborn, and indeed they are. Launched under what seem to me false pretenses, the Mental Hygiene Movement has had no ameliorative effect on the plight of the mentally ill in America. I suspect it may even have retarded worthwhile efforts in this field. It is significant, perhaps, that this movement should have been started by a man who admired authority and force, and was contemptuous of human rights.

Like Beers, few mental patients care to think of themselves as mental patients. They prefer to believe that there was never anything wrong with them, or that they have recovered. Beers spoke of having "found his mind." This implies that mental patients *qua* mental patients do indeed deserve the bad treatment that has traditionally been their lot: they deserve something better only if unjustly committed or if recovered. This posture robs the mental patient, and those wishing to help him, of arguing effectively that he is deserving of human rights, even in his role as mental patient.

The mental patient's disdainful attitude toward the mentally ill also robs him of the incentive to unite with his fellows. Benjamin Franklin warned the Founding Fathers that if they fail to hang together, they shall hang separately. Mental hospital patients have consistently failed to hang together. As a result, they have indeed hanged separately. Nevertheless, psychotherapeutic efforts with mental patients—directed at educating them to revolt for independence—might yet instill in them the understanding, and the hope, that their rights may be secured not only by assimilation into the more privileged majority but also by effective protest.

The problem of "liberating" the hospitalized mental patient from his psychosocial, religious, and legal shackles is exceedingly complex and difficult. It calls to mind the socioeconomic problems of so-called underdeveloped nations. Because of a low level of education and industrialization, it is extremely difficult for such nations to get going in a cycle of increasing education, increasing industrialization, and increasing democratization. Similarly, it is often a lack of social feeling or interest that causes a person to become a mental patient. This deficiency prevents him from engaging in organized social activity with his peer group. Hence, he remains isolated, and the benign circle of organizing, learning, acquiring new skills, approaching equality with his superiors, never begins. Like underdeveloped nations, mental patients need "foreign aid." But such "aid" can easily be destructive. The mental hospital patient needs help, but not in the form of housing, food, and tranquilizers. Such aid only perpetuates the infantile, disabled role for the patient.

In my opinion, what the mental hospital patient needs is to acquire the spirit of liberty and, indeed, of revolt. I propose that we supply him with an agency to foster this.

2. *A Watchdog Agency Should Be Created to Protect the Rights of the Mental Patient.* The mental patient needs an agency to counteract the power of the hospital psychiatrists. It should consist of a corps of lawyers, psychiatrists, social workers, and perhaps others, and be independent of the department which operates the state mental hospitals.

This agency would assist persons threatened with commitment and those already hospitalized. For instance, when a wife files a petition to commit her husband, it would be the duty of this agency to provide capable persons to investigate the possible alternatives to commitment. They could help the husband obtain a separation or divorce from his wife, or help him rebut her accusations of mental illness.

This agency would thus be entrusted with the task of promoting the "mental patient's" interests as he defines them. The hospitalized mental patient could call on the resources of this facility if he should wish to leave the hospital, obtain a driver's license, or secure any other lost rights or privileges which he is ill-equipped to regain.*

Lack of commitment to this enterprise, or inadequate financial support for it, could lead only to failure. However, if properly implemented, I am confident that such an agency could foster a significant improvement in the conditions of the mentally ill in America.

3. *Mental Hospitals Should Cease to Be "What Else" Institutions.* When people do not know "what else" to do with, say, a lethargic, withdrawn adolescent, a petty criminal, an exhibitionist, or a difficult grandparent— our society tells them, in effect, to put the "offender" in a mental hospital (Becker, 1962).

---

* There is a similarity between the agency I am proposing and the practice of supplying defense counsel to indigent persons accused of crimes, by the federal courts, by local bar associations, and by legal-aid societies. (See in this connection Gellhorn [1961, p. 38].)

To overcome this, we shall have to create an increasing number of humane and rational alternatives to involuntary mental hospitalization. Old-age homes, workshops, temporary homes for indigent persons whose family ties have disintegrated, progressive prison communities—these and many other facilities will be needed to assume the tasks now entrusted to mental hospitals. Some of the money and effort spent on mental hospitals should be devoted to such enterprises. As matters now stand, mental hospitals only waste our valuable human resources and funds. They also endanger our trusted political institutions and our personal liberties.

4. *The Hospitalized Mental Patient Should Retain as Many of His Rights as Possible.* At present, the involuntarily hospitalized mental patient is virtually without any rights. In theory, the committed mental patient is not incompetent. In fact, however, he may be treated as if he werè. If the hospital psychiatrists decide to deprive the patient of a right, there is little he can do about it.

As an alternative, we could experiment with partial deprivation of liberty for the mental patient. In this connection, involuntary military service may serve as a model. A person conscripted for military service loses some of his freedom—for example, the freedom to pursue his occupation, to select his home or clothes, to move about freely, and so forth. He retains, however, the right to marry and divorce, to enter into valid contracts, to vote, and many others. The point is that the conscripted soldier surrenders *only* those rights which are required by the duties of soldiering. The deprivation of rights that cannot be justified on this ground—for example, censoring the serviceman's mail or reading materials—offends our sensibilities. It would also be unconstitutional.

The same principles should apply to the loss of freedom incurred by the involuntarily hospitalized mental patient. Let us suspend only those freedoms which are necessary for settling the dispute that caused him to be defined as mentally ill. For example, instead of committing the alcoholic husband who abuses his wife, the court could order him to cease annoying her. Subsequent violations of such orders could be treated by judicial, not psychiatric, penalties. The court would thus regulate only the patient's relationship with his wife. His liberty would remain otherwise unimpaired. Accordingly, the husband would not be forced to submit to psychiatric treatments he does not want; nor would he be prevented from working, making telephone calls, writing letters, and so forth. Current commitment laws deprive such a person of all these freedoms. In sum, the committed patient's loss of rights should be partial rather than almost total.

5. *Involuntary Mental Hospitalization Should Be Discouraged.* Frequently, when people do not know what to do about a human problem, they may try to resolve it by committing one of the parties to the conflict to a mental hospital. Thus, husbands may prefer committing their wives to legally separating from them or divorcing them. Physicians may prefer committing a difficult patient to withdrawing from the case. Policemen and

district attorneys may prefer committing certain offenders to prosecuting them. And so forth.

In each of these instances, commitment offers—at least temporarily—an easy solution to a difficult situation. If, however, we consider involuntary mental hospitalization a serious evil, we should search for more effective means of coping with these problems. Moreover, if we do not discourage easy commitment, there will never develop the social tension which may be necessary for creating adequate facilities for, say, indigent old people.

The present practice of admitting to the state mental hospitals people of all sorts, whether "mentally ill" or not, represents the persistence of an old habit: this was the function of the insane asylum in the eighteenth century. This practice cannot be justified any longer. Under the same roof, how can psychiatrists provide for the needs of such diverse persons as juvenile schizophrenics and indigent old people dying of cancer, drug addicts and depressed housewives, petty criminals and religious paranoiacs? They cannot—but often justify what they do by humanitarian motives and the pressure of social needs. In the long run, however, inadequate or misdirected stopgap measures of this kind serve only the self-seeking interests of psychiatrists, for whose services such tactics generate an ever increasing demand. At the same time, the welfare of the sufferers is sacrificed.

6. *People Should Be Educated About the Dangers of Mental Hospitalization.* My final proposal, if adopted, would reverse many current practices in mental health education. Instead of comparing mental health to physical health, and exhorting people to use psychiatric services as much as possible, I suggest clarifying and emphasizing the differences between them. These I consider the more significant. Likewise, I suggest stressing the similarities between the roles of prisoner and mental hospital patient. If we expect people to conduct themselves responsibly, we must tell them not what is "good" for them, but what is true.

I believe, further, that so long as our mental health facilities are inadequate, we should not urge people to use psychiatric help as much as possible. Instead, we should emphasize the risks. Curiously, psychiatrists seem to be quite immune to the hazards that threaten nonpsychiatric physicians and various medical facilities (such as hospitals and pharmaceutical companies). Radiologists and surgeons, for example, who do not inform a patient of the dangers of a procedure, fail to secure "informed consent" (Hirsch, 1961). This renders them liable for damages if the patient is harmed as a result of their actions. In other words, the physician will be liable for damages even if his performance was faultless, and the patient suffered merely as a result of risks inherent in the procedure.[*]

[*] I think this is entirely reasonable. A person cannot intelligently decide whether to avail himself of medical help if he is apprised only of the potential benefits, but not of the dangers, of the treatment to which he contemplates submitting himself. The physician who exaggerates the beneficial effects of a particular form of therapy, and

This principle was the basis for awarding compensation to the persons who contracted poliomyelitis from injections of Salk vaccine manufactured by the Cutter Laboratories. "In the Cutter suit, no judge or jury has found the laboratory negligent in its manufacture of the vaccine, but damages were awarded on the grounds that *Cutter had breached an implied warranty since the vaccine caused the disease it was intended to prevent.*" (Italics added. *Modern Medicine*, December 11, 1961, p. 2.) Because the public was not warned of the risk of contracting polio from the vaccine, the court held the manufacturer responsible for an "implied warranty."

The Cutter affair, tragic though it was, is a relatively minor instance of injuries incurred by patients as a result of their having been misinformed. The faulty polio vaccine affected less than fifty persons, some only slightly. Compared to the thousands, perhaps hundreds of thousands, who have been injured by mental hospitalization—without having been fully apprised of the risks inherent in this form of "treatment"—the Cutter affair will seem like a raindrop in the ocean. Approximately a quarter-million people are hospitalized in mental institutions every year. A significant proportion is injured as a result. Nevertheless, contemporary mental health propaganda (it cannot very well be called "education") is silent about the hazards to which a person exposes himself when he enters a mental hospital, or to which he exposes those whom he causes to be hospitalized. It may be argued that there are certain unavoidable risks inherent in mental hospitalization. Indeed there are. But this only emphasizes that all those responsible for recommending or providing this type of care ought to be duty-bound to inform the patients, and the public, of the exact dimensions of this risk. If, instead of providing accurate information, they indulge in spreading propaganda—then, I submit, they should be held legally responsible for the damages that may result from mental hospitalization.

Indeed, this may be the best way to improve the social position of the mental patient. For attorneys specializing in cases of personal injury resulting from medical procedures, there is a large, unexploited field for suits for damages caused by psychiatric action. To be sure, suits for false commitment are almost always ineffective. In such cases, compliance with the form of the law protects the psychiatrist. However, there is no such protection for the psychiatrist whose patient enters the hospital voluntarily, and then discovers he cannot leave, or is otherwise injured. It is against the rules of the psychiatric hospital game, as it is currently played, to give prospective patients, or their relatives, accurate information about the social dangers (for example, from loss of civil rights, injury to chances for future employment, and so on) inherent in mental hospitalization. Hence, patients incurring such injuries would, I think, have valid cause for civil action against the psychiatrists responsible for not informing them.

---

minimizes or withholds information about its dangers, misleads his patient. If, as a consequence, the patient is injured, it is only fair to hold the physician responsible.

Conclusions

Pinel may have struck the chains of iron from the hospitalized mental patient, but the chains of the law are still fastened on him. Who shall sever these legal restraints? Perhaps it will be attorneys. They have already helped the medical patient in his struggle against coercive practices by (nonpsychiatric) physicians. Although unpleasant for doctors, malpractice suits fulfill two important functions. First, they secure money damages for patients injured as a result of certain medical procedures. Second, they underscore the fact that a person's body belongs to himself, not to his physician. The latter assumes paternalistic control over it at his own peril.

In psychiatry, and especially in the hospital practice of it, physicians frequently exert paternalistic control over their patients. Perhaps through litigation, attorneys could dislodge this oppressive relationship. An individual's personality, no less than his body, should belong to him, not to his self-appointed psychiatric guardians. Anything that would move us toward this goal would contribute immensely to the furtherance of human liberties, and hence, in my view, to better "mental health" as well.

Summary and Conclusions

American society had not the faintest idea of what it was doing or where it was going. . . . It had not yet got a glimpse of the elementary truth which was so clear to the mind of Mr. Jefferson, that in proportion as you give the State power to do things for you, you give it power to do things to you; and that the State invariably makes as little as it can of the one power, and as much as it can of the other.
—ALBERT J. NOCK (1943)

Psychiatry as a Science

The Nature and Scope of Psychiatry. Psychiatry is one of the sciences concerned with the study of human social behavior. It is generally distinguished from other sciences studying the same phenomena—that is, from anthropology, economics, politics, psychology, and sociology—by the claim that psychiatry is both a biological and a social science. Its scope is thus often said to extend all the way from biochemical studies of cellular metabolism at one end, to studies of child-rearing practices or religions at the other. So long as these studies are undertaken for the ostensible purpose of shedding light on mental health and illness, all are considered contributions to psychiatry. Although at first glance such an approach may seem an expression of laudable eclecticism and broad-mindedness, it is objectionable for two reasons. First, if psychiatry is so defined, few activities having any bearing on man—and there are few that have none—will fall outside its scope. However, if a class contains too many members, its value as a logical device will be proportionately small. Second,

237

such a broad definition of psychiatry is useless in actual practice. Workers engaged in research on the cellular metabolism of erythrocytes in schizophrenics do not speak the same language as psychiatrists who testify as expert witnesses in criminal trials. To refer to both as psychiatrists, and to believe that they are engaged in a kindred enterprise, is as accurate as calling both mathematicians and automobile mechanics "physicists."

It may be thought that the precise nature and scientific status of psychiatry concern only psychiatrists and workers in allied fields. But this is not so. Through the fabric of law—and specifically through mental health legislation—the definitions of mental health and illness, and the activities of psychiatrists, become matters of vital import for everyone. Hence, a clear understanding of the nature and uses of psychiatry is indispensable for any rational inquiry into the relationship between psychiatry and jurisprudence.

Although a few psychiatrists are engaged in research in biochemistry or genetics, the work of most psychiatrists is quite different. Generally, psychiatrists study human behavior and also try to alter it. The purpose of the law is similar: it is to regulate, and sometimes to change, human behavior. Thus, the practical activities of psychiatrists and of lawyers—as legislators, judges, or practicing attorneys—have much in common.

Psychiatry and Language. Since verbal communication is one of the principal methods psychiatrists use for changing behavior, words play an important role in this discipline. Indeed, even the basic question of deciding whether certain types of social behavior should or should not be considered manifestations of an *illness* illustrates the significance of language in behavioral science, and also in so-called psychological treatment. For whether we consider a person sick, sinful, criminal, or none of these, will, of course, affect profoundly our attitude toward him as a social being. Accordingly, the efforts of psychiatrists to define increasing numbers of human conditions as sickness were not dictated by purely scientific considerations. Originally they were due to a wish to enlist a therapeutic, rather than a punitive, attitude toward certain persons. Later, however— and this may be the case today—they stemmed from a desire, on the part of psychiatrists, to gain social control over increasing areas of human conduct.

An illuminating way to say some of these things has been suggested by Hardin (1961). To display the differences between the natural and behavioral (or social) sciences, he proposed that we distinguish three classes of truth: (1) that which is unaltered by being said; (2) that made true by being said; and (3) that destroyed, or falsified, by being said.

The first type of truth is characteristic of natural science. The proposition that "Apples fall to the earth" is unaffected by my belief or disbelief in it.

The second type of truth, which is made true by being said, has long been familiar to social scientists. For example, a stock will increase in value following the prediction of its rise by an influential investment advisory service. This sort of thing has been called the self-fulfilling prophecy. Almost every significant communication may bring about this effect. For this reason, psychiatric, social, and economic diagnoses or prognoses may profoundly influence the predicted events. Consider such psychiatric terms as "predelinquent" or "addict." The former is an invitation to the delinquent role. The latter implies an uncontrollable craving for a drug, and a need for it or for external supervision of the craving.

The third type of truth, which is destroyed by being said, is exemplified by mystical, poetic, or religious "truths." We call a myth a "myth" in order to destroy it. When Marx called religion an "opiate of the people," and Freud described it an "illusion," they wanted to discredit, by semantic methods, what many regarded as truths.

The destruction of certain "truths" (of type three) by words is particularly relevant to our problems in psychiatry and law. Hardin suggested that this process may be a kind of semantic therapy that "seeks to cure diseases of words with words. If we represent 'diseased words' by words$_d$, and 'therapeutic words' by words$_t$, we may say that words$_d$ are cured by words$_t$. The disturbing question is this: in the course of time, will words$_t$ metamorphose into words$_d$?" (page 18).

The answer is an emphatic Yes! For example, malingerers were originally renamed hysterics, in an effort to improve their lot. Soon, however, the word "hysteria" was just as damaging as the word "malingering" had been. In brief, a word$_t$ had become a word$_d$. In our day, this happened to the entire conception of mental illness. Although this transformation of "diseased" words into "therapeutic" ones, and back to "diseased" again, is of minor importance in the private practice of psychoanalysis, in institutional and legal psychiatry it has far-reaching consequences.

Psychiatry as a Social Institution

The private psychotherapeutic situation must be distinguished from institutional psychiatry, just as private religious belief must be distinguished from organized religion. Institutional psychiatry is similar to other social institutions. Simultaneously it strives to discharge its official duties and to extend its own power and rewards. The success of every social institution depends largely on the encouragement and protection, or the enmity, of other social institutions, the law especially. Traditionally, psychiatric hospitals have been jails. Thus, to say that they have received legal protection would be a vast understatement. They have been, and continue to be, an integral part of the legal order.

Psychiatrists are entrusted by society, through its legislators and laws, to apprehend and confine, as well as to "diagnose" and "treat," persons considered mentally ill. This fact confronts us, once more, with the crucial role of mental illness as a conceptual and semantic bridge between psychiatry as theoretical science and as social engineering.

There is a crucial difference between medical and mental hospitalization. As a rule, the former requires the patient's consent, while the latter does not. Involuntary mental hospitalization, diagnosis, and treatment are usually justified on two separate grounds: therapy and social protection. It is alleged that in mental illness the disease deprives the patient of the capacity to appreciate his own needs; hence, involuntary treatment is called for. It is held, further, that the mentally sick person is dangerous; hence, the patient's restraint is necessary for the protection of those around him—his family, friends, society generally.

In my opinion, the therapeutic justification is almost completely untenable. Institutional psychiatry should only make "help" available to people. The argument that so-called mentally ill persons do not know what they "really" need for their own welfare is deceptive. Everyone, not only so-called mental patients, may want things which, in terms of other values, may not be good for him. To select one group of persons and treat them as incapable of defining their own interests can only be harmful to them. In this respect, I agree with Mill (1859) that "each person is the proper guardian of his own health, whether bodily, or mental and spiritual. Mankind are greater gainers by suffering each other to live as seems good to themselves, than by compelling each to live as seems good to the rest" (page 18).

Against this argument, the advocates of involuntary mental hospitalization raise the second justification: protection of the public. This, of course, is a legitimate interest. But, following in the libertarian tradition, I hold that a person should be deprived of his liberty only if he is proved guilty of breaking the law. No one should be deprived of his freedom for the sake of his "mental health."

My criticism of psychiatry, as a form of social control, is intended to reach beyond the harm it has actually caused. It seeks to alert the reader to the spirit of do-goodism which animates contemporary psychiatric reforms. It is against this spirit that I direct the main force of my criticism. Why? Because I do not believe that we can effectively promote "mental health"—unless this term be a euphemism for psychiatric despotism—with coercion and deceit. And yet, coercion and deceit are rampant in the legal and social uses of psychiatry—beginning with the pseudomedical definitions of mental illness, and ending with the tyrannical abuses of psychiatric power in cases of political and other offenses. Again, Mill was prophetic when he wrote that "the spirit of improvement is not always a spirit of liberty, for it may aim at *forcing* improvements on an unwilling people; and the spirit of liberty, insofar as it resists such attempts, may ally itself locally and temporarily with the opponents of improvement; but the only unfailing and permanent source of improvement is liberty, since by it there are as many possible independent centers of improvement as there are individuals" (page 102).

Psychiatry and the Criminal Law

Psychiatric participation may be invited at every point in the criminal procedure. What are the reasons for this eagerness to involve psychiatry in the criminal law?

Two main reasons were suggested: first, to escape from the guilt feelings associated with meting out punishment; second, to improve the administration of justice. The first motive is easy to understand; and its effects are not difficult to trace. The second deserves further comment.

Lawyers, psychiatrists, and laymen seem to agree nowadays that the role of psychiatry in criminology is to improve the administration of justice. This is a noble cause. But how does psychiatry help to promote it?

The principal weapon in psychiatry's alleged struggle to improve justice has been the battle cry that criminals are mentally sick. Hence, they need treatment, not punishment. In my judgment, this has not been an effective method of social reform.

Formerly, insanity was an excusing condition. A person "temporarily insane" was acquitted of the crime with which he was charged. He thus escaped punishment. Nor was he forced to submit to psychiatric hospitalization or treatment after acquittal. Here we recognize "insanity" as what Hardin called a therapeutic word. The therapeutic word "insanity" was intended to cure the diseased word "criminal." In this it was often successful. In the Leopold and Loeb case, for example, Darrow introduced the issue of mental illness to save the defendants from the death sentence. Instead of being executed, they were sentenced to life imprisonment. After thirty-three years in prison, Leopold regained his freedom. (Loeb was killed in jail by a fellow prisoner.)

Rarely is mental illness used any more as a therapeutic word. It has become a diseased word. Inasmuch as offenders incarcerated in mental hospitals are likely to serve a longer term than those sentenced to prison, the word "insanity" has changed from an excusing condition to an incriminating one. In the past, defendants used to "plead" insanity in the hope of ameliorating their fate. Today they are often "charged" with it. The fundamental transformation of insanity from an excusing into an incriminating condition explains an important current problem: Defendants may wish to plead guilty, but may be prevented from doing so by district attorneys and judges who insist on charging them with insanity instead. The force of this semantic metamorphosis is sustained by the time-honored practice of confining indefinitely in mental hospitals those who are considered mentally ill.

In addition to the punitive functions that psychiatrists serve, the psychiatric attempt to improve criminology is bound to fail for a more basic reason. The focus on the mental state of the offender distracts attention from many nonpsychiatric, especially moral and social, aspects of crime and from efforts to deal with them.

For example, psychiatrists have succeeded in diverting attention from the fact that, in the United States, the scope of criminal activity is so vast that defining criminality as mental illness is tantamount to classifying everyone as mentally ill. This cannot help matters. However, by considering certain types of criminality as symptoms of mental illness, but not others, the psychiatrists are allowed, in effect, to be arbiters of law and morals.

If society wishes to provide prisoners with decent food, or a library, or psychological counseling, it ought to do so directly, by acknowledging the need as well as the wish to supply it. If there is a need for better penal care—and no doubt there is—psychiatrists should lobby for its recognition, and not for a redefinition of all criminality as sickness.

But even these considerations skirt the most pressing issues. Our criminal statutes contain many provisions which mock not only our elementary concepts of human psychology, but our sense of decency. Most of the states have not abolished the death penalty. In sixteen states it is legally possible to execute children as young as seven; in three the minimum age is eight; and in three others, ten (Gavzer, 1962).

Consider, further, the laws governing divorce and birth control. In New York State it is possible to obtain a divorce legally only by committing perjury. Who is to judge these laws, and by what standards? We should not confuse law with morality, nor believe naïvely that obeying a law is necessarily good, and breaking it bad. By concentrating on the offender, psychiatrists imply, perhaps unwittingly, that nothing else in society requires psychiatric analysis or attention. However, as social scientists and critics, psychiatrists should, it seems to me, begin by stating the sort of legal order they desire. They should then use ordinary channels of communication and persuasion, used by other moral and social forces in society—for instance, the organized religions—to enlist support for their brand of morality. Should it be a humanistic ethic, psychiatric efforts to attain it could be considered truly liberal. As it is, so-called psychiatric liberalizations—for instance, of abortion laws, commitment procedures, or the disposition of criminals—are attempts to medicalize, not to liberalize. Such measures give doctors, and especially psychiatrists, the power to control aspects of personal conduct that, according to the liberal ethic, should be in the hands of self-responsible individuals. As a result, people are no freer than they were before. Their constraint has merely been transferred from judicial to psychiatric authorities.

Psychiatry and Constitutional Rights

Historically, the Constitution and the Bill of Rights were designed to regulate the relationship between the people and the government. As a rule, therefore, problems of constitutionality arise only if there is a conflict of interests between these two parties. Conflicts between individuals—for example, between husband and wife, or physician and patient—are generally regarded as problems of civil law. The Constitution is essentially irrelevant in settling such disputes.

But what is a purely interpersonal transaction, of no concern to the government? Through the years, there have been many interpretations. Slavery was considered constitutional until the Thirteenth Amendment became the law in 1865. Similarly, before 1890, certain oppressive business practices were constitutional; after the passage of the Sherman Act, they were not. The constitutionality, or lack of it, of certain kinds of psychiatric practices will thus depend on our conceptions of the nature of these acts and on our moral judgments of them. If we accept the claim that psychiatric actions are, by definition, therapeutic, we foreclose the possibility of rational inquiry into the potential conflicts between coercive psychiatric "therapies" and individual liberties. The Constitution does not frown on "doctors treating patients." Hence if psychiatric practices can be brought within the meaning of this phrase, psychiatrists will have carte blanche to violate constitutional rights.

And yet, both legal and psychiatric arguments can support the thesis that constitutional protection is pertinent and that it should apply to the treatment of hospitalized mental patients.

First, the legal argument. Although it is true that constitutions generally speak to governments, rather than to individuals, the conduct of the latter is regulated by laws and statutes that enforce the "will" of the constitution. One of the central problems of constitutional law is to decide if an action is governmental or private. In hospital psychiatry the difficulty is not very great, for the majority of psychiatric institutions are owned and operated by state and federal governments. On this basis alone, psychiatric "treatment" in these buildings should be regarded as instances of governmental action.

Certain psychiatric actions—like the indefinite sentencing of some persons to mental institutions—have been held constitutional on the ground that deprivation of liberty was incidental to therapy, and not intended as punishment. But is this not a misinterpretation of the Constitution? In a discussion of the problem, not of mental illness, but of persons injured by being labeled "security risks," Pfeffer (1956) emphasized that it was "only because of historical accident that the procedural safeguards developed in criminal proceedings; there is nothing inherent in criminal proceedings that makes procedural safeguards relevant only there" (page 162). Accordingly, such safeguards should apply to persons hounded by congressional committees, but legally innocent of wrongdoing; and also, to persons "hounded" by psychiatrists. Why should this be necessary? Because, as Pfeffer so aptly stated, "democracy differs from despotism in that in the former the government deals fairly with the people in *all its relations with them—not in a selected few*. A government that adheres to fair play only part of the time is only a part-time democracy" (italics added; page 162). Psychiatric practices, especially with hospitalized patients, violate my concept of fair play.

The psychiatric argument against the thesis that the Constitution is irrelevant to the way the mental patient is handled is briefly this. It was suggested earlier that what we call mental illnesses are not diseases; nor, for the most part, are psychiatric actions treatments. This is not to say that psychiatrists may not do much to help people. However, not everything that helps a person is *ipso facto* a form of *medical treatment*. For example, many Americans might consider it helpful if divorce could be obtained by mutual consent; if abortion and gambling were legalized; or if the capital gains tax were abolished; and so forth. Yet, we do not regard these as medical therapeutic measures.

When Is Social Action Therapy? The crux of our problem is not only the constitutionality of recent mental health laws, but of our traditional mental health practices. Involuntary mental hospitalization has always been considered constitutional, for people have believed it was right to segregate so-called mentally sick persons from the rest of the population, both for their own welfare and that of society. Just as the Dred Scott decision of the Supreme Court betrayed, in 1857, the people's sense of value about slavery, so our traditional acceptance of involuntary mental hospitalization as constitutional reflects the current sense of value about the mentally ill.

There are many similarities between the discrimination against Negroes and against mentally ill persons. So long as the Negro was considered an inferior being, it was reasonable to treat him as a ward of the state, instead of as a citizen. Hence, slavery could be justified on what were essentially therapeutic grounds; and it could thereby be made compatible with the Constitution. Similarly, if we accept the idea that the hospitalized mentally ill are, on account of their "mental disease," significantly inferior to others, we shall rob them of their constitutional rights in the name of taking care of them.

What seems to emerge is the realization that certain so-called therapeutic ventures have gradually assumed a supralegal existence in our society. Many public acts in the mental health field are accepted as legal, and constitutionally valid, solely because they are regarded as therapeutic. Laws sanctioning involuntary mental hospitalization and the control of so-called sexual psychopaths are two examples. However, these measures, and others like them, should raise this question: When do ostensibly remedial social actions serve the purpose of moral reform, and when those of medical therapy? Only the former must comply with the legal requirements of constitutionality; the latter need not. Let us consider some examples.

The Eighteenth Amendment to the Constitution (1920) regulated the manufacture, sale, and consumption of alcoholic beverages. If its aim was to combat alcoholism, why was it not presented as a therapeutic measure? Had this been done, no constitutional Amendment would have been necessary. Instead, people who contributed to the "disease" called "alcoholism" could have been treated by the same repressive measures by which mental patients were treated, and continue to be treated today. This, of course, would have been recognized as a totalitarian invasion of civil liberties.

We might consider the Supreme Court's desegregation decision in 1954 in the same light. The purpose of this decision was moral and social reform. It reflected the view that the Negro is an American citizen, and therefore the federal government should not tolerate discrimination against him in public schools. But if we assumed a therapeutic rather than a moral attitude toward this issue, we could circumvent the whole problem of constitutionality. We could then claim that separate but equal public schools for Negroes are pathogenic, in a quasi-medical sense: they make the Negro mentally sick. Having gained this foothold, we could reason that it is the duty of the government to intervene, to protect a group of people from being "made sick"—as it were "poisoned"—by certain social arrangements. Governmental interference with segregation would then be similar to governmental interference with the distribution of, say, contaminated milk. Desegregation could thus be advocated as a therapeutic measure, to which the Constitution is irrelevant.

Of course, one could also argue that segregation should be maintained for reasons of health—that is, to prevent white people in the South from becoming "mentally sick." Hence, Negroes should be segregated—perhaps even reduced to slavery—to preserve the "mental health" of the whites.

I hope these examples illustrate that so-called therapeutic actions, especially in the mental health field, always involve moral values and constitutional rights. The therapeutic mold in which such actions are cast serves only to hide the political and socioethical aspects of both the dilemma and the remedy for it.

Freedom in Games and Rules of Irrelevance. One of the distinguishing features of a democracy is its legal recognition of a *minimum* of relevant distinctions among people. This is what we mean when we say that before the law all men are equal. Thus, such variables as age (assuming that the person is an adult), education, economic status, race, and religion are irrelevant in judging a man's conduct. Goffman (1961b) suggested that we call this feature of games "the rules of irrelevance." It matters not, for example, "whether checkers are played with bottle tops on a piece of squared linoleum, with gold figurines on inlaid marble, or with uniformed men standing on colored flagstones in a specially arranged court square, the pairs of players can start with the same positions, employ the same sequence of strategic moves and countermoves, and generate the same contour of excitement" (pages 19–20).

The Rule of Law is an attempt to use the rules of irrelevance to the full for personal distinctions in the legal game. The contrary principles— such as administrative law or the therapeutically oriented laws of the United States and Soviet Russia—seek to reduce these rules, and to recognize *as relevant* an increasing range of personal distinctions. Such differences will thus possess the power to modify the legal encounter.

This is a fundamental issue. All the evidence—political, psychological, and social—points to the fact that the integrity of the game as well as the liberty of the players to move freely within the rules are promoted by everything that increases the rules of personal irrelevance. In opposition to this point of view, there are those who argue, on allegedly humanitarian grounds, that such arrangements are "unfair" to some of the players. The adherents of this view try to alter the game by handicapping the stronger players, in order to give a "more equal" chance to the weaker ones. This procedure is fraught with many dangers, not the least of which is giving great discretionary powers to the handicappers.

In this discussion, I have advocated that we follow the classic traditions of Anglo-American legal thinking, and try to increase, not diminish, the rules of irrelevance in our legal system. At present, the greatest violation of these rules occurs in connection with the issue of mental illness. In matters of law and public policy, a person's race, religion, occupation, marital status, and so forth, are usually not considered significant, but his mental status is. I believe the rules of irrelevance in these games should include the person's mental status as well. Except perhaps in cases of the grossest kinds of defect—which in practice would make it impossible for a person to participate in games such as marriage, work, or crime—people should be treated seriously in the activity in which they are engaged. This means that they should be held responsible for whatever moves they make in the games they play. A person's mental condition should be relevant only to his own attempts to improve it, but irrelevant to our judgment of his social conduct.

Psychiatry and Public Policy

Because the concept of mental illness is infinitely elastic, almost any moral, political, or social problem can be cast into a psychiatric mold. Thus, despite the fact that in a free society public policy should be determined by democratic political methods within a framework of constitutional guarantees, this process may easily become transformed into a bureaucratic administration of public health measures.

In recent decades, outstanding psychiatrists have included among the symptoms of mental illness such things as a dislike of Negroes and Jews, or a preference for Fascism over democracy. Every ethical principle has thus been interpreted as a sign of either mental health or sickness. Unfortunately, many people have accepted this view.

The State as Therapist. The main result of our escape from moral and political responsibility has been to bestow magical expectations on the health professions, especially psychiatry. At the same time, our image of the nature and function of government has changed profoundly. We have come to look on the state as parent and physician. Just as children expect their parents to take care of them, and patients expect their physicians to cure them, so people have come to expect their government to take care of them when they are in need, and to cure them when they are sick. The concept of sickness, moreover, is so broadly interpreted that there is an expectation of therapeutic assistance from the government not only for medical illness, but for moral, political, and social discomforts as well.

When, for instance, an outstanding antisegregationist leader is physically attacked by a Negro woman, her act is judged insane. When a famous American poet embraces Fascism, and is charged with treason, he is considered mentally ill and is imprisoned in a mental hospital. The examples could be multiplied.

Why do we act this way? Why do people let psychiatrists sell them the shoddy pseudomorality of a mental health ethic? In his celebrated work *Escape from Freedom,* Erich Fromm (1941) suggested an answer. He described how, in the aftermath of the First World War, many people, especially in Germany and Italy, did not want political freedom. Instead, they yearned for the security which they believed a totalitarian government could provide.

It seems to me that the increasing intrusion of psychiatry into public policy is both the cause and the result of a similar situation. People seem tired of their moral responsibilities. They try to escape from their moral freedom by delegating their responsibility for moral decisions to the experts in human relations, especially the psychiatrists. Of course, this is self-deception. But just as counterfeit money, if accepted as real, can buy many things, so this type of moral counterfeiting may work, and may be a powerful social force, until it is unmasked.

Where is this moral counterfeiting leading us? In controversies over public policy, we substitute judgments of mental health for judgments of moral value. I believe we are thus heading toward moral Fascism. Unlike political Fascism, which sought its justification in the value of the "good of the state," and subordinated everything else to it, the moral Fascism we have been cultivating subordinates all to the value of the "welfare of the people." The expression "welfare state" is an understatement. For the state is fast becoming not merely an administrator of the general welfare, but a veritable therapist. Recently, a psychiatrist (Hume, 1961) proudly extolled the promise of "community psychiatry," the ultimate purpose of which is to "transform a state into a great therapeutic community."

Herein lies the gravest danger to personal liberties. For, in its therapeutic aspirations, the government is not content to offer help. In the classic spirit of "doctor knows best," it is ready and willing to coerce the "patient" to submit to treatment if he refuses to cooperate. Thus, the parallel between political and moral Fascism is close. Each offers a kind of protection. And upon those unwilling to heed peaceful persuasion, the values of the state will be imposed by force: in political Fascism by the military and the police; in moral Fascism by therapists, especially psychiatrists. I think that we are rapidly heading toward the Therapeutic State. Perhaps we are there already, and have not realized it.

What is the evidence that the state is assuming therapeutic functions? Two examples were cited to support this thesis: statutes that affect the sexual psychopath, and the notion that the hospitalized mental patient should have a right to treatment. I should like to amplify my previous arguments on this subject.

Sexual Activity Between Consenting Adults: Should It Be a Crime or a Right? Our attitudes toward sexual practices illustrate our profound moral indecision. Do we wish to favor personal autonomy and responsibility or conformity to a strict moral code? If the former, we should regard an adult person's body as his own property, so long as his behavior does not directly injure his neighbor (Szasz, 1960b). This would require us to abstain from interfering, legally or psychiatrically, with sexual activities between consenting adults, even though they may violate our personal or collective judgment of the nature of normal sexual conduct.

If we favor social conformity to a moral code, we shall accept responsibility not only for our own moral conduct but also for our neighbor's. It will then be proper to punish a person if his sexual activity, though not directly injurious to anyone else, violates our standard of normal sexuality.

We often claim, and perhaps even believe, that we favor the former ethic. But both our laws and our psychiatric practices contradict this. Thus, in the United States, not only homosexuality but all kinds of sexual acts deemed "unnatural" are also illegal, even between consenting adults. In many states, some sexual acts between husband and wife are prohibited by law. Of course, many of these laws are not enforced. But that should not blind us to some important facts.

Legislators are notoriously wary of trying to repeal laws prohibitive of sexual conduct. It is bad politics to do so. Furthermore, the so-called sexual-psychopath laws *are* enforced. This means that certain sexual activities between consenting adults may be grounds for apprehending a person and sentencing him to a penal institution disguised as a therapeutic one. Once again, this procedure is justified on the basis that it is necessary both for the protection of society and for the well-being of the "patient." This is an instance of coercive psychiatric "treatment," modeled after the fashion of public health measures. But since this sort of danger is quite unlike the plague or smallpox, these laws are therapeutic deceptions. They are the manifestations of what I call moral Fascism: certain types of conduct are prohibited, and violations are punished not by penal but by so-called therapeutic sanctions.

If the state were to favor the ethic of personal autonomy and responsibility, it would be compelled to adopt a less restrictive attitude toward adult citizens whose social conduct, though perhaps morally offensive, is harmful to no one. Indeed, such an attitude toward homosexuality was advocated in England by the Wolfenden Report (Home Office, 1957). This study criticized the view that homosexuality was a disease, and proposed "that homosexual behavior between consenting adults in private should no longer be a criminal offense" (page 25). This is in the tradition of libertarian political thinking, which holds that "unless a deliberate attempt is to be made by society, acting through the agency of law, to equate the sphere of crime with that of sin, there must remain a realm of private morality and immorality which is, in brief and crude terms, not the law's business" (page 24).

Contemporary American mental health legislation is moving in exactly the opposite direction. It seeks to impose close supervision on personal conduct, as if so-called mental sickness were a serious public health hazard.

Only in this light can we understand why people advocate, justify, and perpetuate widespread infringements of personal liberties in the name of mental health. Today, the desire to achieve mental health justifies almost any measure, just as in the Middle Ages the goal of true faith justified the Inquisition. The guardians of this precious "health" have wide discretionary powers. In Massachusetts, for example, a person may be committed to a mental hospital—to be cared for by *doctors*—if psychiatrists testify that he "is likely to conduct himself in a manner which clearly violates the established laws, ordinances, conventions, or morals of the community." Is there anyone who could be shown *not* to belong in this class of persons? Ostensibly, this is a piece of rational legislation. So far as I know, the psychiatrists in Massachusetts have not criticized it. Perhaps they were even instrumental in drafting it. Many other states have similar statutes. I submit that such laws are scientifically absurd. Moreover, it is alarming how similar they are to certain legislative acts in Nazi Germany, about which Justice Robert Jackson (1946) wrote: "Laws were enacted of such ambiguity that they could be used to punish almost any innocent act. It was, for example, made a crime to provoke 'any act contrary to the public welfare'" (page 472). Is the Massachusetts law punishing social deviance by commitment less ambiguous?

Psychiatric Treatment: Opportunity, Punishment, or Right? The proposition that hospitalized mental patients should have a right to psychiatric treatment is another manifestation of the image of the state as therapist. Having parentified the state, and infantilized the citizen, it follows logically that the mentally sick person—who is considered even more childish than his healthy counterpart—should be entitled to treatment by the state. In this way, the model of the juvenile court is extended to the mental hospital, and potentially to the entire community.

The juvenile court, however, is not a court at all. Rather, it is like a surrogate parent to the child whose parents have defaulted on their job. The juvenile court takes over, and tries to do what is supposedly best for the child. The adult mental patient in the state hospital is treated in a similar way. As representatives of the state, the state hospital physicians assume custody over him, and ostensibly try to do what is best for him.

Unfortunately, all this is pure hypocrisy. Most people find it hard enough to be decent parents to their own children. When they assume parental functions toward others, they are apt to coerce, exploit, and oppress them.

There is still another difficulty. How could an enterprise as poorly defined as psychiatric treatment be considered a legal right? Who would decide what is therapeutic and what is noxious? It is widely accepted today that involuntary mental hospitalization may itself be therapeutic. But, might it not be harmful sometimes? Moreover, might it not be therapeutic for some hospitalized mental patients to be set free? These are crucial considerations. For if we define as "therapeutic" acts which restrict a person's freedom, we shall establish the conditions for therapeutic Fascism. The question can now be clearly posed: Should individual liberties be guaranteed by laws, or should they be contingent on meeting certain standards of mental health?

Finally, we must realize that the moral character of the concept of mental illness influences the so-called treatment methods of psychiatry. If the mentally healthy person is one who is independent and rational, how can methods employing deceit and fostering submission be "therapeutic"?

Psychiatry and Law as Instruments of Social Change. In committing people to mental hospitals, or testifying concerning their mental fitness, psychiatrists act as agents of social control, comparable to policemen, judges, or prison personnel. The point to remember, once more, is that this is done under medical auspices. Although the Massachusetts statute, cited above, defines mental illness in entirely nonmedical terms, it empowers physicians to diagnose and manage this condition. This is an arbitrary act, justifiable only on grounds of social expediency.

The same State defines contraception as a moral and legal matter, not a medical one. Actually, if the laws of the Commonwealth of Massachusetts were seriously enforced, a physician prescribing a contraceptive diaphragm to a married woman with fifteen children could be considered a law-breaker, and hence, under the statute, mentally sick. He could thus be committed to a mental hospital, for "treatment" for his misguided ideas on the ethics of contraception.

Absurd? Of course. It would be a mistake, however, to dismiss lightly the satirical description of an existing situation. Satire is intended to expose the inner workings of a social mechanism which people prefer to ignore. The mechanism here is the use of ostensibly psychiatric interventions serving as technics of social control.

Where Do We Go from Here?

Most issues have at least two sides. Problems of psychiatry and law are no exception. Proponents of current mental health practices, and the self-styled liberals who advocate a far-reaching psychiatrization not only of our criminal law but of the whole fabric of our society, are well able to defend their side of the argument.

In this book, I have tried to present my views. I made every effort to be accurate, but I doubt if I succeeded in being impartial. I think the cause of impartiality is better served by expressing one's ideas conscientiously and forcefully, and then letting people have free access to other points of view and reasoning. Where we, as a people, shall go from here will depend on the ultimate interplay of the information available on this subject and its use.

We should guard against two basic mistakes in our relations with so-called mental patients. One is the fear that they may harm us. If strong enough, this fear can easily justify segregating and punishing those whom we consider "dangerous." The other is the discomfort that the mental patient's behavior may cause us. If intense enough, it may justify intolerance toward personal idiosyncrasies and so-called aberrations of behavior. And yet, labeling conduct as sick merely because it differs from our own may be nothing more than discrimination disguised as medical judgment.

In brief, we should not be carried away by our therapeutic ambition, even though it may be animated by generous motives. If people are evil, it is fair to judge them so, and to protect ourselves from their evil deeds; but not by evil means. If people commit crimes, we are justified in apprehending them, and, if guilty, punishing them; but not by criminal methods of crime detection and punishment. If people are sick—let us say mentally sick —we should protect ourselves from the effects of their sickness; but not by means which, when employed by others, we consider sick.

Before taking leave of the reader, I should like to supplement these general considerations about our attitude toward reforms in the mental health field with a brief outline of a more practical suggestion.

Fashions in Litigation. Fashions change not only in women's wear, but in most human pursuits. The law is no exception. In the early decades of the century, the public was dazzled by the heroic defense of unpopular causes and people. The great Clarence Darrow was the outstanding example of this legal fashion. He defended atheistic Darwinists against devout fundamentalists; labor organizers against industrialists; the pampered sons of millionaires who killed for fun against outraged public opinion; the rights of Negro "agitators" against a predominantly white citizenry; and so forth. In the 1920's and 1930's, it was the fashion to be the legal champion of the underdog. Darrow was its Dior.

The next major trend started in the 1940's, and has been the vogue since then. The outstanding designer of this legal pattern is Melvin Belli. He became the champion of another kind of underdog—the person disabled by personal injury. Suits seeking compensation for injuries in automobile accidents, industrial mishaps, or in the course of medical diagnoses and treatments attracted increasing public attention. This kind of litigation became the vogue.

Physicians and medical organizations often regard the attorney who specializes in malpractice cases as their enemy. This is a parochial view. In my opinion, this type of litigation and the widespread attention it has attracted have improved the relationship between physician and patient. Like institutional psychiatrists today, physicians in the past tended to treat their patients as children. They acted as if the patient's body had been entrusted to them, to treat as their professional consciences saw fit. Accordingly, physicians felt little or no obligation to inform their patients of their diagnoses or the treatments planned.

Following one's conscience, especially if it is reliable, is still a good policy, but the threat of legal penalties has reminded physicians that this is not enough. They must also respect the wishes of their patients. Malpractice suits against physicians have thus succeeded in making a traditionally despotic kind of relationship more democratic.

Regardless of how sound physicians consider their medical actions, or how many colleagues agree with them, they can no longer treat patients without first obtaining their "informed consent." If we value the patient's personal autonomy and his responsibility for his health care, then the achievements of Belli and his colleagues are comparable to those of Darrow.

It is desirable not only for medical patients but also for so-called mental patients to assume maximal responsibility for their health care. Physicians who interfere with their medical patients' autonomy by treatir.g them involuntarily are guilty of an offense, punishable by both civil and criminal statutes. Why should this not apply to similar offenses against mental patients? Surely, at least in some cases, people have the right to be informed about their own mental condition, and to decide if they wish to submit to mental treatment. If they do possess these rights, then their infringement—by treating patients against their wishes, even though the treatment may be medically correct—should be considered an offense punishable by law.

It is often said that in a democracy a person can secure his legal rights only if he is prepared to fight for them. Like the Jews in Nazi Germany or, until recently, the Negroes in the South, mental patients have been afraid to stand up and fight for their liberty. This, more than anything else, may have made them, and may continue to make them, convenient scapegoats. Instead of protecting their own integrity, they have, as the psychoanalysts put it, identified with the aggressor. Perhaps the most effective method for securing the mental patient's liberty—not to become mentally well, but, if need be, to remain as he is and yet enjoy the rights of an American—lies in legal action against his oppressors.

Epilogue

MORE THAN ever before, men are preoccupied with the question: What is the good life? Usually they have no answer. But even when men know the answer, or think they do, there remains the question: How can we achieve the conditions for the good life?

Man has made little progress toward mastering these challenges. We, in the West, who perhaps have been the most troubled by them, have taken refuge in certain solutions, which are not answers to the questions, but distractions from them. I refer to the solutions contained in words such as *help, progress, security, therapy,* and last but not least, *welfare.* The main attraction of marching under the banner of these words is that the marchers need not trouble themselves about where they are headed.

For Americans, even the First World War was a therapeutic enterprise. They fought not just to win it, but to make the world safe for democracy. Since then, the idea of helpfulness has run amok, not only in the United States but apparently throughout the world. This is not altogether new. The medieval witch-hunters were also animated by motives of helpfulness. But in those days, people were more clearheaded about what they wanted to help others achieve. For instance, it was obvious that the inquisitors were not medical therapists. They sought to improve only the spiritual well-being of their "clients"; for their bodily health they cared nothing. Today, however, many therapeutic enterprises are undertaken without either the helpers or the potential helpees having the foggiest idea of what they are up to. To be sure, words like *democracy* or *mental health* may be waved about like flags on the Fourth of July, and for the same reasons. Such symbols make people feel well, but do not make them wiser.

Most modern ventures in social therapy have left the "patient" sicker than he was. And for good reason. Man seeks "therapy" from experts as if he were an anesthetized surgical patient. In human affairs, however, this does not work. In morals, politics, and psychiatry, experts are useful only

254

as sources of information. They can advise or inform a society, but they cannot govern it.

What I am trying to say is that achieving dignity and individuality is always a personal affair. It can be facilitated or hindered; but, in the end, each person must do it for himself.

In a sense, an individual is the end product of the *decisions* he has made. He who fails to make decisions, for the consequences of which he is responsible, is not a person. The ego, the self, the personality—call it what you will—comes into being and grows through the process of making responsible decisions. This, it seems to me, is also the point of the parable of Man's fall from Divine Grace.

Let us regard the story of Adam and Eve not as literal history but as a poetic hint at the psychosocial transformation of man and human nature. What does it tell us? After indulging in his morally expensive meal, Adam was never the same again: Henceforth he knew right from wrong! In brief, his self developed from irresponsibility and naïve trust in God, to responsibility and, let us hope, skepticism toward authority.

Did Adam have a *choice* in deciding whether or not to eat the apple? The parable implies that he had. Why, then, did he choose to accept the serpent's offer rather than God's? If Adam were a patient and I his analyst, I would probably tell him that he decided as he had because he preferred that course to its alternative. In other words, might we not say that Adam *chose* knowledge and responsibility, and, to gain these, rejected God's seductive offer of a perpetual vacation in His garden? He thus refused help, tranquillity, welfare—even psychiatric therapy, in a sense—if these benefits could be obtained only at the cost of sacrificing truth and responsibility. Instead, he chose the joys of knowledge and mastery, and the sorrows of loneliness and guilt. What had been God's plaything became a *person*.

If Adam had committed his crime in England after 1843, his offense might have been exculpated on the basis of the M'Naghten formula. For clearly Adam did not know right from wrong. He became aware of that distinction only *after* the crime. And yet, if he could not distinguish one of his interests from another, why did he choose venturesome knowledge in preference to secure ignorance?

Adam rejected God's offer of irresponsible bliss. If Adam refused to be seduced by God—who tempted him no less than did the serpent—why should we accept our fellowman's offer of much shoddier therapies, intended to relieve us of our moral burdens, which, in our ignorance, we fail to recognize as our very humanity.

Many modern psychotherapists have adopted, as their credo, Socrates' declaration that the unexamined life is not worth living. But for modern man this is not enough. We should pledge ourselves to the proposition that the irresponsible life is not worth living either.

Bibliography

Acton, J. E. E. D. (1887). Acton-Creighton Correspondence. In Acton, J. E. E. D.: *Essays on Freedom and Power.* (Selected and with a New Introduction by Gertrude Himmelfarb.) Pp. 328–345. New York: Meridian, 1955.

Alexander, F., and Staub, H. (1929). *The Criminal, the Judge, and the Public: A Psychological Analysis.* (Revised Edition with New Chapters by F. Alexander. Original Edition Translated by G. Zilboorg.) Glencoe, Ill.: The Free Press and the Falcon's Wing Press, 1956.

Alexander, L. (1954). The commitment and suicide of King Ludwig II of Bavaria. *Amer. J. Psychiat.,* 111: 100.

American Civil Liberties Union (1962). Goals for 1962. With a Review of 1961 (an information sheet).

Arens, R. (1961). Statement. In *Constitutional Rights of the Mentally Ill* (1961), pp. 207–217.

Baily v. *McGill* (1957). 247 N.C. 286, 100 S.E. 2d 860.

Baldwin, J. (1959). In Baldwin, J. (1961), p. 115.

Baldwin, J. (1961). *Nobody Knows My Name: More Notes of a Native Son.* New York: Dial Press.

Barzun, J. (1959). *The House of Intellect.* New York: Harper, p. 260.

Bazelon, D. L. (1960). The awesome decision. *Saturday Evening Post,* Jan. 23, pp. 32 ff.

Bazelon, D. L. (1961). *Equal Justice for the Unequal.* (The Isaac Ray Award Lecture.) Mimeographed.

Becker, E. (1962). *The Birth and Death of Meaning: A Perspective in Psychiatry and Anthropology.* New York: The Free Press of Glencoe.

Beers, C. W. (1908). *A Mind That Found Itself: An Autobiography.* Seventh Edition. Garden City, N.Y.: Doubleday, 1956.

Belknap, I. (1956). *Human Problems of a State Mental Hospital.* New York: McGraw-Hill.

Berman, H. J. (1948). The challenge of Soviet law. Parts I and II. *Harvard Law Rev.,* 62: 220.

Berman, H. J. (1949). The challenge of Soviet law. Part III. *Harvard Law Rev.,* 62: 449.

Bettelheim, B. (1960). *The Informed Heart: Autonomy in a Mass Age.* New York: The Free Press of Glencoe.

Biddle, F. (1960). *Justice Holmes, Natural Law, and the Supreme Court.* (The Oliver Wendell Holmes Devise Lectures, 1960.) New York: Macmillan, 1961, p. 71.

Birnbaum, M. (1960). The right to treatment. *Amer. Bar Assoc. J.* 46: 499.

Bixby, F. L. (1961). Treating the prisoner: A lesson from Europe. *Federal Probation,* 25: 7.

Bloomberg, W. (1960). A proposal for a community-based hospital as a branch of a state hospital. *Amer. J. Psychiat.,* 116: 814.

Bok, C. (1959). *Star Wormwood.* New York: Knopf.

Bowman, K. M., and Rose, M. (1951). A criticism of the terms "psychosis," "psychoneurosis," and "neurosis." *Amer. J. Psychiat.,* 108: 161.

Braceland, F. J. (1961). Statement. In *Constitutional Rights of the Mentally Ill* (1961), pp. 63–74.

Braceland, F. J., and Ewalt, J. R. (1961). Excerpts from testimony presented on behalf of the American Psychiatric Association. In *Constitutional Rights of the Mentally Ill* (1961), pp. 79–84.

Brandeis, L. D. (1928). *Olmstead* v. *United States,* 277 U.S. 438, 479. In Jackson, P. E. (Editor) (1962), p. 169.

Brecka v. *State of New York* (1958). 14 Misc. 2d 317, 179 N.Y.S. 2d 469 (Ct. Claims).

Brown, J. A. C. (1961). *Freud and the Post-Freudians.* Baltimore: Penguin.

Cahn, E. (1956). *The Moral Decision: Right and Wrong in the Light of American Law.* Bloomington, Ind.: Indiana University Press.

Cahn, E. (1961). *The Predicament of Democratic Man.* New York: Macmillan.

Carter v. *General Motors Corp.* (1960). 361 Mich. 577, 106 N.W. 2d 105.

Castiglioni, A. (1941). *A History of Medicine.* Translated by E. B. Krumbhaar. New York: Knopf.

Chandler, S. S. (1961). Statement. In *Constitutional Rights of the Mentally Ill* (1961), pp. 247–260.

Chasan, R. H. (1961). Statement. In *Constitutional Rights of the Mentally Ill* (1961), pp. 217–233.

Chisholm, G. B. (1946). The psychiatry of enduring peace and social progress. *Psychiatry,* 9: 3.

Cohen, M. R. (1931). Reason in Social Science. In Feigl, H., and Brodbeck, M. (Editors): *Readings in the Philosophy of Science,* pp. 663–673. New York: Appleton-Century-Crofts, 1953, p. 667.

Constitutional Rights of the Mentally Ill (1961). Hearings before the Subcommittee on Constitutional Rights of the Committee of the Judiciary, United States Senate. Eighty-seventh Congress, First Session. March 28, 29, and 30, 1961: Part 1—Civil Aspects. May 2, 4, and 5, 1961: Part 2—Criminal Aspects. Washington, D.C.: U.S. Government Printing Office.

Corwin, E. S. (1928–29). *The Higher Law Background of American Constitutional Law.* Ithaca, N.Y.: Great Seals Books Division of the Cornell University Press, 1955.

Corwin, E. S. (1948). *Liberty Against Government: The Rise, Flowering and Decline of a Famous Juridical Concept.* Baton Rouge: Louisiana State University Press.

Creekmore, H. (1961). Poet and disciple. *New York Times Book Review,* October 15, p. 32.

Davidson, H. A. (1952). *Forensic Psychiatry.* New York: Ronald Press.

De Jouvenel, B. (1953). A discussion of freedom. *Cambridge Journal,* 6: 707.

Deutsch, A. (1949). *The Mentally Ill in America: A History of their Care and Treatment from Colonial Times.* Second Edition Revised and Enlarged. New York: Columbia University Press.

Dewar, R. (1961). Escapes from a mental hospital. *Mental Hygiene,* 45: 450.

Diamond, B. L. (1956). Isaac Ray and the trial of Daniel M'Naghten. *Amer. J. Psychiat.,* 112: 651.

Dicey, A. V. (1914). *Lectures on the Relation Between Law and Public Opinion in England During the Nineteenth Century.* Second Edition. London: Macmillan, 1920, p. 264.

Diethelm, O. (1953). The fallacy of the concept: psychosis. In Hoch, P. H., and Zubin, J. (Editors): *Current Problems in Psychiatric Diagnosis,* pp. 24–32. New York: Grune & Stratton.

Douglas, W. O. (1954). *An Almanac of Liberty.* Garden City, N.Y.: Doubleday.

Douglas, W. O. (1961). *A Living Bill of Rights.* Garden City, N.Y.: Doubleday.

Durham v. *United States* (1954). 214 F. 2d, 862 (D.C. Circ.).

Eisendorfer, A. (1959). The selection of candidates applying for psychoanalytic training. *Psychoanalyt. Quart.,* 28: 374.

Eissler, K. R. (1953). Effect of the structure of the ego on psychoanalytic technique. *J. Am. Psychoanalyt. Assoc.,* 1: 104.

Fairbairn, W. R. D. (1952). *Psycho-Analytic Studies of the Personality.* London: Tavistock.

Federal Security Agency. U.S. Public Health Service (1952). *A Draft Act Governing Hospitalization of the Mentally Ill.* Public Health Service Publication No. 51. Washington, D.C.: U.S. Government Printing Office.

Feibleman, J. K. (1956). *The Institutions of Society.* London: George Allen and Unwin.

Felix, R. H. (1961). Psychiatrist, medicinae doctor. *Amer. J. Psychiat.,* 118: 1.

Ferenczi, S. (1913). A Lecture for Judges and Barristers. In Ferenczi, S.: *Further Contributions to the Theory and Technique of Psycho-Analysis,* pp. 424–434. London: Hogarth Press, Ltd., 1950.

Ferenczi, S. (1919). Psycho-Analysis and Criminology. In Ferenczi, S.: *Further Contributions to the Theory and Technique of Psycho-Analysis,* pp. 434–436. London: Hogarth Press, Ltd., 1950.

Field, S. J. (1873). *Galpin* v. *Page,* 85 U.S. 350, 368. In Jackson, P. E. (Editor) (1962), p. 197.

Fortas, A. (1957). Implications of Durham's Case. *Amer. J. Psychiat.,* 113: 577.

Frankfurter, F. (1947). *United States* v. *Paramount Pictures,* 334 U.S. 131, 180. In Jackson, P. E. (Editor) (1962), p. 390.

Freud, S. (1893). Charcot. In *Collected Papers,* Vol. I, pp. 9–23. London: Hogarth Press, 1948.

Freud, S. (1906). Psycho-Analysis and the Establishment of the Facts in Legal Proceedings. In *The Standard Edition of the Complete Psychological Works of Sigmund Freud,* Vol. IX, pp. 97–114. London: Hogarth Press, 1959.

Freud, S. (1909). Leonardo da Vinci and a Memory of his Childhood. In *The Standard Edition of the Complete Psychological Works of Sigmund Freud*, Vol. XI, pp. 57–137. London: Hogarth Press, 1957.

Freud, S. (1927). The Future of an Illusion. In *The Standard Edition of the Complete Psychological Works of Sigmund Freud*, Vol. XXI, pp. 1–56. London: Hogarth Press, 1961.

Freud, S. (1931). The Expert Opinion in the Halsmann Case. In *The Standard Edition of the Complete Psychological Works of Sigmund Freud*, Vol. XXI, pp. 251–253. London: Hogarth Press, 1961.

Fromm, E. (1941). *Escape from Freedom*. New York: Rinehart.

Fromm, E. (1958). Freud, friends, and feuds: I. Scientism or fanaticism? *Saturday Review*, June 14, p. 11.

Gavzer, B. (1962). Even a 7-year old could get death penalty in 16 states. *Syracuse Herald-American*, Jan. 7, p. 33.

Gellhorn, W. (1961). *American Rights: The Constitution in Action*. New York: Macmillan.

Glueck, S. S. (1925). *Mental Disorder and the Criminal Law: A Study in Medico-Sociological Jurisprudence*. Boston: Little, Brown.

Goffman, E. (1957). On the Characteristics of Total Institutions. In Goffman, E. (1961a), pp. 1–124.

Goffman, E. (1959). The Moral Career of the Mental Patient. In Goffman, E. (1961a), pp. 125–170.

Goffman, E. (1961a). *Asylums: Essays on the Social Situation of Mental Patients and Other Inmates*. Garden City, N.Y.: Doubleday.

Goffman, E. (1961b). *Encounters: Two Studies in the Sociology of Interaction*. Indianapolis: Bobbs-Merrill.

Goldman, R. P., and Ross, S. (1956). Our forgotten mental patients—Who are they? Part II. *Parade*, November 18, pp. 18 ff.

Goldstein, J., and Katz, J. (1960). Dangerousness and mental illness: Some observations on the decision to release persons acquitted by reason of insanity. *Yale Law J.*, 70: 225.

Goldstein, J., and Katz, J. (1962). Psychiatrist-patient privilege: The GAP proposal and the Connecticut statute. *Amer. J. Psychiat.*, 118: 733.

Goldstein, K. (1948). *After effects of Brain Injuries in War*. New York: Grune & Stratton.

Goldstein, K. (1951). *Human Nature in the Light of Psychopathology*. Cambridge, Mass.: Harvard University Press.

Goldstein, K., and Scheerer, M. (1941). Abstract and Concrete Behavior: An Experimental Study with Special Tests. *Psychological Monograph*, 53: No. 2 (Whole No. 239).

Gregory, T. (1960). A new right. *Amer. Bar. Assoc. J.*, 46: 516.

Grotjahn, M. (1960). *Psychoanalysis and the Family Neurosis*. New York: Norton.

Group for the Advancement of Psychiatry (1948). *Commitment Procedures*. Report No. 4. Topeka, Kans.

Guillain, G. (1959). *J.-M. Charcot, 1825–1893: His Life—His Works*. Edited and Translated by Pearce Bailey. New York: Paul B. Hoeber.

Guttmacher, M. (1954). The quest for a test of criminal responsibility. *Amer. J. Psychiat.*, 11: 428.

Guttmacher, M. (1961). Statement. In *Constitutional Rights of the Mentally Ill* (1961), pp. 143–160.

Guttmacher, M. S., and Weihofen, H. (1952). *Psychiatry and the Law.* New York: Norton.

Guzy v. Guzy (1959). 16 Misc. 2d 975, 184 N.Y.S. 2d, 161 (S. Ct. Queens Co.).

Hakeem, M. (1958). A critique of the psychiatric approach to crime and correction. *Law and Contemporary Problems,* 23: 650.

Hall, J. (1958). Mental disease and criminal responsibility: M'Naghten versus Durham and the American Law Institute's tentative draft. *Indiana Law J.,* 33: 212.

Hall, J. (1960). *General Principles of Criminal Law.* Second Edition, Revised. Indianapolis: Bobbs-Merrill.

Hall, L., and Glueck, S. (1958). *Cases on Criminal Law and Its Enforcement.* Second Edition (American Casebook Series, Griswold, E. H., General Editor). St. Paul, Minn.: West Publishing Co.

Hardin, G. (1956). Meaninglessness of the word protoplasm. *Sci. Monthly,* 82: 112.

Hardin, G. (1961). Three classes of truth: Their implication for the behavioral sciences. *Etc.: Rev. of Gen. Semantics,* 18: 5.

Hart, H. L. A. (1958). Legal Responsibility and Excuses. In Hook, S. (Editor): *Determinism and Freedom in the Age of Modern Science,* pp. 81–104. New York: New York University Press.

Hartmann, H. (1960). *Psychoanalysis and Moral Values.* New York: International Universities Press.

Hayek, F. A. (1957). *The Road to Serfdom.* Chicago: Phoenix Books.

Hayek, F. A. (1960). *The Constitution of Liberty.* Chicago: University of Chicago Press.

Hazard, J. H. (1949). Soviet Law and Its Assumptions. In Northrop, F. S. C. (Editor): *Ideological Differences and World Order: Studies in the Philosophy and Science of the World's Cultures,* pp. 192–207. New Haven: Yale University Press.

Henderson, D., and Gillespie, R. D. (1950). *A Textbook of Psychiatry.* Seventh Edition. London: Oxford University Press.

Hewart, L. (1929). *The New Despotism.* New York: Cosmopolitan Book Corp.

Hillenbrand, M. J. (1949). *Power and Morals.* New York: Columbia University Press, p. 22.

Hirsch, B. D. (1961). Informed consent to treatment. Medicolegal comment. In Averbach, A., and Belli, M. M. (Editors): *Tort and Medical Yearbook,* Vol. 1, pp. 631–638. Indianapolis: Bobbs-Merrill.

Hobbes, T. (1651). *Leviathan.* Part I. Introduction by Russell Kirk. Chicago: Henry Regnery, 1956, p. 27.

Hollingshead, A. B., and Redlich, F. C. (1958). *Social Class and Mental Illness: A Community Study.* New York: Wiley.

Home Office (1957). *Report of the Committee on Homosexual Offences and Prostitution* (The Wolfenden Report). London: Her Majesty's Stationery Office.

Hough v. *United States* (1959). 271 F. 2d, 458 (D.C. Cir.).

Hume, P. B. (1961). Lecture delivered at the Annual Meeting of the Southern California Psychiatric Society. Quoted in *The American Psychiatric Association Newsletter*, Vol. 14, No. 4, p. 4.

Jackson, P. E. (Editor) (1962). *The Wisdom of the Supreme Court*. Norman, Okla.: University of Oklahoma Press.

Jackson, R. H. (1946). Closing address in the Nuremberg Trial. In London, E. (Editor): *The World of Law*, Vol. II, pp. 467–506. New York: Simon and Schuster, 1960.

Jefferson, T. (1800). From a letter to Benjamin Rush. In Schachner, N.: *Thomas Jefferson: A Biography*, p. 642. New York: Thomas Yoseloff, 1951.

Jones, E. (1953, 1955, 1957). *The Life and Work of Sigmund Freud*. Vols. 1, 2, 3. New York: Basic Books.

Kecskemeti, P. (1952). *Meaning, Communication, and Value*. Chicago: University of Chicago Press.

Kennedy, R. F. (1961). Justice is found in the hearts and minds of free men. *Federal Probation*, 25: 3.

King, L. S. (1954). What is disease? *Philosophy of Science*, 21: 193.

Krash, A. (1961a). The Durham rule and judicial administration of the insanity defense in the District of Columbia. *Yale Law Journal*, 70: 905.

Krash, A. (1961b). Statement. In *Constitutional Rights of the Mentally Ill* (1961), pp. 601–624.

Krim, S. (1959). The Insanity Bit. In Krim, S. (Editor). *The Beats*, pp. 60–77. New York: Fawcett, 1960, p. 77.

Langer, S. K. (1942). *Philosophy in a New Key*. New York: Mentor Books, 1953.

Lea, H. C. (1887). *The Inquisition of the Middle Ages: Its Organization and Operation*. New York: Citadel Press, 1961.

Lebensohn, Z. M. (1955). Contributions of St. Elizabeths Hospital to a century of medicolegal progress. *Med. Ann. Dist. Columbia*, 24: 469, and 542.

Lemert, E. (1946). Legal commitment and social control. *Sociology and Social Research*, 30: 370.

Lemert, E. (1951). *Social Pathology: A Systematic Approach to the Theory of Sociopathic Behavior*. New York: McGraw-Hill.

Levine, M. (1942). *Psychotherapy in Medical Practice*. New York: Macmillan.

Lief, A. (1948). *The Commonsense Psychiatry of Adolf Meyer*. New York: McGraw-Hill.

Lindman, F. T., and McIntyre, D. M., Jr. (Editors) (1961). *The Mentally Disabled and the Law: The Report of the American Bar Foundation on the Rights of the Mentally Ill*. Chicago: University of Chicago Press.

Linn, L. (1955). *A Handbook of Hospital Psychiatry: A Practical Guide to Therapy*. New York: International Universities Press.

Llewellyn, K. N. (1950). The Anthropology of Criminal Guilt. In Llewellyn, K. N.: *Jurisprudence: Realism in Theory and Practice*, pp. 439–450. Chicago: University of Chicago Press, 1962.

Mabbott, J. D. (1939). Punishment. In Olafson, F. A. (Editor): *Justice and Social Policy: A Collection of Essays*, pp. 39–54. Englewood Cliffs, N.J.: Prentice-Hall, 1961.

McGee, H. J. (1961). Statements. In *Constitutional Rights of the Mentally Ill* (1961), pp. 54–63 and pp. 656–669.

M'Naghten's Case (1843). 10 Cl. & F. 200, 8 Eng. Rep. 718 (H.L.).

Maine, Sir H. (1861a). *Ancient Law*. In Everyman's Library, No. 734. London: J. M. Dent & Sons, n.d.

Maine, Sir H. (1861b). Quoted in *The Encyclopaedia Britannica*, Vol. VI, p. 710. Chicago: University of Chicago Press, 1948.

Masserman, J. (1955). *The Practice of Dynamic Psychiatry*. Philadelphia: Saunders.

Menninger, K. (1954). Psychological aspects of the organism under stress. Parts I and II. *J. Amer. Psychoanalyt. Assoc.*, 2: 67 and 280.

Menninger, K. (1960). In Bazelon, D. L. (1960), p. 32.

Mental Health Act (1959). 7 & 8 Eliz. 2. Ch. 72. London: Her Majesty's Stationery Office.

Meyer, A. (1926). Genetic-dynamic psychology versus nosology. In Winters, E. F. (General Editor): *The Collected Papers of Adolf Meyer*, Vol. III, pp. 57–73. Baltimore: Johns Hopkins Press, 1951.

Meyer, A. (1933). Preparation for psychiatry. In Winters, E. F. (General Editor): *The Collected Papers of Adolf Meyer*, Vol. III, pp. 74–86. Baltimore: Johns Hopkins Press, 1951.

Mihm, F. P. (1954). A re-examination of the validity of our sex psychopath statutes in the light of recent appeal cases and experience. *J. Crim. Law and Criminology*, 44: 716.

Mill, J. S. (1859). *On Liberty*. Chicago: Henry Regnery, 1955.

Mullins, E. (1961). *This Difficult Individual, Ezra Pound*. New York: Fleet.

Nock, A. J. (1943). *Memoirs of a Superfluous Man*. New York: Harper, pp. 175–176.

Norman, C. (1960). *Ezra Pound*. New York: Macmillan.

Noyes, A. P. (1953). *Modern Clinical Psychiatry*. Fourth Edition. Philadelphia: Saunders.

Noyes, A. P., and Kolb, L. C. (1958). *Modern Clinical Psychiatry*. Fifth Edition. Philadelphia: Saunders.

Orwell, G. (1943). Looking back on the Spanish War. In Orwell, G.: *Such, Such Were the Joys*, pp. 129–153. New York: Harcourt, Brace, 1953.

Orwell, G. (1949). *Nineteen Eighty-four*. New York: Harcourt, Brace.

Overholser, W. (1948). Foreword. In Schweitzer, A.: *The Psychiatric Study of Jesus*, pp. 11–15. Boston: Beacon Press.

Overholser, W. (1953). *The Psychiatrist and the Law*. New York: Harcourt, Brace.

Overholser, W. (1959). Major Principles of Forensic Psychiatry. In Arieti, S., *et al.* (Editors). *American Handbook of Psychiatry*, Vol. II, Chapter 95, pp. 1887–1901. New York: Basic Books.

Overholser, W. (1961). Statement. In *Constitutional Rights of the Mentally Ill* (1961), pp. 19–40.

Overstreet, H. A. (1952). *The Great Enterprise: Relating Ourselves to the World*. New York: Norton.

Packard, E. P. W. (1868). *The Prisoner's Hidden Life, Or Insane Asylums Unveiled. As Demonstrated by the Report of the Investigating Committee of the Legislature of Illinois, together with Mrs. Packard's Co-adjutor's Testimony.* Published by the Author. Chicago: A. B. Case, Printer.

Packard, E. P. W. (1873a). *Modern Persecution, or Insane Asylums Unveiled. As Demonstrated by the Report of the Investigating Committee of the Legislature of Illinois.* Vol. I. Published by the Authoress. Hartford: Case, Lockwood and Brainard, Printers and Binders.

Packard, E. P. W. (1873b). *Modern Persecution, or Married Woman's Liabilities. As Demonstrated by the Action of the Illinois Legislature.* Vol. II. Published by the Authoress. Hartford: Case, Lockwood, and Brainard, Printers and Binders.

Perceval, J. (1838). In Bateson, G. (Editor): *Perceval's Narrative: A Patient's Account of His Psychosis, 1830–1832.* Stanford, Calif.: Stanford University Press (1961), pp. 3–4.

Peters, R. S. (1958). *The Concept of Motivation.* London: Routledge & Kegan Paul.

Pfeffer, L. (1956). *The Liberties of an American: The Supreme Court Speaks.* Boston: Beacon Press.

Pitts, J. R. (1961). Introduction. In Parson, T.; Shils, E.; Naegele, K. D.; and Pitts, J. R. (Editors): *Theories of Society,* Vol. II, pp. 685–716. New York: The Free Press of Glencoe.

Ploscowe, M. (1951). *Sex and the Law.* New York: Prentice-Hall.

Popper, K. R. (1944–45). *The Poverty of Historicism.* Boston: Beacon Press, 1957.

Popper, K. R. (1945). *The Open Society and Its Enemies.* Princeton, N.J.: Princeton University Press, 1950.

Pound, E. (1914). Salutation the third. In Pound, E.: *Personae: The Collected Poems of Ezra Pound,* p. 145. New York: New Directions, 1926.

Ragsdale v. *Overholser* (1960). 281 F. 2d, 943 (D.C. Cir.).

Ray, I. (1838). *A Treatise on the Medical Jurisprudence of Insanity.* Fifth Edition. 1871. (Edited by Winfred Overholser.) Cambridge, Mass.: Harvard University Press, 1962.

Reich, W. (1954). Response. In Reich, W.: *Selected Writings,* pp. 539–544. New York: Noonday Press, 1961.

Reichard, S. (1956). A re-examination of "Studies in Hysteria." *Psychoanalyt. Quart.* 25: 155.

Reichenbach, H. (1947). *Elements of Symbolic Logic.* New York: Macmillan.

Richter, W. (1954). *The Mad Monarch: The Life and Times of Ludwig II of Bavaria.* Translated from the German by William S. Schlamm. Chicago: Henry Regnery.

Roche, P. Q. (1955). Criminality and mental illness: Two faces of the same coin. *Univ. of Chicago Law Rev.,* 22: 320.

Roche, P. Q. (1958). *The Criminal Mind: A Study of Communication Between Criminal Law and Psychiatry.* New York: Farrar, Straus, and Cudahy.

Ross, H. A. (1959). Commitment of the mentally ill: Problems of law and policy. *Michigan Law Rev.,* 57: 945.

Ross, H. A. (1961). Statement. In *Constitutional Rights of the Mentally Ill* (1961), pp. 183–199.

Rossiter, C. (1955). Prefatory Note. In Corwin, E. S. (1928–29), pp. v–viii.

Russell, B. (1953). The cult of 'common usage.' *Brit. J. Phil. Science*, 3: 303.

Russell, B. (1956). Symptoms of Orwell's 1984. In Russell, B.: *Portraits from Memory and Other Essays*, pp. 202–210. London: George Allen & Unwin, p. 205.

Ryle, G. (1949). *The Concept of Mind*. London: Hutchinson's University Library.

Schelling, T. C. (1960). *The Strategy of Conflict*. Cambridge, Mass.: Harvard University Press.

Schweitzer, A. (1913). *The Psychiatric Study of Jesus: Exposition and Criticism*. Translation and Introduction by Charles R. Joy. Foreword by Winfred Overholser. Boston: Beacon Press, 1948.

Stanton, A. H., and Schwartz, M. S. (1954). *The Mental Hospital: A Study of Institutional Participation in Psychiatric Illness and Treatment*. New York: Basic Books.

Stason, E. B. (1961). Foreword. In Lindman, F. T., and McIntyre, D. M., Jr. (Editors): *The Mentally Disabled and the Law*, p. vii. Chicago: University of Chicago Press.

State of New York, Department of Mental Hygiene (1957). *Laws Relating Mental Hygiene*. Utica, N.Y.: State Hospital Press.

State of New York, Department of Mental Hygiene (1959). *Official Directory of State and Licensed Mental Institutions*. Data compiled as of April 1, 1959. Utica, N.Y.: State Hospital Press.

State v. Jones (1871). 50 N.H. 369.

Stoljar, S. (1959). Ascriptive and prescriptive responsibility. *Mind*, 68: 350.

Strachey, J. (1959). Editor's Note. In *The Standard Edition of the Complete Psychological Works of Sigmund Freud*, Vol. IX, pp. 99–102. London: Hogarth Press.

Sullivan, H. S. (1953). *The Interpersonal Theory of Psychiatry*. New York: Norton.

Szasz, T. S. (1956). Some observations on the relationship between psychiatry and the law. *A.M.A. Arch. Neurol. & Psychiat.*, 75: 297.

Szasz, T. S. (1957a). A contribution to the psychology of schizophrenia. *A.M.A. Arch. Neurol. & Psychiat.*, 77: 420.

Szasz, T. S. (1957b). *Pain and Pleasure: A Study of Bodily Feelings*. New York: Basic Books.

Szasz, T. S. (1959). Psychiatry, psychotherapy, and psychology. *A.M.A. Arch. Gen. Psychiat.*, 1: 455.

Szasz, T. S. (1960a). Three problems in contemporary psychoanalytic training. *A.M.A. Arch. Gen. Psychiat.*, 3: 82.

Szasz, T. S. (1960b). The ethics of birth control. *The Humanist*, 20: 332.

Szasz, T. S. (1961). *The Myth of Mental Illness: Foundations of a Theory of Personal Conduct*. New York: Hoeber-Harper.

Szasz, T. S. (1962). Human nature and psychotherapy: A further contribution to the theory of autonomous psychotherapy. *Comprehensive Psychiat.*, 3: 268.

Taft, J. (1958). *Otto Rank: A Biographical Study Based on Notebooks, Letters, Collected Writings, Therapeutic Achievements, and Personal Associations*. New York: Julian Press.

Traver, R. (1958). *Anatomy of a Murder*. New York: St. Martin's Press.

Turton, W. (1802). *A Medical Glossary.* Second Edition. London: Lackington, Allen.

van den Berg, J. H. (1955). *The Phenomenological Approach to Psychiatry: An Introduction to Recent Phenomenological Psychopathology.* Springfield, Ill.: Charles C. Thomas.

Webster, D. (1834). Quoted by Corwin, E. S. (1948), p. 8.

Weihofen, H. (1933). *Insanity as a Defense in Criminal Law.* New York: The Commonwealth Fund.

Weihofen, H. (1956). *The Urge to Punish.* New York: Farrar, Straus, and Cudahy.

Weinstock, H. I. (1957). *Report of the Central Fact-Gathering Committee of the American Psychoanalytic Association.* (Mimeographed.) New York: American Psychoanalytic Association.

Wertham, F. (1949). The road to Rapallo: A psychiatric study. *Amer. J. Psychotherapy,* 3: 585.

Wertham, F. (1955a). Psychoauthoritarianism and the law. *Univ. of Chicago Law Rev.,* 22: 336.

Wertham, F. (1955b). Review of *The Psychology of the Criminal Act and Punishment,* by Gregory Zilboorg. New York: Harcourt, Brace, 1954. *Univ. of Chicago Law Rev.,* 22: 569.

Wertham, F. (1957). Review of *The Criminal, the Judge, and the Public,* by Franz Alexander and Hugo Staub. Revised Edition. Glencoe, Ill.: The Free Press and the Falcon's Wing Press, 1956. *Scientific Monthly,* 85: 101.

White, W. A. (1938). *The Autobiography of a Purpose.* Garden City, N.Y.: Doubleday.

Williams, G. (1953). *The Criminal Law.* London: Stevens.

Wiseman, F. (1961). Psychiatry and law: Use and abuse of psychiatry in a murder case. *Amer. J. Psychiat.,* 118: 289.

Wootton, B. (1959). *Social Science and Social Pathology.* London: George Allen & Unwin.

Wootton, B. (1960). The image of the social worker (review article). *Brit. J. Sociology,* 11: 373.

Wouk, H. (1951). *The Caine Mutiny: A Novel of World War II.* Garden City, N.Y.: Doubleday, 1954.

Zilboorg, G. (1954). *The Psychology of the Criminal Act and Punishment.* New York: Harcourt, Brace.

Index

Bleuler, Eugen, 31, 32, 34
Blind, the, attitude toward, 44
Bloom, Victor, on Welch, 210
Bloomberg, W., on chronic patients, 180
Bok, Curtis
  on criminal rehabilitation, 220
  on punishment, 119, 120
Bowman, K. M., on diagnosis of psychosis, 27
Braceland, F. J.
  quoted, 65
  on railroading, and restraints, 60, 61
Brandeis, Louis D.
  on constitutional rights, 160
  on liberty, 212
Brecka v. *State of New York*, 66
Brill, A. A., and Frink, 20
Brous, Bernard, case of, 164
Brown, J. A. C., 17
Browne, Sir Thomas, on witches, 100

Cahn, E., on the blind, 44; on democracy, 121
The Caine Mutiny (Wouk), 52
Carter v. *General Motors Corporation*, 152
Castiglioni, A., on Galen, 34
Castro, Fidel, 168, 200
  jailed for political offenses, 206
  as psychiatric case, 17
Chandler, Stephen S., views on law and psychiatry, 162–164
Charcot, Jean-Martin, 23, 98, 185
  and psychiatric vocabulary, 19
Chasan, Raymond H.
  on false commitment, 63, 64
  on involuntary servitude in public mental hospitals, 189
Chisholm, Brock, 3, 4
Choice
  and burden of good and evil, 4, 255
  and liberty, 3
  psychiatry, responsibility and, 16
Chomentowski, Michael L., case of, 165–166
Civil liberties, conflict between psychiatric therapy and, 101–103
Civil rights, commitment, and loss of, 40–41
Classification, in psychiatry, 24–36

Coercion
  and commitment, 42–43
  and mental health, 4–6
  and mental hospitalization, 97
Cohen, Morris R., on psychiatry and technical terms, 138
Commitment. *See also* Hospitalization
  civil, 40
    versus criminal, 142–144
  coercion and, 42, 43
  criminal, 40
  defined, 39
  false, 57–71
    contemporary, 57–71
    examples of, 62–65
    and habeas corpus, 66–69
    legal nonrecognition of, 65–66
    in nineteenth century, 57–59
  emergency, 40
  as grossly discriminatory sanction, 47–48
  Group for Advancement of Psychiatry on, 43
  indefinite, 40
  Iowa Supreme Court on, 42
  justifications for, 45–46
  and loss of civil rights, 40–41
  of mentally ill, 39–56
  psychiatric positions on, 41–45
  and psychiatry and social control, 39–56
  psychosis and behavior justifying, 46–47
  as psychotherapy, 45
  as punishment, 142
  right of patient to resist, 60
  and slavery, 55
  as social restraint, 46–48
  and social role, 47
  suits for false, 235
  therapeutic paternalism and, 43
  types of, and their scope, 40–41
Common usage, cult of, and concepts of mental health and mental illness, 205
Communication, language, psychiatry and, 238–239
Competency. *See also* Commitment
  and mental hospitalization, 40
Connecticut, statute protecting psychiatrist-patient privilege, 81
Consent, informed, 234
Constitutionalism, and liberty, 7

Maine, Sir Henry (*Cont.*):
on "unity of person," 152
Malingering, and hysteria, 19
Malpractice suits, 236, 252
Man, refusal to treat as contracting individual, 154–158
Marx, Karl, on religion, 239
Massachusetts
Briggs Law, 155
and Cooper case, 154–158
mental illness laws in, 249–251
Masserman, J., on commitment, 41
Matteawan State Hospital, N. Y., legal definition of function of, 83–84
Medical diagnosis, social and legal consequences of, 224
Medical hospital, and mental, contrasted, 87–88
Menninger, Karl
on nosology, 32
quoted on Durham decision, 98
Mental disease. *See also* Mental illness
as fact and theory, 133–134
Mental disorder, concept of generally recognized, 99–100
Mental health. *See also* Mental hospitalization; Mental illness; Mental patient; Mentally ill
autonomy, coercion and, 4–6
concept of, and cult of common usage, 205
long-range goals for, 226–230
proposals for reform in field of, 223–226
and social engineering, 4
Soviet law as instrument of, 218–221
Mental hospital. *See also* Hospitalization; Mental hospitalization; Mental illness; Mentally ill
admissions to, 81–84
elimination as "what else" institutions, 232–233
escapes from, 179–181
involuntary servitude in, 189
legal structure of, 80, 81–83
and medical, contrasted, 87–88
and punishment, 96
as total institution, 53–56
treatments in, 55–56
voluntary and involuntary admissions to, 83–84

The Mental Hospital (Stanton and Schwartz), 45
Mental hospitalization. *See also* Hospitalization; Mental health; Mental illness; Mental patient; Mentally ill
alternative to involuntary, 233
coercive, 97
discouragement of, 233–234
education to dangers of, 234–235
the individual, family and, 153–154
involuntary
as constitutional, 244, 245
elimination of, 225, 226–227
justification of, 240
legal aspects of, 62–63
as new kind of institution, 227–228
as punishment, 70, 189
role of deceit in involuntary, 54–55
Mental illness. *See also* Hospitalization; Mental health; Mental patient; Mentally ill
confusion between criminality and, 229
and contract and status, 149–158
and crime as social deviation, 105–108
and criminality, 143–144
dangerousness and, 144–145
as deviation from norm, 14
as disease or derogation, 18–23
as diseased word, 241
early psychoanalytic views on crime and, 103–105
as excusing condition, 135–137
main uses of concept of, 12–17
Massachusetts laws on, 249–250, 251
myth of, 11–12, 16–17
as name for problems in living, 13–16
and nonconformity, 205–206
presumption of crime and of, 223–226
as sign of brain disease, 12–13
similarities between crime and committable, 47
and social deviation, 205–206
and social disharmony, 13–16
as socially deviant behavior, 14, 22

Psychiatric testimony, in cases of political offense, 206
Psychiatric therapy, conflict between civil liberties and, 101–103
Psychiatric treatment. *See also* Psychiatrist; Psychiatry
 American Bar Association Journal on, 215
 defining of, 215
 implications of right to, 215–216
 as opportunity, punishment, or right, 250
Psychiatrist. *See also* Psychiatric treatment; Psychiatry
 antagonistic relationship of mental patient and, 230–232
 definition of task of, 145–146
 double role of institutional, 169–170
 expert testimony of, 112–116
 forensic, 109–122
 and inheritance game, 74–76, 78
 and lawyer, attitudes of, 41
 legal powers of, 87
 moral dilemmas of, 4–6
 and obscurantism, 73
 parallels between medieval inquisitor and institutional, 76–78
 prisoners' fear of, 107
 as social tranquilizer, 196–197
 statement of desired legal order, 242
Psychiatry. *See also* Psychiatric treatment; Psychiatrist
 as administrative law, 216–217, 221
 birth of modern, 2
 choice, responsibility and, 16
 classification in, 24–36
 and commitment and social control, 39–56
 and common sense, 35–36
 community, 248
 and constitutional rights, 146–190, 243–246
 and criminal law, 91–146, 241–243
 criticized as form of social control, 240–241
 and ethics, 15
 game-model analysis of forensic, 109–122
 influence on American criminal law, 161
 institutional, 240

Psychiatry *(Cont.)*:
 as institutional force, 86–87
 and language, 238–239
 and law, 1–2
  as instruments of social change, 250–251
 liberty against, 6–7
 modern, and political action, 86
 and morality, 3
 nature and scope of, 237–239
 and norms of conduct, 2
 operational approach to classification in, 26–31
 organized, in U.S.A., as favored institution, 79–88
 origin of, and concept of liberty, 1–2
 panchrestons in, 33, 34
 and paternalistic control, 236
 and penology, 119–120
 and politics, 199–211
 power of, and social action, 79–88
 and prestige in association with medicine, 23
 private, vii, 91
  and public policy, 191–198
 and promotive uses of language, 18–19
 propagandistic, 35
 as science, 237–239
 and semantic conversion and reconversion, 19–22
 and social control, 2
 as social engineering, vii
 as social institution, 39–88, 239–241
 social and legal uses of, vii–viii
 subject, method, and aim of, 26
Psychiatry and the Law (Guttmacher and Weihofen), 73, 82–83
Psychoanalysis (*see also* Alexander F.; Ferenczi; Freud; Jones), 73, 82–83
 as basis for criminology and penology, 93
"Psycho-Analysis and the Establishment of Facts in Legal Proceedings" (Freud), 103–104
Psychoauthoritarianism, 92, 101
Psychopathology. *See also* Mental illness
 assessment of, in analytic candidates, 21
 crime as, 93–103

Schizophrenia (*Cont.*):
as panchreston, 34
Schwartz, M. S., on mental hospitals, 45
Schweitzer, Albert, on Jesus, 199, 208–209
Segregation, and desegregation, 245
Self-incrimination, protection against, violated, 187
Semantic conversion, and reconversion, 19–22
Semantic reconversion, and anti-Semitism, 22, 23
Semantic therapy, 239, 241–242
Sentence, indeterminate, 212–213
Servitude, invountary, in mental hospitals, 189
Sexual activity, between consenting adults, as crime or right, 248–249
Sexual-psychopath laws, 213–214, 245
American Bar Foundation and, 214
enforcement of, 249
Shaw, George Bernard, and Fascism, 207
Sherman Act, and business relations, 184, 243
Slavery, and commitment, 55–56
Social action
power of psychiatry and, 79–88
scientific judgment and, 17
and therapy, 244
Social change
psychiatry and law as instruments of, 250–251
social engineering and, 225
Social control
psychiatric commitment, and, 39–56
psychiatry as, 240–241
Social disturbance, and commitment, 47
Social deviation
crime and mental illness as, 105–108
and mental illness, 205–206
Social engineering
and mental health, 4
piecemeal, and social change, 225
Social oppression, 185
Social Pathology (Lemert), 106
Social restraint, commitment as, 46–48

Social role, and commitment, 47
Social Science and Social Pathology (Wootton), 102–103
Social therapy, Marxist, 219
Social tranquilization, 196–197
Society, 150
Socrates, 207, 255
Soviet law, as instrument of mental health, 218–221
Stalin, Joseph
discredited by Khrushchev, 221
on freedom, 218
Standard Nomenclature (American Psychiatric Association), 25
Stanton, A. H., on mental hospitals, 45
Stason, E. B., 179
State
as *parens patriae,* 151–153
and personal autonomy, 249
power to commit mentally ill, 184
the therapeutic, 211–222
as therapist, 247
State hospitals, abuse of mental patients, 47
State v. *Jones,* 130
Status, concepts of contract and, 149–151
Staub, H.
on crime and mental illness, 92, 93, 94, 95
The Criminal, the Judge, and the Public, 93–95
Stoljar, S., on responsibility, 124
Strachey, J., on Freud, 104
Sukarno, A., 168
jailed for political offenses, 207
Sullivan, H. S., concept of nosology, 33
Syracuse Herald-Journal
on Chomentowski Case, 166
report on suicide of David B. Pratt, 84–85
Syracuse Post-Standard, on Chomentowski Case, 166
Szasz, Thomas S., previous works referred to
on assessment of psychoanalytic candidates, 21
on autonomous psychotherapy, 15, 52, 97, 197
on Charcot and Freud, 19, 186